A CALENDAR
OF GREATNESS

September 7, 1892
Gentleman Jim Corbett knocks out champion John L. Sullivan to win the world heavyweight boxing title.

★

July 15, 1912
Jim Thorpe wins the decathlon gold medal accumulating nearly 800 more points than his closest competitor.

★

July 18, 1924
Swimmer Johnny Weissmuller wins the 400 meter freestyle gold medal at the Paris Olympics.

★

August 3, 1936
With Adolf Hitler looking on, American Jesse Owens wins the 100 meter gold medal at the Berlin Olympics.

★

October 8, 1956
Don Larsen pitches the only perfect game in World Series history as the New York Yankees defeat the Brooklyn Dodgers 2–0.

★

March 6, 1976
Dorothy Hamill wins the World Figure Skating Championships in Göteborg, Sweden.

★

JUST PICK A DAY.
THERE'S MORE INSIDE...

THIS DATE IN SPORTS HISTORY

THIS DATE IN SPORTS HISTORY

FLOYD CONNER

WARNER BOOKS

A Warner Communications Company

WARNER BOOKS EDITION

Copyright © 1989 by Floyd Conner
All rights reserved.

Warner Books, Inc.
666 Fifth Avenue
New York, N.Y. 10103

Cover design by Anthony Russo
Cover photos by *Focus on Sports*

 A Warner Communications Company

Printed in the United States of America

First Printing: August, 1989

10 9 8 7 6 5 4 3 2 1

THIS DATE IN SPORTS HISTORY

JANUARY 1

January 1, 1902: Michigan routs Stanford 49–0, in the first Rose Bowl. Tournament of Roses officials are so disappointed with the gate receipts of the game that they discontinue the Rose Bowl for 13 years, replacing it with various spectacles such as chariot races, polo, and a match race between a camel and an elephant.

January 1, 1929: California's captain, Roy Riegels, runs 60 yards the wrong way after scooping up a fumble recovery in the Rose Bowl against Georgia Tech.

January 1, 1942: Because the tournament officials fear a sneak attack by the Japanese is possible if the game is played in Pasadena, the Rose Bowl is held in Durham, North Carolina. Despite having the home field advantage, Duke loses to Oregon by the score of 20 to 16.

January 1, 1944: Army defeats Navy, 10–7, in the so-called Arab Bowl. The teams, stationed in Oran, North Africa, play the game on the sands of the desert. The halftime show includes camel races.

January 1, 1967: The Green Bay Packers defeat the Dallas Cowboys, 34–27, in the NFL championship game.

JANUARY 2

January 2, 1939: Duke enters the Rose Bowl game against Southern California undefeated and unscored upon. Duke is leading, 3–0, with less than a minute to play when fourth-string quarterback Doyle Nave throws the game-winning touchdown pass to substitute end Al Krueger to give the Trojans an upset 7–3 victory.

January 2, 1965: The Green Bay Packers defeat the Cleveland Browns, 23–12, in the NFL championship game.

January 2, 1982: San Diego defeats Miami, 41–38, in overtime in a memorable AFC playoff game. The explosive Chargers jump out to a 24–0 lead, only to have the Dolphins come back to tie the game.

January 2, 1983: Cincinnati quarterback Ken Anderson

completes 20 consecutive passes in a game against Houston to set an NFL record for passing accuracy.

January 2, 1985: The University of Nevada-Las Vegas defeats Utah, 142–140, in triple overtime in the highest-scoring college basketball game in history. The game marks coach Jerry Tarkanian's 600th career victory.

JANUARY 3

January 3, 1865: Boxers Con Orem and Hugh O'Neill fight for 193 rounds in Virginia City, Montana, before the bout is halted because of darkness.

January 3, 1920: Boston Red Sox owner Harry Frazee sells slugger Babe Ruth to the New York Yankees for $125,000. Ruth had led the Red Sox to three pennants, primarily as their star pitcher. The Yankees recognized his slugging potential and the Babe hits 54 home runs in 1920 as compared to only 22 for the entire Red Sox team. Ruth leads the Yankees to seven pennants, while Boston will not win another pennant for 26 years.

January 3, 1931: Nels Stewart of the Montreal Maroons sets a National Hockey League record by scoring two goals in four seconds. The outburst wipes out a 3–1 Boston lead as Montreal goes on to defeat the Bruins, 5–3.

January 3, 1983: Dallas's Tony Dorsett runs for a 99-yard touchdown, the longest in NFL history, during a Monday-night game won by the Minnesota Vikings, 31–27.

JANUARY 4

January 4, 1987: Thomas Stevens pedals into San Francisco to become the first person to bicycle around the world. Stevens's odyssey takes 2 years, 8 months, and 12 days for him to complete.

January 4, 1967: Daredevil Donald Campbell is killed while attempting to become the first man to travel over 300 miles per hour on water. He appears on his way to success when his jet-engined powerboat, *Bluebird*, becomes airborne at 310 miles per hour and disintegrates on Coniston Lake in England. Campbell's body was never found.

January 4, 1981: The Dallas Cowboys score a thrilling come-from-behind victory over the Atlanta Falcons in an NFL playoff game. Dallas scores 20 points in the final quarter to beat the Falcons, 30–27.

January 4, 1984: The Edmonton Oilers defeat the Minnesota North Stars, 12–8, in the highest-scoring game in modern National Hockey League history. Edmonton center Wayne Gretzky leads the scoring parade with four goals and four assists.

JANUARY 5

January 5, 1957: Jackie Robinson announces his retirement from baseball. Robinson decided to retire rather than accept being traded from the Brooklyn Dodgers to the New York Giants. The major leagues' first black player accepts a position as a vice-president with Chock Full o' Nuts.

January 5, 1963: The San Diego Chargers roll up 610 yards in offense as they bury the Boston Patriots, 51–10, in the American Football League championship game.

January 5, 1971: The Harlem Globetrotters lose to the New Jersey Reds, 100–99, to snap their consecutive winning streak at 2,495 games.

January 5, 1975: Twenty-nine-year-old Houston pitcher Don Wilson dies of carbon monoxide poisoning at his home. Wilson pitched two no-hitters during his career.

January 5, 1988: Pete Maravich collapses and dies after a pickup basketball game in Pasadena, California. Maravich set an NCAA record by averaging 44.2 points during his college career.

JANUARY 6

January 6, 1920: Hall of Fame pitcher Early Wynn is born in Hartford, Alabama.

January 6, 1951: Indianapolis defeats Rochester, 75–73, in a six-overtime National Basketball Association game.

January 6, 1957: Golfer Nancy Lopez is born in Torrance, California.

January 6, 1964: Controversial baseball owner Charlie Finley announces his intention to move his Athletics from Kansas City to Louisville. American League owners will vote overwhelmingly to reject the move, but four years later Finley moves the A's to

Oakland, where they will win three consecutive world championships beginning in 1972.

January 6, 1976: Millionaire businessman Ted Turner purchases the Atlanta Braves for a reported 12 million dollars.

January 6, 1987: Lady's Secret wins the Eclipse Award as Horse of the Year.

JANUARY 7

January 7, 1899: Walter Camp publishes his first All-American football team in *Collier's Weekly*.

January 7, 1927: Before a crowd of 300, in a high-school gymnasium in Hinckley, Illinois, the Harlem Globetrotters play their first game.

January 7, 1936: Women's tennis champion Helen Wills Moody and American Davis Cupper Howard Kinsey volley 2,001 times without a miss. The rally, lasting 1 hour and 18 minutes, may never have ended if Kinsey didn't have to leave to teach a lesson.

January 7, 1964: Dick Weber rolls the highest game in bowling history in a Boeing 707 Starstream Astrojet.

January 7, 1972: The Los Angeles Lakers bury the Atlanta Hawks, 134-90, for their 33rd consecutive win. The Lakers, led by Wilt Chamberlain and Jerry West, finish the season with a 69–13 record and win the NBA championship.

January 7, 1980: In the NHL, Minnesota defeats Philadelphia, 7–1, to stop the Flyers' record streak of 35 games without a loss.

JANUARY 8

January 8, 1955: The University of Kentucky loses to Georgia Tech, 59–58, to suffer their first defeat at home since January 2, 1943. The Wildcats had won 130 consecutive games at home during that span. The same day, Furman established an NCAA record by scoring 154 points in a game.

January 8, 1985: John Henry wins his sixth Eclipse Award. Champion three-year-old colt Swale and champion sprinter Eillo receive their Eclipse Awards posthumously.

January 8, 1986: Willie McCovey is elected by baseball writers to the Baseball Hall of Fame on the first ballot. "Stretch," one of the most feared left-handed batters in baseball history, hit 521 home runs in his major league career.

JANUARY 9

January 9, 1903: Two businessmen from New York, Frank Farrell and Bill Devery, buy the struggling Baltimore baseball franchise for $18,000 and move it to New York City. They name the team the New York Highlanders, but years later they will change the name to the Yankees. It will become the most successful franchise in baseball history.

January 9, 1953: Bevo Francis of Rio Grande College scores 116 points in a basketball game against Ashland College.

January 9, 1958: University of Cincinnati sophomore Oscar Robertson outscores the entire Seton Hall basketball team as the Bearcats win, 118–54. Robertson's 56 points is at the time the most points ever scored in Madison Square Garden.

January 9, 1977: The Oakland Raiders overwhelm the Minnesota Vikings, 32–14, in Super Bowl XI. The Vikings suffer their fourth consecutive Super Bowl loss.

January 9, 1979: New Orleans high-school student Daryl Moreau sinks his 126th consecutive free throw. Moreau had not missed a free throw in nearly a year.

JANUARY 10

January 10, 1907: Feisty New York Giants manager John McGraw saves his wife and another passenger from a team of runaway horses. A trolley collides with the carriage the McGraws are riding in, spooking the horses. McGraw is dragged two blocks through the streets before he is able to bring the team to a halt.

January 10, 1920: Montreal blasts Toronto, 14–7, in a wild National Hockey League encounter.

January 10, 1931: The Philadelphia Quakers defeat the Montreal Maroons, 4–3, to end their 15-game losing streak, the longest in National Hockey League history.

January 10, 1982: The Cincinnati Bengals defeat the San Diego Chargers, 27–7, in the AFC championship game. The game is played in frigid conditions with the wind-chill factor at game time a bitter 59 degrees below zero. That afternoon, the San

Francisco 49ers nip the Dallas Cowboys, 28–27, in the NFL championship game on a fingertip catch in the end zone by Dwight Clark with 51 seconds left to play.

JANUARY 11

January 11, 1953: J. Edgar Hoover, head of the FBI, declines a six-figure offer to become the president of the International Boxing Club.

January 11, 1960: In a bout in Las Vegas, heavyweight boxer Lamar Clark records his 44th consecutive knockout.

January 11, 1970: The Kansas City Chiefs, a two-touchdown underdog, surprise the Minnesota Vikings, 23–7, in Super Bowl IV.

January 11, 1971: Detroit Tigers ace reliever John Hiller suffers a heart attack at his home in Duluth, Minnesota. The 27-year-old pitcher will make one of the most remarkable comebacks in baseball history. Two years later, Hiller will set a major league record with 38 saves.

January 11, 1976: In Colorado Springs, Colorado, Dorothy Hamill wins her third consecutive national figure skating championship.

January 11, 1984: The Denver Nuggets defeat the San Antonio Spurs, 163–155, in the highest-scoring regulation game in NBA history.

JANUARY 12

January 12, 1930: The Boston Bruins win their 14th consecutive game, a streak dating back to December 3, 1929.

January 12, 1944: Former heavyweight boxing champion Joe Frazier is born in Beaufort, South Carolina.

January 12, 1946: The Cleveland Rams football team announce they are moving their National Football League franchise to Los Angeles.

January 12, 1969: In one of the most shocking upsets in professional football history, the New York Jets defeat the Baltimore Colts, 16–7, in Super Bowl III. "Broadway" Joe Namath had brashly guaranteed a Jet victory even though the Colts were three-touchdown favorites. Running back Matt Snell rushes for 121 yards and end George Sauer catches eight passes for 133 yards.

January 12, 1975: The Pittsburgh Steelers defeat the Minnesota Vikings, 16–6, in Super Bowl IX. The Steel Curtain defense limits the Vikings to 17 yards rushing and a mere 119 total yards.

JANUARY 13

January 13, 1962: Wilt Chamberlain establishes an NBA record by scoring 73 points in a game.

January 13, 1968: Minnesota North Stars center Bill Masterton is fatally injured when he is checked into the boards and falls heavily to the ice.

January 13, 1974: The Miami Dolphins become Super Bowl champions for the second year in a row as they defeat the Minnesota Vikings, 24–7, in Super Bowl VIII. The Dolphins' Larry Csonka rushes for 145 yards and quarterback Bob Griese, although throwing only seven passes, completes six.

January 13, 1982: Baseball greats Hank Aaron and Frank Robinson are elected to the Baseball Hall of Fame in their first year of eligibility.

January 13, 1985: Ninety-nine-year-old Otto Bucher scores a hole in one on the 12th hole of the La Manga golf course in Spain.

JANUARY 14

January 14, 1951: The American Conference defeats the National Conference, 28–27, in the first NFL Pro Bowl.

January 14, 1954: Baseball immortal Joe DiMaggio marries movie star Marilyn Monroe. The marriage will last only one year. DiMaggio will send roses to Monroe's grave three times a week after her death in 1962.

January 14, 1968: The Green Bay Packers win the Super Bowl for the second consecutive year as they defeat the Oakland Raiders, 33–14, in Super Bowl II. This is Green Bay coach Vince Lombardi's last game and marks the end of the Packer dynasty.

January 14, 1973: The Miami Dolphins defeat the Washington Redskins, 14–7, in Super Bowl VII to become the first NFL team to finish the season undefeated. The lone Washington score comes with two minutes left in the game when Miami kicker Garo Yepremian makes a feeble attempt to pass the ball after his

CBS for racial remarks he made during a television interview in Washington.

JANUARY 17

January 17, 1942: Cassius Marcellus Clay is born in Louisville, Kentucky. After he wins the heavyweight title in 1964, he will change his name to Muhammad Ali.

January 17, 1971: In a comedy of errors, the Baltimore Colts defeat the Dallas Cowboys, 16–13, in Super Bowl V. The game is marred by 11 turnovers and numerous penalties. The game's most spectacular play occurs in the second quarter, when Baltimore tight end John Mackey catches a tipped pass and romps 75 yards for a touchdown. Jim O'Brien boots a 32-yard field goal with five seconds remaining to give Baltimore the victory.

January 17, 1986: "Terrible" Tim Witherspoon wins a close 15-round decision over champion Tony Tubbs to regain the World Boxing Association heavyweight title.

JANUARY 18

January 18, 1976: The Pittsburgh Steelers defeat the Dallas Cowboys, 21–17, in Super Bowl X. The game clincher comes in the fourth quarter when Pittsburgh quarterback Terry Bradshaw hooks up with Lynn Swann for a 64-yard completion. Bradshaw is knocked unconscious on the play and doesn't learn of the touchdown until he comes to in the dressing room.

January 18, 1983: Seventy years after the International Olympic Committee had stripped Jim Thorpe of his gold medals, the medals are returned to Thorpe's children. Thorpe's medals had been taken from him in 1913 when it was learned that he had been paid $25 a week for playing semipro baseball.

JANUARY 19

January 19, 1898: Brown defeats Harvard, 6–0, in the first college hockey game.

January 19, 1900: Boston catcher Marty Bergen goes berserk and murders his wife and two children with an ax and razor in his

North Brookfield, Massachusetts, home before committing suicide.

January 19, 1937: Cy Young, Tris Speaker, and Nap Lajoie are elected to the Baseball Hall of Fame.

January 19, 1972: Sandy Koufax, Yogi Berra, and Early Wynn are elected to the Baseball Hall of Fame.

January 19, 1974: Notre Dame defeats UCLA, 71–70, to snap the Bruins' record 88-game winning streak. The winning basket comes on a jumper from the corner by Dwight Clay with 21 seconds remaining. Notre Dame had been the last team to defeat UCLA, a feat they accomplished in 1970.

January 19, 1981: Muhammad Ali talks a despondent 21-year-old youth out of committing suicide. The youth was threatening to jump from the ledge of an office building in Los Angeles.

JANUARY 20

January 20, 1892: Students at the International YMCA Training School in Springfield, Massachusetts, play the first organized basketball game. The game was invented by Canadian-born James Naismith, who installed peach baskets in the gymnasium. After each goal, someone had to climb up and remove the ball from the basket. The bottomless basket will not be invented until 1905.

January 20, 1968: Houston defeats UCLA, 71–69, before 52,693 basketball fans in the Astrodome. The loss snaps UCLA's 47-game winning streak. The game is billed as a matchup between UCLA's Lew Alcindor and Houston's Elvin Hayes. Hayes outscores Alcindor, who is playing with a painful eye injury, 39 to 15.

January 20, 1974: Essex Community College blows out Englewood Cliffs College, 210–67, in small-college basketball action.

January 20, 1980: The Pittsburgh Steelers score a come-from-behind 31–19 victory over the Los Angeles Rams in Super Bowl XIV.

January 20, 1985: The San Francisco 49ers defeat the Miami Dolphins, 38–16, in Super Bowl XIX.

JANUARY 21

January 21, 1940: Golfing legend Jack Nicklaus is born in Columbus, Ohio.

January 21, 1979: In Super Bowl XIII, one of the most exciting, the Pittsburgh Steelers defeat the Dallas Cowboys, 35–31. The turning point comes in the third quarter when veteran Dallas tight end Jackie Smith drops a sure touchdown pass while all alone in the end zone.

January 21, 1980: Les Henson of Virginia Tech makes a desperation length-of-the-floor shot at the buzzer to give his team a thrilling 79–77 victory over Florida State. The shot is estimated to have traveled 89 feet.

January 21, 1985: Dennis Potvin ties Bobby Orr's career record for defensemen with his 270th NHL goal.

January 21, 1986: Over 100 Purdue University students participate in the annual Nude Olympics race. Thousands of spectators line the streets of West Lafayette, Indiana, to watch the nude runners brave the frigid 38-degree temperature.

JANUARY 22

January 22, 1857: The National Association of Baseball Players is founded in New York. Several rules are adopted, including the nine-inning game. Previously, the first team to score 21 runs was declared the winner.

January 22, 1951: Fidel Castro is ejected from a Winter League game after beaning Don Hoak. Castro will give up baseball for politics and by the end of the decade is the prime minister of Cuba.

January 22, 1973: Three-to-one underdog George Foreman knocks down champion Joe Frazier six times in two rounds to win the heavyweight boxing title.

January 22, 1984: The Los Angeles Raiders destroy the Washington Redskins, 38–9, in Super Bowl XVIII.

January 22, 1984: Annette Kennedy of the State University of New York sets a women's collegiate record when she scores 70 points in a basketball game against Pratt Institute.

January 22, 1988: Heavyweight champion Mike Tyson knocks out former champion Larry Holmes in the fourth round.

JANUARY 23

January 23, 1944: The hapless New York Rangers lose to the Detroit Red Wings, 15–0, the most lopsided score in NHL history. The Rangers will not win another game until November 11, losing 21 games and tying four during the drought.

January 23, 1965: Center Bill Russell, closely guarded by the towering Wilt Chamberlain, misses all 14 shots he attempts as the Philadelphia Warriors defeat Boston, 104–100, ending the Celtics 16-game winning streak.

January 23, 1983: At the height of his career, five-time Wimbledon champion Bjorn Borg announces his retirement from tennis.

January 23, 1983: Portland scores all 17 points in the overtime period to defeat the Houston Rockets, 113–96, in NBA action.

January 23, 1988: Bob Benoit bowls a perfect game to defeat Mark Roth, 300–255, to win the Quaker State Open and a $100,000 bonus. It is the first time a perfect game has been bowled on television in a title match.

JANUARY 24

January 24, 1968: Olympic gold medalist Mary Lou Retton is born.

January 24, 1971: The NFC defeats the AFC, 27–6, in the first NFL Pro Bowl.

January 24, 1976: George Foreman knocks out Ron Lyle in the fifth round in one of the greatest slugfests in boxing history. In the wild fourth round, the two boxers exchange knockdowns, and near the end of the round Lyle sends the former champion to the canvas once again. Somehow Foreman manages to beat the count, and in the next round he traps Lyle in the corner and knocks him out.

January 24, 1982: The San Francisco 49ers hold on to defeat the Cincinnati Bengals, 26–21, in Super Bowl XVI. Ray Wersching kicks four field goals for the 49ers, while Ken Anderson passes for 300 yards and Dan Ross catches 11 passes for the Bengals.

January 24, 1984: Hulk Hogan pins the Iron Sheik to win the World Wrestling Federation title. The 302-pound Hogan had gained fame as Thunderlips in *Rocky III*.

JANUARY 25

January 25, 1924: The first Winter Olympic Games are inaugurated in Chamonix, France.

January 25, 1955: Skier Jill Kinmont breaks her back when she strikes a tree during the Snow Cup Ski Race in Utah. As a result of the accident, Kinmont is almost totally paralyzed. Twenty years later her life story will be depicted in the film *The Other Side of the Mountain.*

January 25, 1972: Ohio State center Luke Witte is injured in an ugly incident during a game with Minnesota. The 7-footer suffers facial injuries when he is stomped during a donnybrook.

January 25, 1981: The Oakland Raiders defeat the Philadelphia Eagles, 27–10, to become the first wild-card team to win the Super Bowl. Oakland's Kenny King catches an 80-yard touchdown pass from Jim Plunkett.

January 25, 1987: The New York Giants defeat the Denver Broncos, 39–20, in Super Bowl XXI. The Giants trail, 10–9, at halftime before exploding for 30 second-half points.

JANUARY 26

January 26, 1924: Charles Jewtraw of the United States wins the 500-meter speed skating event to become the first gold medalist in Winter Olympic history.

January 26, 1935: Television star and former major league catcher Bob Uecker is born in Milwaukee. Uecker's baseball skills were so meager that he once boasted that his greatest thrill in baseball was walking with the bases loaded in spring training.

January 26, 1960: Pete Rozelle is elected commissioner of the National Football League on the 23rd ballot.

January 26, 1960: High-school basketball sensation Danny Heater scores 135 points as Burnsville defeats Widen, 173–43.

January 26, 1961: Hockey great Wayne Gretzky is born.

January 26, 1983: Paul "Bear" Bryant, the winningest coach in college football history with 322 victories, dies of a heart attack at the age of 69.

January 26, 1986: The Chicago Bears humble the New England Patriots, 46–10, the most lopsided score in Super Bowl history.

JANUARY 27

January 27, 1894: The University of Chicago defeats the Chicago YMCA Training School, 19–11, in the first basketball game involving a college team.

January 27, 1973: Basketball powerhouse UCLA defeats Notre Dame for its 61st consecutive victory, breaking the NCAA record.

January 27, 1973: Janet Lynn wins her fifth consecutive national figure skating championship.

January 27, 1984: Wayne Gretzky is held scoreless by the Los Angeles Kings, the first time in 51 games that the Edmonton superstar had not scored—an NHL record.

January 27, 1986: The Dow Jones Industrial Average reaches an all-time high, once again confirming one of the strangest but most reliable economic indicators: When the National Conference representative wins the Super Bowl, stocks close up for the year, and when the American Conference team prevails, the stock market goes down. Strange as this may seem, this indicator has held true for 19 of the 20 years the Super Bowl has been in existence.

JANUARY 28

January 28, 1943: Forward Doug Bentley, with the help of four assists from his brother, Max, sets an NHL record with five points in a single period.

January 28, 1958: Dodgers catcher Roy Campanella is seriously injured in an automobile accident.

January 28, 1959: The Soviet Union defeats the United States, 62–37, marking the first time an American basketball team had ever lost a game in international competition.

January 28, 1961: An indoor high-school basketball game between West Hazleton and McAdoo in Pennsylvania is rained out. West Hazleton is leading, 31–29, when an open window causes condensation on the floor of the heated gym, making it impossible to continue play.

January 28, 1969: Barbara Jo Rubin rides favored Fly Away to a three-length victory at Hobby Horse Track in Nassau to become the first female jockey to win a race in North America.

January 28, 1973: Henry Boucha of the Detroit Red Wings sets an NHL record for the fastest goal scored at the beginning of a game when he scores at the six-second mark against Montreal.

JANUARY 29

January 29, 1936: Ty Cobb, Babe Ruth, Honus Wagner, Christy Mathewson, and Walter Johnson are the first inductees to the Baseball Hall of Fame.

January 29, 1956: Austrian Toni Sailer wins the giant slalom by an incredible six-second margin at the Winter Olympics in Cortina D'Ampezzo, Italy. It is a sign of things to come, as Sailer becomes the first skier to sweep the alpine events.

January 29, 1960: Olympic diving gold medalist Greg Louganis is born.

January 29, 1964: Grand Avenue High School, of De Quincy, Louisiana, humiliates Audrey Memorial High School of Cameron, Louisiana, 211–29, the most lopsided high-school basketball score in American history.

January 29, 1982: Old Dominion defeats Louisiana Tech, 61–58, to snap their 54-game winning streak, the longest in women's college basketball history.

JANUARY 30

January 30, 1936: Fans of the Boston Braves are asked to select a new name for the team after they lose a record 115 games in 1935. The team's name is changed to the Boston Bees, but after five more seasons in the second division the name is changed back to the Braves.

January 30, 1955: Golfer Curtis Strange is born.

January 30, 1971: Guard Russell Thompson scores 25 points as Birmingham Southern State College defeats Florence State University, 55–46. What makes the feat special is that all of Thompson's points come from the foul line. Thompson makes 25 of 28 shots from the charity stripe while being held scoreless from the field.

January 30, 1983: The Washington Redskins defeat the Miami Dolphins, 27–17, in Super Bowl XVII. The star of the game is Washington's John Riggins, who rushes for 166 yards, including a 43-yard touchdown run in the fourth quarter.

JANUARY 31

January 31, 1919: Jackie Robinson is born in Cairo, Georgia.

January 31, 1920: Quebec's Joe Malone scores seven goals in a Stanley Cup playoff game against Toronto. Malone outscores the entire Toronto team as Quebec wins by the score of 10 to 6.

January 31, 1931: Chicago Cub great Ernie Banks is born in Dallas, Texas.

January 31, 1947: Strikeout king Nolan Ryan is born in Refugio, Texas.

January 31, 1958: *Jackpot Bowling* debuts on NBC with Leo Durocher as host. Two years later, Milton Berle, "Mr. Television," will become the program's emcee.

January 31, 1974: McDonald's chairman Ray Kroc buys the San Diego Padres.

January 31, 1988: The Washington Redskins trounce the Denver Broncos, 42–10, in Super Bowl XXII. The Redskins explode for five touchdowns in the second quarter to put the game out of reach. Washington quarterback Doug Williams passes for a record 340 yards. Ricky Sanders rushes for 193 yards and Tim Smith sets a receiving record with 204 yards.

FEBRUARY 1

February 1, 1914: The New York Giants and Chicago White Sox play an exhibition game in Egypt, using the Great Pyramid as a backstop. The game is part of a 56-game world tour to promote baseball. The game ends in a 3–3 tie.

February 1, 1956: American Hayes Jenkins wins the gold medal in figure skating at the Winter Olympics. Americans sweep the medals as Ronnie Robertson, perhaps the greatest spinner of all time, wins the silver medal, and Hayes's brother, David, wins the bronze.

February 1, 1968: The legendary Vince Lombardi resigns as head coach of the Green Bay Packers. In nine seasons with the Packers, he won five NFL titles and two Super Bowls.

February 1, 1977: Hillsdale High School defeats Person High School, 2–0, in a low-scoring basketball game.

February 1, 1979: Steve Cauthen, who had ridden Affirmed to victory in the 1978 Triple Crown, wins on Father Duffy at Santa Anita, snapping a 110-race losing streak. A few days later, Cauthen announces that he will ride in Europe. There he becomes a champion jockey.

FEBRUARY 2

February 2, 1949: Golfer Ben Hogan has a near-fatal automobile accident when the car he is driving is hit head-on by a Greyhound bus. Hogan will make a miraculous recovery and win the U.S. Open 17 months later.

February 2, 1956: American Tenley Albright wins the Olympic gold medal in figure skating, besting rival Carol Heiss.

February 2, 1962: Pole vaulter John Uelses clears 16 feet, ¼ inch for an apparent world record. As officials attempt to verify the bar height, fans congratulating Uelses accidentally knock over the standards supporting the bar, negating the world record. The next day Uelses vaults 16 feet, ¾ inch for a new world record.

February 2, 1977: In a game against the Detroit Red Wings, Toronto's Ian Turnbull scores five goals to set an NHL record for defensemen.

February 2, 1985: Rock singer Huey Lewis fulfills a lifelong fantasy by playing against former major league baseball players in a Dream Camp in Tempe, Arizona. Lewis's team loses, 5–4, to a team composed of former players from the Giants, Dodgers, Yankees, and Orioles. Lewis bats cleanup and pitches a complete game.

FEBRUARY 3

February 3, 1940: Fran Tarkenton is born in Richmond, Virginia.

February 3, 1945: Miami Dolphins quarterback Bob Griese is born.

February 3, 1948: Dick Button becomes the first American to win the world figure skating championship.

February 3, 1952: Baseball star Fred Lynn is born in Chicago, Illinois.

February 3, 1956: Toni Sailer wins the Olympic downhill to become the first skier to sweep the three alpine events.

February 3, 1964: Sister Marielle and Christine Goitschel of France win the gold and silver medals in the Olympic giant slalom in Innsbruck, Austria.

February 3, 1979: The Minnesota Twins trade seven-time batting champion Rod Carew to the California Angels in exchange for four players.

FEBRUARY 4

February 4, 1916: Sixty-three-year-old Walter Edgerton knocks out John Johnson in the fourth round of their fight at the Broadway Athletic Club in New York to become the oldest boxer ever to win a professional prizefight.

February 4, 1937: Jim Murgie, an amateur bowler, rolls three consecutive perfect games in Philadelphia, Pennsylvania.

February 4, 1962: The Soviet newspaper *Izvestia* publishes an article claiming the game of baseball was invented in Russia.

February 4, 1964: Terry McDermott, a barber by profession, pulls off a major upset as he wins the 500-meter speed skating gold medal at the Innsbruck Olympics. To make the scenario even more implausible, he wins the race on borrowed skates.

February 4, 1969: Thirty-three-year-old John Madden is named head coach of the Oakland Raiders.

February 4, 1987: *Stars & Stripes*, skippered by Dennis Conner, regains the America's Cup from Australia by winning four straight races. Four years earlier, Conner had become the first skipper to lose the Cup, which had been successfully defended by Americans for all of the yachting classic's 132-year history.

FEBRUARY 5

February 5, 1934: All-time home-run king Hank Aaron is born in Mobile, Alabama.

February 5, 1948: Dick Button becomes the first American to win an Olympic gold medal in figure skating. During his program he lands the first double axel in competition.

February 5, 1974: In one of sports' greatest oddities, Swedish teenager Mats Wermelin scores 272 points in a basketball game played in Stockholm. Even more incredible is that no other points are scored by either team during the game.

February 5, 1976: Austrian Franz Klammer thrills millions of television viewers by winning the Olympic downhill in Innsbruck, Austria. Elsewhere at the Olympics, Bill Koch becomes the first American to win a medal in the Nordic events when he finishes second in the 30-kilometer race.

February 5, 1988: Andre the Giant pins champion Hulk Hogan to win the World Wrestling Federation title. It is the first time in over 30 years that a wrestling match has been televised in prime time.

FEBRUARY 6

February 6, 1895: Babe Ruth is born in Baltimore, Maryland.

February 6, 1925: Passaic High School has its 159-game winning streak snapped when they are defeated by Hackensack High, 39–35. Passaic had not lost a game since December 17, 1919.

February 6, 1948: Barbara Ann Scott of Canada wins the Olympic gold medal in figure skating.

February 6, 1971: Astronaut Alan Shepard demonstrates how weak the gravitational pull on the moon is by hitting a 6-iron shot on the lunar surface. Shepard claims the ball travels miles and miles, but several hundred yards is a more reliable estimate.

February 6, 1972: The Japanese, who had won only one Winter Olympic medal before the Sapporo Games, sweep the medals in the 70-meter ski jump. The medalists are Yukio Kasaya, Akitsuga Konno, and Seiji Aochi.

February 6, 1976: Sheila Young of the United States wins a gold medal in the 500-meter speed skating competition at the Innsbruck Olympics.

FEBRUARY 7

February 7, 1882: John L. Sullivan knocks out Paddy Ryan in the ninth round to become the first universally recognized bareknuckle heavyweight champion.

February 7, 1949: Joe DiMaggio signs a contract with the New York Yankees making him the first $100,000-a-year baseball player.

February 7, 1972: In an eventful day at the Winter Olympics at Sapporo, Japan, Bernhard Russi of Switzerland wins the men's downhill. In women's figure skating, Beatrix Schuba of Austria builds up an insurmountable lead in school figures and wins the gold medal despite a lackluster seventh-place finish in the freestyle. American Janet Lynn wins the freestyle portion with an unforgettable performance, but finishes only third overall.

February 7, 1976: Toronto's Darryl Sittler scores six goals and four assists in an NHL game against Boston, setting a record for most points in an NHL game.

February 7, 1988: Michael Jordan scores 40 points as the East defeats the West, 138–133, in the NBA all-star game in Chicago.

FEBRUARY 8

February 8, 1887: The first ski jumping tournament is held at the Aurora Ski Club in Red Wing, Minnesota. Mikkel Hemmestvedt wins the event with a jump of 37 feet.

February 8, 1936: University of Chicago halfback Jay Berwanger is the first player selected in the first NFL draft of college players.

February 8, 1983: Wayne Gretzky scores four goals as the Campbell Conference defeats the Wales Conference, 9–3, in the NHL all-star game.

February 8, 1983: Champion thoroughbred Shergar is kidnapped from the Aga Khan's Ballymary Stud, near Dublin. Shergar was never found.

February 8, 1985: Marshall University guard Bruce Morris sinks the longest in-court shot in basketball history in a game against Appalachian State. The length of the shot is measured at 92 feet, 5¼ inches.

February 8, 1986: Spud Webb of the Atlanta Hawks proves he has the right stuff as he wins the NBA Slam Dunk Competition. The 5-foot-7-inch Webb, the shortest player in the NBA, outslams teammate Dominique Wilkins, who stands over a foot taller.

FEBRUARY 9

February 9, 1895: The Minnesota School of Agriculture defeats Hamline College, 9–3, in the first college basketball game.

February 9, 1971: Leroy "Satchel" Paige becomes the first player from the Negro Leagues to be elected to the Baseball Hall of Fame.

February 9, 1968: Jean-Claude Killy of France wins the downhill at the Grenoble Winter Olympics, finishing .08 of a second ahead of countryman Guy Perillat.

February 9, 1972: American Dianne Holum wins the Olympic 1,500-meter speed skating event at the Sapporo Winter Olympics.

February 9, 1980: Houston's Rick Barry makes eight three-point shots in an NBA game against Utah.

February 9, 1986: Marvin Johnson stops previously unbeaten Leslie Stewart to win the light heavyweight boxing title for a record third time.

February 9, 1988: Mario Lemieux scores three goals and has three assists, leading the Wales Conference to a 6–5 overtime victory in the NHL all-star game.

FEBRUARY 10

February 10, 1920: Major league baseball adopts a rule that bars the spitball, shine ball, emery ball, and other doctored pitches.

February 10, 1950: Swimmer Mark Spitz, winner of nine Olympic gold medals, is born in Modesto, California.

February 10, 1953: Gustave Brickner goes for his daily dip in the ice-clogged Monogahela River. Brickner, known as "The Human Polar Bear," ignores the fact that the temperature at the time is 18 degrees below zero with a windchill factor a frigid 85 degrees below zero.

February 10, 1955: Australian golfer Greg Norman is born.

February 10, 1962: Jim Beatty runs the first sub-four-minute mile indoors when he is clocked at 3:58.9 at the *Los Angeles Times* Indoor meet in Los Angeles.

February 10, 1971: Former first baseman Bill White becomes the first black baseball announcer when he joins the New York Yankees' broadcasting team.

FEBRUARY 11

February 11, 1905: James Blackstone of Seattle, Washington, misses bowling a perfect game by the smallest of margins. He is credited with a 299½ when, on his final delivery in the tenth frame, a pin breaks in half and remains standing.

February 11, 1949: "Clever" Willie Pep outboxes Sandy Saddler to regain the world featherweight boxing title in a 15-round decision at Madison Square Garden.

February 11, 1968: Peggy Fleming wins the Olympic figure skating gold medal at Grenoble, France.

February 11, 1969: Diana Crump rides Bridle 'n' Bit in the fourth race at Hialeah Racetrack to become the first female jockey to ride against males in the United States. Crump's mount finishes fifth.

February 11, 1973: The Philadelphia 76ers lose their 20th game in a row. Philadelphia finishes the season with a dreadful 9-73 record, the worst in NBA history.

February 11, 1976: John Curry of Great Britain wins the gold medal in figure skating at the Innsbruck Winter Olympics.

FEBRUARY 12

February 12, 1926: Broadcaster and former major league catcher Joe Garagiola is born in St. Louis, Missouri.

February 12, 1934: Former Boston Celtics great Bill Russell is born in Monroe, Louisiana.

February 12, 1949: Canada annihilates Denmark, 47–0, in the most lopsided international hockey match in history. The mismatch occurs during the world championships, which will be won by Canada.

February 12, 1949: Villanova's Paul Arizin scores 85 points in a college basketball game against the Philadelphia Naval Air Command.

February 12, 1968: Jean-Claude Killy wins the giant slalom at the Grenoble Winter Olympics by a margin of over two seconds.

February 12, 1986: Don Mattingly, an insurance salesman

from Evansville, Indiana, sinks a 31-foot jump shot to win the Million-Dollar Easy Street Shootout during halftime of the Continental Basketball League all-star game. The million-dollar bonus is offered to the fan who can make the longest shot. Although he shares the same name, Mattingly is not related to the New York Yankees' all-star first baseman.

FEBRUARY 13

February 13, 1937: Maribel Vinson wins her ninth United States figure skating championship.

February 13, 1954: Furman basketball star Frank Selvy scores 100 points in a game against Newberry.

February 13, 1964: Twenty-two-year-old Ken Hubbs is killed in a plane crash near Provo, Utah. The Chicago Cub second baseman had been named the National League Rookie of the Year in 1962.

February 13, 1971: Vice-President Spiro Agnew, playing in a golf exhibition at Palm Springs, California, hits a tee shot into the crowd, striking two spectators. After a second shot also goes into the crowd, Agnew calls it quits for the day.

February 13, 1976: Dorothy Hamill wins the gold medal in figure skating at the Innsbruck Winter Olympics.

February 13, 1983: Golfer Isao Aoki pitches in a 128-yard wedge shot for an eagle 3 on the final hole to snatch victory from Jack Renner in the Hawaiian Open. It is poetic justice that Renner will win the tournament the next year.

FEBRUARY 14

February 14, 1951: Sugar Ray Robinson scores a 13th-round technical knockout over Jake LaMotta to win the undisputed middleweight title.

February 14, 1977: Al Hill makes an auspicious debut as he scores five points in his first National Hockey League game. Hill scores two goals and three assists as his Philadelphia Flyers defeat the St. Louis Blues, 6–4.

February 14, 1978: Chicago Latin overpowers Havard St. George, 117–1, in girls' high-school basketball action. Havard St.

George is handicapped by the fact that only ten girls attend the school and only one player on the team can dribble.

February 14, 1980: Leonhard Stock of Austria wins the Olympic downhill gold medal at Lake Placid. Prior to his surprise victory, Stock had never won a World Cup downhill.

February 14, 1984: Ice dancers Jayne Torvill and Christopher Dean of Great Britain win the gold medal at the Winter Olympics at Sarajevo.

February 14, 1988: Fifty-year-old grandfather Bobby Allison holds off son, Davey, by two car lengths to win the Daytona 500, thus becoming the oldest driver to win a 500-mile race.

FEBRUARY 15

February 15, 1932: Eddie Eagan wins a gold medal as a member of the victorious American four-man bobsled team, becoming the only athlete ever to win gold medals in both the Winter and Summer Olympics. Eagan had been the Olympic light heavyweight boxing champion in 1920.

February 15, 1936: Sonja Henie of Norway wins her third consecutive Olympic gold medal in figure skating.

February 15, 1961: The entire 18-member U.S. figure skating team is killed in a plane crash near Berg, Belgium.

February 15, 1968: Anaheim's Les Salvage makes ten three-point baskets in an ABA game against Denver.

February 15, 1973: Friendsville Academy (Tennessee) defeats St. Camillus Academy (Kentucky), 64–43, to end a 138-game losing streak.

February 15, 1978: Leon Spinks upsets Muhammad Ali to win the world heavyweight boxing title.

February 15, 1980: Wayne Gretzky hands out seven assists as Edmonton defeats Washington, 8–2, in NHL action.

February 15, 1988: Pirmin Zurbriggen of Switzerland wins the Olympic downhill at the Calgary Winter Olympics.

FEBRUARY 16

February 16, 1959: John McEnroe is born in Wiesbaden, West Germany.

February 16, 1970: Joe Frazier knocks out Jimmy Ellis in the fifth round to become the undisputed heavyweight boxing champion.

February 16, 1984: Bill Johnson becomes the first American to win the Olympic downhill. Johnson had brashly predicted that he would win after having the fastest training runs. That evening, American Scott Hamilton holds off a strong challenge by Canadian Brian Orser to win the gold medal in figure skating.

February 16, 1986: Major league baseball stars compete in a slow-pitch softball game. The American League stars score eight runs in the first inning and go on to defeat the National League by the score of 20 to 5.

February 16, 1988: Craig Logan, a pastry chef from Melbourne, Australia, wins the Eleventh Annual Empire State Building Run-Up. Logan runs up the 102 flights of steps of the Empire State Building in 11 minutes and 29 seconds.

FEBRUARY 17

February 17, 1926: Suzanne Lenglen of France defeats American Helen Wills, 6–3, 8–6, in a match played in Cannes, France. It is to be the only meeting between these two tennis greats.

February 17, 1931: The first telecast of a sporting event occurs in Japan during a Waseda University baseball game. The signal is transmitted by closed circuit television from the Tozuka baseball stadium to an electronics laboratory, where the image is viewed on a three-foot screen.

February 17, 1953: The Panther Jet that is being piloted by baseball star Ted Williams over Korea is shot down. Williams manages to successfully crash-land the plane and escape injury.

February 17, 1955: Professional golfer Mike Souchak shoots an amazing 27 on the back nine of a round of the Texas Open. Souchak shoots 60 for the round and posts a winning 72-hole score of 257, a PGA record.

February 17, 1968: Jean-Claude Killy wins his third Olympic alpine gold medal of the Grenoble Winter Games.

February 17, 1985: John Walker of New Zealand breaks the four-minute-mile mark for an unprecedented 100th time.

FEBRUARY 18

February 18, 1928: Sixteen-year-old Sonja Henie of Norway wins her first Olympic gold medal in figure skating.

February 18, 1951: The biggest scandal in college basketball history begins to unravel when three players from the defending national champion, City College of New York, confess to accepting bribes to fix games.

February 18, 1965: Frank Gifford announces his retirement from football in order to begin a broadcasting career.

February 18, 1967: Softball pitcher Eddie Feigner strikes out Willie Mays, Willie McCovey, Brooks Robinson, Roberto Clemente, Maury Wills, and Harmon Killebrew in succession during a celebrity exhibition game.

February 18, 1984: Beautiful East German Katarina Witt wins the Olympic gold medal in figure skating at the Sarajevo Winter Olympics.

FEBRUARY 19

February 19, 1928: At St. Moritz, the powerful Canadian Olympic hockey team wins its third consecutive gold medal. The Canadians do not allow a goal during the competition, while averaging 13 goals a game.

February 19, 1962: Tennis star Hana Mandlikova is born in Prague, Czechoslovakia.

February 19, 1982: Bowler Sharie Langford of Whittier, California, sets a women's record when she rolls an 853 series in the qualifying round of the Clearwater Bowling Classic.

February 19, 1984: Brothers Phil and Steve Mahre win the gold and silver medals in the Olympic slalom at Sarajevo. Steve has the fastest first run, but Phil's combined two-run time is .21 of a second better than his brother's.

February 19, 1986: Tennis star Billie Jean King has a mountain named in her honor. The peak in upstate New York is christened Ms. King Mountain.

FEBRUARY 20

February 20, 1952: American skier Andrea Mead Lawrence wins the Olympic gold medal in the women's slalom despite a fall in the first run.

February 20, 1974: Gordie Howe comes out of retirement to sign a million-dollar contract with the Houston Aeros of the World Hockey Association. One of Howe's reasons for returning to the ice is that his sons, Mark and Marty, also play for the Aeros.

February 20, 1982: The New York Islanders set an NHL record by defeating the Colorado Rockies, 3–2, for their 15th consecutive victory.

February 20, 1985: WBC flyweight champion Sot Chitalada of Thailand successfully defends his title with a fourth-round knockout of Charlie Magri of Great Britain. His joy is short-lived, however, when he discovers that his check for $104,000, the winner's share of the purse, has been stolen by a ringside pickpocket.

February 20, 1988: American Brian Boitano wins the Olympic gold medal in figure skating at the Calgary Winter Olympics. Boitano, probably the greatest jumper in figure skating history, narrowly defeats rival Brian Orser of Canada in the long-awaited "Battle of the Brians."

FEBRUARY 21

February 21, 1952: At the Oslo Winter Olympic Games, Dick Button wins his second consecutive gold medal in figure skating. During his long program, Button lands a triple loop, the first time that a triple jump had ever been completed in competition.

February 21, 1953: Niagara College defeats Siena College, 88–81, in a six-overtime basketball game.

February 21, 1979: A girls' high-school basketball game between Melvin and Sibley ends after four quarters in a scoreless tie. The two Sheldon, Iowa, schools battle for four overtimes before Melvin finally prevails by the score of 4 to 2.

February 21, 1980: In a memorable day at the Lake Placid Winter Olympics, Robin Cousins of Great Britain wins the gold medal in men's figure skating. Eric Heiden wins another gold medal in the 1,500-meter speed skating competition. Hanni Wenzel of Liechtenstein wins the women's giant slalom. Wenzel becomes the first athlete from tiny Liechtenstein, a country with a population of less than 30,000, to win a gold medal.

FEBRUARY 22

February 22, 1950: Basketball's Julius "Dr. J" Erving is born in Roosevelt, New York.

February 22, 1958: Australian swimmer Jon Konrads sets six world records in two days at a swim meet in Melbourne.

February 22, 1959: The first Daytona 500 is won by Lee Petty.

February 22, 1969: Barbara Jo Rubin rides Cohesian to a neck victory at Charlestown Racetrack to become the first woman jockey to win a race in the United States.

February 22, 1980: The underdog United States Olympic hockey team defeats the Russian squad, 4–3, to set off a national celebration. A few weeks earlier, the Russians had humiliated the Americans by seven goals.

February 22, 1981: Oh, brother! Brothers Anton and Peter Stastny score eight points apiece as the Quebec Nordiques rout Washington, 11–7. Peter has four goals and four assists, while Anton scores three goals and five assists.

February 22, 1988: American Bonnie Blair wins the 500-meter speed skating gold medal at the Calgary Winter Olympics.

FEBRUARY 23

February 23, 1906: Canadian Tommy Burns wins the world heavyweight boxing title with a 20-round decision over champion Marvin Hart.

February 23, 1958: Five-time world driving champion Juan Fangio is kidnapped by Cuban rebels prior to the Gran Premio de Havana race. Fangio will be released unharmed and shortly thereafter retire from racing.

February 23, 1960: American Carol Heiss wins the gold medal in figure skating at the Squaw Valley Winter Olympics. Heiss will later marry 1956 gold medal winner Hayes Jenkins.

February 23, 1960: Historic Ebbets Field, home of the

Brooklyn Dodgers for over 40 years, is demolished by a wrecking ball painted like a baseball.

February 23, 1980: Eric Heiden wins the grueling 10,000-meter speed skating event at the Lake Placid Winter Olympics to sweep all five speed skating gold medals.

February 23, 1985: Fiery Indiana basketball coach Bobby Knight throws a chair across the court during a loss to archrival Purdue.

FEBRUARY 24

February 24, 1978: Kevin Porter of the New Jersey Nets hands out a record 29 assists in an NBA game against Houston.

February 24, 1980: The impossible dream comes true as the United States Olympic hockey team defeats Finland, 4–2, to clinch the gold medal at the Lake Placid Winter Olympics.

February 24, 1982: In a game against Buffalo, Wayne Gretzky of the Edmonton Oilers scores his 78th goal of the season to break Phil Esposito's single-season NHL scoring record.

February 24, 1985: Quarterback Jim Kelly of the Houston Gamblers throws five touchdown passes during a 34–33 win over the Los Angeles Express. Kelly passes for 574 yards, breaking Norm Van Brocklin's yardage record for a single game. Kelly will also set a professional record by throwing 52 touchdown passes in a season.

February 24, 1988: Ski jumping superstar Matti Nykanen of Finland wins his third gold medal of the Calgary Winter Olympic Games in the team combined event. Earlier, Nykanen had won the 70- and 90-meter jumps.

FEBRUARY 25

February 25, 1929: Marie Boyd sets a girls' high-school scoring record in a game against Ursuline Academy. Boyd scores 156 points as Central demolishes Ursuline Academy, 163–3.

February 25, 1961: St. Bonaventure loses to Niagara, 87–77, and snap their 99-game winning streak at home.

February 25, 1964: Cassius Clay, a seven-to-one underdog, stops champion Sonny Liston in the seventh round to win the world heavyweight title.

field-goal attempt is blocked and Washington's Mike Bass picks off the pass and runs 49 yards for a touchdown.

JANUARY 15

January 15, 1841: Lord Frederick Stanley, the man for whom the Stanley Cup is named, is born. In 1893, as governor general of Canada, Stanley presented the first Stanley Cup to Canada's premier amateur hockey team.

January 15, 1967: The Green Bay Packers defeat the Kansas City Chiefs, 35–10, in the first Super Bowl. The unlikely star of the game is veteran receiver Max McGee, who had caught only four passes all·season but in this game catches seven passes for 138 yards and two touchdowns. One interesting footnote: the game was officially known as the AFL-NFL World Championship Game and wouldn't be called the Super Bowl until 1971.

January 15, 1978: The Dallas Doomsday Defense forces seven turnovers as the Cowboys defeat the Denver Broncos, 27–10, in Super Bowl XII.

January 15, 1984: Hana Mandlikova defeats Martina Navratilova, 7–6, 3–6, 6–4, to snap Navratilova's 54-match winning streak.

JANUARY 16

January 16, 1905: Outfielder Frank Huelsman is traded from the Boston Red Sox to the Washington Senators, marking the sixth time he was traded in eight months.

January 16, 1970: Steve Myers of Pacific Lutheran University makes the longest shot in basketball history when he sinks a basket while standing out of bounds at the other end of the court. The amazing shot is later measured at 92 feet, 3½ inches.

January 16, 1972: Dallas defeats Miami, 24–3, in Super Bowl VI. The Cowboys' running game, led by Duane Thomas, rushes for a Super Bowl record 252 yards.

January 16, 1981: Leon Spinks, the former heavyweight boxing champion, is found unconscious in Detroit. The former champ had been assailed by muggers, who got away with an undisclosed amount of loot, including Spinks's gold front teeth.

January 16, 1988: Jimmy "The Greek" Snyder is fired by

Lakers, 173–139. Boston guard Bob Cousy sets NBA records by handing out 28 assists in the game, including 19 in one half.

February 27, 1982: Earl Anthony becomes the first bowler ever to win over a million dollars on the Professional Bowlers' Tour. Anthony reaches the milestone after recovering from a heart attack that nearly ended his career.

February 27, 1988: Dazzling East German Katarina Witt wins the gold medal in women's figure skating at the Calgary Winter Olympic Games. Witt becomes the first woman figure skater since Sonja Henie to win a gold medal in two consecutive Winter Olympic Games.

FEBRUARY 28

February 28, 1940: College basketball is televised for the first time by station WZXBS. The first half of the doubleheader played at Madison Square Garden features Pittsburgh and Fordham, while the second game matches New York University and Georgetown.

February 28, 1940: Race driver Mario Andretti is born in Trieste, Italy.

February 28, 1960: The underdog United States Olympic hockey team scores six consecutive goals in the third period to defeat Czechoslovakia, 9–4, to clinch the gold medal at the Squaw Valley, California, Winter Games. The victory comes one day after the Americans defeat the Soviets in hockey for the first time.

February 28, 1967: Center Wilt Chamberlain establishes an NBA record by making his 35th consecutive field goal.

February 28, 1981: Houston guard Calvin Murphy sets an NBA record by sinking his 78th consecutive free throw.

FEBRUARY 29

February 29, 1952: Dick Button wins his fifth consecutive world figure skating championship at Paris.

February 29, 1964: In a high school game played in Mamers, North Carolina, Boone Trail defeats Angier, 56–54, in 13 overtimes.

February 29, 1964: Frank Rugani sets a world record in badminton when he drives a shuttlecock 79 feet, 8½ inches in San Jose, California.

February 29, 1972: Superstar Hank Aaron signs a contract with the Atlanta Braves making him the first major leaguer to earn $200,000 in a year.

February 29, 1980: Gordie Howe becomes the first NHL player to score 800 career goals.

MARCH 1

March 1, 1954: On his first day back from service in the Korean War, Ted Williams fractures his collarbone while diving for a sinking line drive during spring training. Ironically, Williams had flown 39 combat missions in Korea without a scratch.

March 1, 1969: New York Yankee great Mickey Mantle announces his retirement from baseball. Mantle hit 536 home runs during his storied career.

March 1, 1973: Robyn Smith becomes the first female jockey to win a major stakes race when she rides North Sea to victory in the Paumanauk Handicap at Aqueduct Racetrack. Smith will give up a promising riding career to become Mrs. Fred Astaire.

March 1, 1983: Tamara McKinney wins the giant slalom race in Vail, Colorado, to become the first American woman skier to win the World Cup overall championship.

March 1, 1988: In a 5–3 victory over Los Angeles, Wayne Gretzky of the Edmonton Oilers breaks Gordie Howe's career NHL record of 1,049 assists.

MARCH 2

March 2, 1951: The West defeats the East, 111–94, in the first NBA all-star game.

March 2, 1962: Wilt Chamberlain scores an NBA single-game record 100 points. Chamberlain scores 31 points in the final quarter to reach the milestone. Wilt the Stilt has 36 field goals and a record 28 free throws as Philadelphia defeats New York, 169–147.

March 2, 1985: In his first fight for Sylvester Stallone's Tiger Eye Productions, IBF junior welterweight champion Aaron Pryor wins a split decision over Gary Hinton at the Sands Hotel in Atlantic City. Stallone, who rose to fame as Rocky Balboa in the *Rocky* movies, is present to offer encouragement to his fighter, who remains unbeaten as a professional.

March 2, 1986: Greinton, trained by Charlie Whittingham and ridden by Laffit Pincay, catches 157-to-1 long shot Herat in the final strides to win the Santa Anita Handicap by three-quarters of a length. The race marks the first time a million-dollar purse is offered for a handicap.

MARCH 3

March 3, 1875: At the Victoria Skating Rink in Montreal, the first recorded hockey game is played.

March 3, 1920: The Montreal Canadiens overpower the Quebec Bulldogs, 16–3, in a National Hockey League contest. The 16 goals are the most ever scored by a team in an NHL game.

March 3, 1966: Buckpasser wins the so-called ''Chicken Flamingo'' at Hialeah Racetrack. Buckpasser is such an overwhelming favorite for the Flamingo Stakes that Hialeah makes the unpopular decision to run the race as a betless exhibition rather than risk losing money. Long shot Abe's Hope passes Buckpasser in the stretch and actually opens a two-length lead before the champion digs in and prevails in a photo finish.

March 3, 1985: A record crowd of 85,327 cheer as 53-year-old Bill Shoemaker rides Lord at War to victory in the $500,000 Santa Anita Handicap to become the first jockey to surpass 100 million dollars in career earnings.

MARCH 4

March 4, 1928: Nearly 200 runners begin a cross-country race from Los Angeles to New York affectionately known as the ''Bunion Derby.'' The winner is the appropriately named Andy Payne, who covers the distance in 573 hours.

March 4, 1930: Emma Fahning of the Germain Cleaning Team bowls the first sanctioned 300 game ever by a woman. The milestone takes place in Buffalo, New York.

March 4, 1941: Chicago Black Hawks goaltender Sam LoPresti sets an NHL record by stopping 80 shots during a game against Boston. Despite his heroics, the Bruins defeat the Black Hawks, 3–2.

March 4, 1968: Joe Frazier stops Buster Mathis in the 11th round of their heavyweight fight in New York. Frazier avenges a loss to Mathis in the 1964 Olympic Trials. Luckily for Frazier, Mathis broke a knuckle in training, giving Frazier the opportunity to win the gold medal.

March 4, 1970: Jacksonville defeats Miami, 101–97, to become the first college basketball team to average over 100 points a game for an entire season.

MARCH 5

March 5, 1973: New York Yankees pitchers Mike Kekich and Fritz Peterson announce the strangest trade in baseball history when they admit that they swapped wives during the off season.

March 5, 1983: Cincinnati Bengals All-Pro wide receiver Cris Collinsworth challenges thoroughbred Mr. Hurry to a match race at Latonia Racetrack in Florence, Kentucky. Mr. Hurry, who had lost 106 of 108 races during his less-than-illustrious career, for once lives up to his name and defeats Collinsworth easily in the 35-yard race. The stunt is the idea of track publicist Andy Furman, who had made a reputation conceiving outrageous sporting events.

March 5, 1984: Brigham Young quarterback Steve Young signs a long-term contract worth 40 million dollars with the Los Angeles Express of the United States Football League. According to the terms of the contract, deferred payments will be made to Young until the year 2027.

March 5, 1988: Evonne Goolagong Cawley, one of the most graceful players ever, is elected to the International Tennis Hall of Fame.

MARCH 6

March 6, 1976: Seventeen-year-old Wilfred Benitez wins a 15-round decision over champion Antonio Cervantes to win the world junior welterweight title.

March 6, 1976: Dorothy Hamill wins the world figure skating championship in Goteborg, Sweden.

March 6, 1981: Denise Biellmann of Switzerland wins the world figure skating championship in Hartford, Connecticut.

March 6, 1984: Dale Hawerchuk has five assists in the second period of an NHL game between Winnipeg and Los Angeles. Hawerchuk leads Winnipeg to a 7–3 victory.

March 6, 1988: Julie Krone rides her 1,205th winner to become the winningest female jockey in history.

March 6, 1988: Orville Moody proves that he's not getting older, he's getting better. Moody shoots a 63 in the final round of the Vintage International Seniors golf tournament. His 25-under-par total for 72 holes is a seniors tournament record.

MARCH 7

March 7, 1930: Georgetown High School of Chicago defeats Homer, 1–0, in the lowest-scoring organized basketball game of all time. Georgetown makes a free throw early in the game, then goes into a stall for the remainder of the contest.

March 7, 1950: Dick Button wins his third consecutive world championship in figure skating. It's a great competition for Americans, as Michael McGean and Lois Waring win the first world ice dancing championship and Peter and Karol Kennedy become the first American pairs skaters to win the world championship.

March 7, 1951: Heavyweight Champion Ezzard Charles wins a 15-round decision over Jersey Joe Walcott.

March 7, 1954: The NBA experiments for one game with raising the baskets to 12 feet. Players have difficulty finding the range as Minneapolis defeats Milwaukee by the score of 65 to 63.

March 7, 1960: Tennis star Ivan Lendl is born in Prague, Czechoslovakia.

MARCH 8

March 8, 1930: Babe Ruth signs a contract with the New York Yankees for a reported $80,000 a year. When Ruth is informed that he is making more money than President Herbert Hoover, the Babe replies, ''Why not? I had a better year than he did.''

March 8, 1958: The ultimate come-from-behind horse, Silky Sullivan, wins the Santa Anita Derby after trailing by 40 lengths early in the race.

March 8, 1968: Six-year-old Tommy Moore scores a hole-in-one at the Woodbrier Golf Course in Hagerstown, Maryland.

March 8, 1971: Joe Frazier wins a hard-fought 15-round

decision over Muhammad Ali in their long-awaited match. The fight is close until the 15th round, when a Frazier left hook floors Ali.

March 8, 1982: Ray "Boom Boom" Mancini stops Art Frias in the first round to win the WBA lightweight title.

March 8, 1986: Martina Navratilova becomes the first tennis player to earn more than 10 million dollars in tournament play.

MARCH 9

March 9, 1976: In one of the biggest upsets in boxing history, little-known Willie "The Worm" Monroe wins a 10-round decision over Marvelous Marvin Hagler.

March 9, 1978: American Charlie Tickner wins the world figure skating championship.

March 9, 1980: How sweet it is! Golfer Ray Floyd shoots a 66 in the final round to win the Jackie Gleason Inverrary Classic in Lauderhill, Florida, and a first prize of $45,000.

March 9, 1981: Buffalo scores nine goals in the second period in a 14–4 victory over Toronto.

March 9, 1984: "Terrible" Tim Witherspoon wins a 12-round decision over Greg Page to claim the WBC heavyweight title vacated by Larry Holmes.

MARCH 10

March 10, 1896: The first modern marathon is won by Greek Charilaos Vasilakos in a time of 3 hours and 18 minutes. The idea for the race of 26 miles, 385 yards dates back to the Battle of Marathon, when a messenger named Pheidippides died after running this distance to relay news of the Greek victory over the Persians.

March 10, 1949: Detroit Tigers pitcher Art Houtteman is critically injured when his automobile collides with a fruit truck during spring training in Lakeland, Florida. Houtteman suffers a fractured skull and is given his last rites. Remarkably, he recovers from the injury and wins 15 games in 1949 after winning only 2 of 18 decisions in 1948.

March 10, 1963: Pete Rose debuts by getting hits in his first two at bats in a spring training game against the Chicago White

Sox. Rose enters the game in the ninth inning as a defensive replacement and has the chance to come to bat only because the game goes into extra innings.

March 10, 1966: Five-time Horse of the Year Kelso is retired from racing.

MARCH 11

March 11, 1892: The first public basketball game is played at the Training School of the International YMCA College in Springfield, Massachusetts. Dr. James Naismith invented basketball three months earlier when he placed peach baskets on the balcony of the YMCA gymnasium.

March 11, 1979: Randy Holt receives 67 minutes in penalties in a National Hockey League game between the Los Angeles Kings and the Philadelphia Flyers. What makes this such a remarkable achievement is that there are only 60 minutes in a hockey game. Holt picks up one minor penalty, three majors, two ten-minute misconducts, and three game misconducts—all in the first period!

March 11, 1985: The first annual Bobby Knight Chair-Throwing Contest is held. The idea evolved after the temperamental Indiana coach threw a chair during a game against Purdue.

MARCH 12

March 12, 1956: Dick Farley of the Syracuse Nationals sets an NBA record he'd rather forget when he fouls out of a game against St. Louis only five minutes after entering the game. Despite Farley's efforts, Syracuse manages to win the game by the score of 97 to 92.

March 12, 1956: Atlanta Braves star Dale Murphy is born in Portland, Oregon.

March 12, 1962: New York Mets outfielder Darryl Strawberry is born in Los Angeles.

March 12, 1966: Bobby Hull, "The Golden Jet," scores his 51st goal of the season, breaking the then single-season NHL record.

March 12, 1984: The British ice dancing team of Jayne Torvill and Christopher Dean become the first skaters to receive nine perfect marks of 6.0 during the world championships.

March 12, 1986: Susan Butcher wins the Iditarod Trail Sled Dog Race, a 1,158-mile odyssey from Anchorage, Alaska, to Nome. Butcher earns a top prize of $50,000 in cold cash. The previous year, Butcher lost the race when she and her dog team were trampled by moose.

MARCH 13

March 13, 1915: Brooklyn Dodgers manager Wilbert Robinson attempts to catch a baseball dropped from an airplane during spring training in Daytona Beach, Florida. Robinson is unaware that the pilot has substituted a grapefruit, which splatters when he tries to catch it. Robinson mistakes the grapefruit juice for blood until he is let in on the joke.

March 13, 1954: Milwaukee outfielder Bobby Thomson fractures his ankle during a spring training game and is replaced by a rookie named Hank Aaron, who will eventually become the all-time home run leader. Three years earlier, while with the New York Giants, Thomson had switched positions to make room for another promising rookie. His name was Willie Mays.

March 13, 1961: In their rubber match, Floyd Patterson knocks out Ingemar Johansson in the sixth round to retain his heavyweight title.

March 13, 1982: American Elaine Zayak, in seventh place after the short program, lands six triple jumps in her long program to win the world figure skating championship.

MARCH 14

March 14, 1963: San Francisco guard Guy Rodgers passes out 28 assists in a game against the St. Louis Hawks to tie the NBA record set by Boston's Bob Cousy.

March 14, 1967: Huge Michigan State defensive end Bubba Smith is selected by the Baltimore Colts as the top player in the first combined NFL–AFL draft. Smith will later star in movies, television, and Lite Beer commercials.

March 14, 1980: Twenty-two members of the United States amateur boxing team are killed in a plane crash near Warsaw, Poland.

March 14, 1987: In Cincinnati, Ohio, Katarina Witt of East Germany wins her third world figure skating championship.

MARCH 15

March 15, 1912: Pitcher Cy Young retires from baseball. Young won 511 games during his career, a record.

March 15, 1958: Cincinnati Royals basketball star Maurice Stokes collapses during a playoff game. His condition is diagnosed as encephalitis, a crippling brain disease. Stokes lapses into a coma and is permanently disabled by the disease.

March 15, 1962: Wilt Chamberlain becomes the first and only player in NBA history to score over 4,000 points in a season. Chamberlain will average over 50 points a game for the season.

March 15, 1962: Donald Jackson of Canada makes figure skating history when he becomes the first man ever to land a triple lutz jump. Jackson receives seven perfect marks of 6.0 from the judges en route to winning the world championship.

March 15, 1987: Golfer Dan Pooley scores a hole-in-one on the 17th hole of the Hertz Bay Hill Classic to win a million-dollar bonus. It is more money than Pooley has earned during his entire professional career, and ten times more than the winner of the tournament received.

MARCH 16

March 16, 1876: Nelly Saunders and Rose Harland participate in the first organized boxing match between women. The bout is staged at Hill's Theater in New York, with the winner to receive $200 and a silver-plated butter dish. Saunders wins a close four-round decision.

March 16, 1937: During a scrimmage basketball game between seniors and sophomores at St. Peter's High School in Fairmont, West Virginia, the last senior player except Pat McGee fouls out with the score tied, 32–32. McGee single-handedly holds the entire sophomore team scoreless and scores the winning points as the seniors prevail, 35–32.

March 16, 1938: Temple defeats Colorado, 60–36, to win the first National Invitational Tournament in Madison Square Garden.

March 16, 1947: Billy Taylor of the Detroit Red Wings sets a National Hockey League record with seven assists during a game against Chicago.

March 16, 1964: Pro football stars Paul Hornung and Alex Karras are reinstated after being suspended for a year for betting on NFL games. Karras is asked to call heads or tails during a coin flip before the game to which he replied, "I can't do that, sir. I'm not allowed to gamble."

MARCH 17

March 17, 1897: Bob Fitzsimmons knocks out James "Gentleman Jim" Corbett in the 14th round to win the world heavyweight championship. When asked to explain his victory over his much larger opponent, Fitzsimmons declares, "The bigger they are, the harder they fall."

March 17, 1917: The first bowling tournament exclusively for women, the Women's International Bowling Congress, convenes in St. Louis. A Mrs. Koester is the winner, with a 162 average.

March 17, 1965: College football coaching legend Amos Alonzo Stagg dies in Stockton, California, at the age of 102.

March 17, 1985: Matti Nykanen of Finland sets a world record when he ski jumps 623 feet during a competition in Planica, Yugoslavia.

March 17, 1987: Mike Tyson wins a lackluster 15-round decision over James "Bonecrusher" Smith to become the undisputed heavyweight champion.

MARCH 18

March 18, 1953: Indiana defeats Kansas 69–68, to win the NCAA basketball championship. Indiana is led by Don Schlundt, who scores 30 points, while Kansas is paced by Bertram Born's 26 points.

March 18, 1953: The National League approves a move that will permit the Boston Braves to move to Milwaukee, the first major franchise shift in 50 years. The Braves' attendance will increase over 600 percent during their first year in Milwaukee.

March 18, 1956: Champion skier Ingemar Stenmark is born in Tarnaby, Sweden.

March 18, 1972: Carolina's Larry Miller scores an ABA record 67 points in a game against Memphis.

MARCH 19

March 19, 1938: The Toronto Maple Leafs score eight goals in less than five minutes in an NHL game against New York.

March 19, 1950: In college basketball, the City College of New York defeats Bradley, 69–61, to win the National Invitational Tournament. Nine days later, these same two teams will meet in the NCAA final, with CCNY once again winning.

March 19, 1955: The University of San Francisco dethrones defending national champion La Salle, 77–63, to win the NCAA basketball tournament.

March 19, 1960: Ohio State, led by Jerry Lucas and John Havlicek, defeat defending champion California, 75–55, in the NCAA finals.

March 19, 1966: Paced by Bobby Joe Hill's 20 points, Texas Western defeats Kentucky, 72–65, in the NCAA basketball finals.

March 19, 1972: In the most lopsided game in NBA history, the Los Angeles Lakers humble the Golden State Warriors, 162–99.

March 19, 1988: North Carolina defeats Loyola of California, 123–97, to set NCAA tournament records for the most points scored in a game and the highest field-goal percentage (79 percent).

MARCH 20

March 20, 1897: Yale defeats Penn, 32–10, in the first major college basketball game ever played.

March 20, 1948: Bobby Orr, probably the greatest defenseman in NHL history, is born in Parry Sound, Ontario, Canada.

March 20, 1954: La Salle defeats Bradley, 92–76, to win the NCAA basketball tournament.

March 20, 1965: UCLA defeats Michigan, 91–80, to win its second consecutive NCAA title. Gail Goodrich scores 42 points for the Bruins, while Cazzie Russell nets 28 for Michigan.

March 20, 1966: Philadelphia goes on a rampage, scoring 24 unanswered points in an NBA game against Baltimore.

March 20, 1973: Roberto Clemente is elected to the Baseball Hall of Fame.

March 20, 1984: Butch Carter scores a record 14 points in an overtime period of an NBA game between Indiana and Boston.

MARCH 21

March 21, 1934: Babe Didrikson pitches one inning against the Brooklyn Dodgers in an exhibition game. Didrikson allows two base runners on a walk and a hit batsman, but gets out of the inning when her Philadelphia Athletic teammates turn in a triple play.

March 21, 1953: The Boston Celtics defeat Syracuse, 111–105, in a wild four overtime playoff game. A record 106 personal fouls are whistled and 12 players foul out.

March 21, 1959: California defeats West Virginia, 71–70, in the NCAA finals. Jerry West scores 28 points in a losing cause.

March 21, 1963: Featherweight champion Davey Moore is knocked out in the tenth round by Sugar Ramos. Two days later, Moore will die.

March 21, 1964: UCLA defeats Duke, 98–83, to give coach John Wooden his first national championship.

March 21, 1970: UCLA defeats Jacksonville, 80–69, in the NCAA championship game.

March 21, 1982: Golfer Jerry Pate celebrates winning the Tournament Players' championship by jumping into a water hazard.

MARCH 22

March 22, 1894: Montreal defeats Ottawa, 3–1, in the first Stanley Cup playoff game. Both teams are amateur; the National Hockey League will not be formed until over 20 years later.

March 22, 1929: It's a race caller's nightmare as a record 66 horses run in the Irish Grand National Sweepstakes.

March 22, 1958: Kentucky defeats Seattle, 84–72, to win the NCAA basketball tournament. Vern Hatton scores 30 points for the Wildcats, while Elgin Baylor scores 25 for Seattle.

March 22, 1969: UCLA defeats Purdue, 92–72, for their fifth national championship in six years. The Bruins' towering center, Lew Alcindor, scores 37 points and is named the tournament's Most Valuable Player for the third consecutive year.

March 22, 1986: Debi Thomas of the United States becomes the first black woman to win the world figure skating championship.

March 22, 1986: Canadian Trevor Berbick wins a decision over champion Pinklon Thomas to become the new WBC heavyweight champion.

MARCH 23

March 23, 1944: Maurice "The Rocket" Richard scores all five goals as Montreal defeats Toronto, 5–1, in an NHL Stanley Cup playoff game.

March 23, 1948: The University of Kentucky defeats Baylor, 58–42, to win the NCAA basketball title.

March 23, 1952: Right winger Bill Mosienko records the fastest hat trick in NHL history when he scores three goals in just 21 seconds to lead the Chicago Black Hawks to a 7–6 victory over the New York Rangers.

March 23, 1956: The University of San Francisco defeats Iowa, 83–71, for their second consecutive NCAA basketball title.

March 23, 1957: Unbeaten North Carolina edges Kansas, 54–53, in three overtimes to win the NCAA basketball championship.

March 23, 1963: Loyola of Chicago defeats Cincinnati, 60–58, in overtime to deny the Bearcats their third consecutive national basketball title.

March 23, 1968: UCLA rolls over North Carolina, 78–55, to win another NCAA basketball crown.

March 23, 1974: North Carolina State defeats UCLA, 80–77, in double overtime in the semifinals, ending the Bruins' seven-year reign as NCAA basketball champs.

MARCH 24

March 24, 1936: The Detroit Red Wings defeat Montreal, 1–0, in a Stanley Cup game that lasts six overtimes.

March 24, 1956: A funny thing happens to Devon Loch as he is apparently on his way to winning the Grand National Steeplechase. The horse, owned by the Queen Mother, is leading by six lengths when he attempts to jump a phantom hurdle and lands on his stomach. His jockey, Dick Francis, will later become a best-selling mystery writer.

March 24, 1962: For the second consecutive year, the

University of Cincinnati defeats Ohio State in the finals of the NCAA basketball tournament.

March 24, 1962: Emile Griffith knocks out Benny "Kid" Paret in the 12th round to regain the welterweight title. Ten days later, Paret will die from head injuries sustained in the fight.

March 24, 1980: Darrell Griffith and the "Doctors of Dunk" present coach Denny Crum with his first national championship as Louisville defeats UCLA by the score of 59 to 54.

MARCH 25

March 25, 1916: Heavyweight champion Jess Willard and challenger Frank Moran battle to a ten-round no-decision. It is the first time that women are allowed to attend a boxing match.

March 25, 1934: Golfer Horton Smith wins the first Masters.

March 25, 1947: Holy Cross defeats Oklahoma, 58–47, to win the NCAA basketball title.

March 25, 1961: The University of Cincinnati upsets Ohio State, 70–65, in overtime to win the national championship.

March 25, 1967: UCLA, led by sophomore sensation Lew Alcindor, defeats Dayton, 79–64, to win its third national crown in four years.

March 25, 1972: UCLA wins its sixth consecutive national title with a hard-fought 81–76 victory over a talented Florida State team.

March 25, 1974: North Carolina State defeats Marquette, 76–64, to win the NCAA basketball championship.

March 25, 1988: In Budapest, Hungary, American figure skater Brian Boitano wins his second world title. Canadian Kurt Browning becomes the first skater to successfully land a quadruple jump, a quadruple toe loop.

MARCH 26

March 26, 1931: Leo Bentley bowls three consecutive perfect games in Lorain, Ohio.

March 26, 1946: Oklahoma A & M, coached by Hank Iba, wins their second consecutive NCAA title with a 43–40 victory over North Carolina.

March 26, 1949: Kentucky repeats as national champions as they defeat Oklahoma A & M, 46–36.

March 26, 1973: Another year, another title. UCLA blasts Memphis State, 87–66, for their seventh straight NCAA title. The Bruins extend their record winning streak to 75 games. Bruins center Bill Walton is unstoppable, making 21 of 22 shots and scoring 44 points.

March 26, 1979: The fast-breaking Michigan State Spartans snap Indiana State's 33-game winning streak to claim the national title with a 75–64 victory. Magic Johnson outscores Larry Bird, 24–19, in a rivalry that will carry on into the NBA.

March 26, 1988: In her final amateur performance, East German figure skater Katarina Witt wins her fourth world championship.

MARCH 27

March 27, 1879: Arthur Chambers defeats Johnny Clark for the lightweight championship in a bout held in Chippewa Falls, Canada. The 136-round fight is the longest championship match in boxing history.

March 27, 1917: The Seattle Metropolitans defeat the Montreal Canadiens to win the Stanley Cup. It is the first Stanley Cup awarded since the formation of the National Hockey League. Previously, the Stanley Cup had been awarded to amateur teams.

March 27, 1939: The University of Oregon Webfoots defeat Ohio State, 46–33, to win the first NCAA basketball tournament.

March 27, 1951: Kentucky wins its third NCAA basketball championship with a 68–58 victory over Kansas State.

March 27, 1952: Clyde Lovellette scores 33 points as Kansas defeats St. John's, 80–63, for the NCAA basketball title.

March 27, 1971: UCLA wins their fifth consecutive national basketball title with a 68–62 victory over Villanova.

March 27, 1978: Kentucky defeats Duke, 94–88, for the national college basketball championship. The star of the game is Kentucky's Jack Givens, who scores 41 points.

MARCH 28

March 28, 1906: Tommy Burns, the shortest heavyweight champion in boxing history, shows he can pack a punch by knocking out on the same night both Jim O'Brien and Jim Walker in the first round.

March 28, 1942: Stanford defeats Dartmouth, 53–38, to win the NCAA basketball championship.

March 28, 1944: Herb Wilkinson sinks a basket with three seconds remaining to give Utah a 42–40 victory over Dartmouth and the NCAA basketball title.

March 28, 1950: The City College of New York becomes the first and only college basketball team to win both the NCAA and NIT tournaments in the same year. CCNY accomplishes the unique double by defeating Bradley, 71–68, in the NCAA championship game. Nine days earlier, they had defeated Bradley, 69–61, for the NIT title.

March 28, 1977: Marquette defeats North Carolina, 67–59, to give retiring coach Al McGuire his first national championship.

MARCH 29

March 29, 1917: The legendary race horse Man o' War is foaled in Lexington, Kentucky.

March 29, 1929: The Boston Bruins finish a sweep of the New York Rangers to win the Stanley Cup.

March 29, 1976: Indiana defeats Michigan, 86–68, to win the NCAA basketball title. Scott May scores 26 points while center Kent Benson adds 25 for the Hoosiers, who finish the season with a 32–0 record.

March 29, 1982: North Carolina defeats Georgetown, 63–62, to give coach Dean Smith his first national championship. Georgetown has the ball with five seconds remaining when Fred Brown inexplicably passes the ball to North Carolina's James Worthy to deny the Hoyas a last-second shot.

March 29, 1987: Ninety-three thousand fans, a record for an indoor sporting event, jam the Pontiac Silverdome to witness *Wrestlemania III*. Hulk Hogan defends his World Wrestling Federation title by becoming the first wrestler to defeat Andre the Giant. In his farewell match, Rowdy Roddy Piper defeats Adorable Adrian Adonis.

MARCH 30

March 30, 1889: John T. Reid unveils the nation's first

golf course, a converted Yonkers, New York, cow pasture. The six-hole course is named the St. Andrews Golf Club in honor of the famed Scottish links.

March 30, 1940: Indiana defeats Kansas, 60–42, to win the NCAA basketball championship.

March 30, 1941: Wisconsin defeats Washington State, 39–34, in the NCAA championship game.

March 30, 1943: Wyoming defeats Georgetown, 46–34, to win the NCAA basketball title. Wyoming's Ken Sailors, with 16 points, is the only player in the game to score in double figures.

March 30, 1945: Oklahoma A & M defeats New York University, 49–45, in the NCAA basketball finals.

March 30, 1981: Indiana defeats North Carolina, 63–50, to give coach Bobby Knight his second national basketball title.

March 30, 1987: Keith Smart hits a jumper with five seconds remaining to lift Indiana to a 74–73 victory over Syracuse in the NCAA basketball championship game.

MARCH 31

March 31, 1928: Hockey immortal Gordie Howe is born in Floral Sask, Canada.

March 31, 1931: Notre Dame football coach Knute Rockne is killed in a plane crash in Bazaar, Kansas.

March 31, 1973: Unknown heavyweight Ken Norton breaks Muhammad Ali's jaw en route to a 12-round decision over the former champ.

March 31, 1975: In John Wooden's final game, UCLA defeats Kentucky, 92–85, for their tenth national championship in 12 years.

March 31, 1980: Behind on points, Mike Weaver knocks out champion John Tate with a devastating left hook in the 15th round to win the WBA world heavyweight title.

March 31, 1985: The tag team of Hulk Hogan and Mr. T defeats Paul Orndorff and Rowdy Roddy Piper in the first *Wrestlemania*.

March 31, 1986: Pervis Ellison scores 25 points to lead Louisville to a 72–69 victory over Duke in the NCAA championship game.

APRIL 1

April 1, 1920: The Ottawa Senators defeat the Seattle Metropolitans in the deciding game of the Stanley Cup playoffs.

April 1, 1938: The Baseball Hall of Fame is opened in Cooperstown, New York.

April 1, 1972: Major league baseball players stage their first collective strike in the game's history. The strike is settled 12 days later, but not before 86 games are canceled.

April 1, 1985: Underdog Villanova defeats Georgetown, 66–64, to win the NCAA basketball title. Villanova shoots an unbelievable 79 percent from the field in upsetting the defending national champions.

April 1, 1985: Author George Plimpton pulls a fast one on the readers of *Sports Illustrated*. Plimpton writes a fictional story about Sidd Finch, a New York Mets pitching prospect who can reportedly throw a baseball a phenomenal 168 miles per hour. The article appears in the April Fools' Day issue.

APRIL 2

April 2, 1931: A teenage girl named Jackie Mitchell strikes out Babe Ruth and Lou Gehrig on six pitches in an exhibition game played in Chattanooga, Tennessee.

April 2, 1935: Mary Hirsch, daughter of famed thoroughbred trainer Max Hirsch, becomes the first licensed female trainer.

April 2, 1966: By the luck of the draw, the New York Mets acquire the rights to pitcher Tom Seaver. Originally, the Atlanta Braves had signed Seaver, but the contract was voided by the baseball commissioner, William Eckert, because the agreement was reached before the end of the college season. The Mets, Philadelphia Phillies, and Cleveland Indians bid for Seaver's services, but New York's name is picked out of a hat.

April 2, 1983: Luther Bradley intercepts six passes in a United States Football League game between the Chicago Blitz and the Tampa Bay Bandits. Bradley returns one of the interceptions 93 yards for a touchdown as Chicago blitzes Tampa Bay, 42–3.

April 2, 1984: Georgetown defeats Houston, 84–75, to win the NCAA basketball title.

APRIL 3

April 3, 1868: The highest wave ever ridden on a surf-board, a 50-foot tsunami, is mastered by a Hawaiian named Holua. Holua rides the wave not for sport but in order to save his life from the tidal wave, which struck Minola, Hawaii.

April 3, 1930: Montreal completes a sweep of Boston to win the Stanley Cup.

April 3, 1936: Lightweight Al Carr knocks out Lew Massey with one punch in a bout that only lasts ten seconds.

April 3, 1966: Los Angeles catcher John Roseboro hits a three-run home run off San Francisco's Juan Marichal in his first at bat against the "Dominican Dandy" since Marichal hit him over the head with a baseball bat. The Dodgers win the spring training game by the score of 8 to 4.

April 3, 1985: Vic Elliot pockets 15,780 balls in 24 hours in a pool exhibition in Lincoln, England.

APRIL 4

April 4, 1948: In one of sports' most unusual competitions, 84-year-old Connie Mack challenges 78-year-old Clark Griffith to a footrace. The Philadelphia A's manager and Washington Senators owner run from third base to home plate, a distance of 90 feet. The race ends in a flatfooted tie.

April 4, 1963: Eighteen-year-old boxer Endzio Barelli dies in Brisbane, Australia, two days after his last fight. Ring fatalities are not uncommon, what makes this a special case is that Barelli won his last fight.

April 4, 1974: Hank Aaron of the Atlanta Braves homers off Cincinnati's Jack Billingham to tie Babe Ruth's all-time record of 714 home runs.

April 4, 1983: North Carolina State upsets Houston, 54–52, to win the NCAA basketball championship.

April 4, 1986: Edmonton's Wayne Gretzky scores three assists to break his single-season record in a 9–3 loss to Calgary.

April 4, 1988: Underdog Kansas, led by Danny Manning's

31 points and 18 rebounds, defeats Oklahoma, 83–79, to win the NCAA basketball championship.

APRIL 5

April 5, 1896: The first modern Olympic Games officially open. The United States is represented by an eight-man team. Four of the Americans are from Princeton University and the other four are members of the Boston Athletic Association. The Americans top all nations with 11 gold medals.

April 5, 1915: Jess Willard knocks out champion Jack Johnson in the 26th round to win the world heavyweight title. Johnson later claims that he took a dive, but although it appears that he was shielding his eyes from the sun while laying on the canvas, most boxing experts now believe the knockout was legitimate.

April 5, 1932: Australian champion thoroughbred Phar Lap is struck down with an ailment "officially" diagnosed as colic shortly after winning the Agua Caliente Handicap. Many believe foul play was involved.

April 5, 1984: Kareem Abdul-Jabbar of the Los Angeles Lakers scores on a sky hook to break Wilt Chamberlain's all-time career scoring record of 31,419 points.

APRIL 6

April 6, 1896: American James Connolly wins the first gold medal in the modern Olympic Games when he places first in the triple jump competition. It marks the first time that an Olympic event has been held since the year 392, when Roman Emperor Theodosius canceled the Games because of riots resulting from charges made by Greek athletes that some of the Roman athletes were professionals.

April 6, 1900: In the shortest heavyweight title fight ever, champion Jim Jeffries knocks out challenger Jack Finnegan in 55 seconds.

April 6, 1954: The Montreal Canadiens score three goals in a 56-second span in a Stanley Cup playoff game against Detroit. Montreal does not score the rest of the game, but hangs on to win, 3–1.

April 6, 1973: New York's Ron Blomberg becomes the first designated hitter in major league baseball history.

February 25, 1977: Pete Maravich of the New Orleans Jazz sets an NBA record for a guard by scoring 68 points in a game against the New York Knicks.

February 25, 1988: Fashion designer Oleg Cassini drives ten-to-one long shot Hi Po Bay Myst to victory in the fourth race at Freehold Raceway. The 74-year-old clotheshorse had received his harness driver's license the day before. Cassini earns the princely sum of $67.50 for his victory.

February 25, 1988: Flamboyant Italian Alberto Tomba wins a gold medal in the giant slalom at the Calgary Winter Olympic Games. Tomba has extra motivation, as his father has promised to buy him a new Ferrari if he wins the race.

FEBRUARY 26

February 26, 1887: Baseball Hall of Famer Grover Cleveland Alexander is born in Elba, Nebraska. In 1952, Hollywood will make a movie about his life entitled *The Winning Team*, with Ronald Reagan portraying Alexander.

February 26, 1918: The worst disaster in sports history occurs as 604 spectators are killed when the grandstand of the Hong Kong Jockey Club collapses and burns.

February 26, 1941: It's a real slugfest as both Pat Carroll and his opponent Sammy Secreet are so battered that they are unable to continue their bout. Referee Clarence Rosen rules the fight a double knockout.

February 26, 1960: American David Jenkins wins the Olympic gold medal in figure skating at the Winter Olympic Games in Squaw Valley, California. He follows in the footsteps of his brother, Hayes, who won the gold medal in 1956.

FEBRUARY 27

February 27, 1890: Boxers Danny Needham and Patsy Kerrigan fight to a 100-round draw in San Francisco. The marathon bout lasts 6 hours and 39 minutes.

February 27, 1959: The Chicago Cardinals trade star running back Ollie Matson to the Los Angeles Rams in exchange for nine players.

February 27, 1959: The Boston Celtics rout the Minneapolis

Dodgers, to break Babe Ruth's all-time record. Aaron will retire in 1976 with 755 home runs.

April 8, 1975: Baseball's first black manager, Frank Robinson, makes his debut a winning one. The Cleveland Indians' player-manager hits a home run in a 7–5 victory over the New York Yankees.

April 8, 1982: Steve Bentley of Sacramento, California, tosses a Frisbee 272½ feet for a new world record. What makes the feat more impressive is that Bentley catches his own throw.

APRIL 9

April 9, 1913: Philadelphia defeats Brooklyn, 1–0, in the first game ever played at Ebbets Field. Dodgers owner Charles Ebbets sells peanuts at the game.

April 9, 1959: The Boston Celtics defeat the Minneapolis Lakers, 118–113, to win the NBA championship in four straight games.

April 9, 1960: The Boston Celtics defeat the St. Louis Hawks, 122–103, in the seventh game of the NBA championship series.

April 9, 1965: The Houston Astrodome, baseball's first indoor stadium, opens with an exhibition game between the Astros and the New York Yankees. Mickey Mantle hits baseball's first indoor home run, but Houston wins the game, 2–1.

April 9, 1974: New San Diego Padres owner Ray Kroc grabs the public address microphone and yells, "I've never seen such stupid baseball!" To prove his point, the Padres lose to the Houston Astros, 9–5. During the game Ted Giannoulas makes his debut as the San Diego Chicken.

April 9, 1983: Mike Boit runs a mile in 3:28.36 in Auckland, New Zealand. The time, almost 20 seconds better than the world record, is accomplished because the race is all downhill.

APRIL 10

April 10, 1896: In Athens, Greek runner Spiridon Louis wins the first Olympic marathon. Louis is showered with gifts, including the hand of a Greek millionaire's daughter and a guarantee of free shoeshines for the rest of his life.

April 10, 1953: The Minneapolis Lakers defeat New York, 91–84, to win the NBA championship series in five games.

April 10, 1955: Syracuse defeats Fort Wayne, 92–91, in the deciding game of the NBA championship series.

April 10, 1956: The Montreal Canadiens defeat the Detroit Red Wings in five games to win the Stanley Cup.

April 10, 1961: Gary Player of South Africa becomes the first foreign golfer to win the Masters when he defeats Arnold Palmer by one shot.

April 10, 1971: The era of table tennis diplomacy begins as the United States table tennis team is invited to play the Chinese in Peking.

April 10, 1988: Dallas Cowboys running back Herschel Walker performs with the Forth Worth Ballet.

APRIL 11

April 11, 1907: In a game against Philadelphia, New York Giants catcher Roger Bresnahan becomes the first player to wear shin guards. The Giants are forced to forfeit the game in the eighth inning when New York fans pelt umpire Bill Klem with snowballs. The innovative Bresnahan will also invent the batting helmet, which he calls the pneumatic head protector.

April 11, 1921: Station KDKA transmits from Pittsburgh the first broadcast of, a sporting event on radio, a boxing match between Johnny Dundee and Johnny Ray.

April 11, 1961: The Boston Celtics defeat the St. Louis Hawks, 121–112, to win the NBA championship in five games.

April 11, 1962: The Amazin' New York Mets debut in characteristic fashion by losing to St. Louis, 11–4. At season's end, the Mets will have lost a record 120 games.

April 11, 1965: Jack Nicklaus sets a tournament record by shooting a 17-under-par 271 to win the Masters by nine shots.

APRIL 12

April 12, 1861: Abner Doubleday, the man who, according to legend, invented the game of baseball, fires the first Union shot in defense of Fort Sumter.

April 12, 1951: The day after President Truman relieves him of his command in Korea, General Douglas MacArthur is nominated to become the new baseball commissioner. MacArthur declines the offer.

April 12, 1954: The Minneapolis Lakers defeat the Syracuse Nationals, 87–80, in the seventh game of the NBA championship series.

April 12, 1958: The St. Louis Hawks defeat the Boston Celtics, 110-109, to win the NBA championship series in six games.

April 12, 1962: Making his major league debut in a game against the Cincinnati Reds, Los Angeles Dodgers reliever Pete Richert strikes out the first six batters to face him. Richert also ties a major league record by striking out four batters in an inning.

April 12, 1987: Hometown favorite Larry Mize sinks a 140-foot chip shot on the second hole of sudden death to defeat Greg Norman and win the Masters golf tournament.

APRIL 13

April 13, 1954: In his major league debut, Hank Aaron of the Milwaukee Braves goes hitless in five at bats against Cincinnati.

April 13, 1957: The Boston Celtics defeat the St. Louis Hawks, 125–123, in double overtime in the seventh game of the NBA championship series.

April 13, 1963: Pete Rose of the Cincinnati Reds collects his first major league base hit, a triple off Pittsburgh's Bob Friend.

April 13, 1975: Jack Nicklaus wins his fifth Masters, edging Johnny Miller and Tom Weiskopf by one shot. Lee Elder becomes the first black golfer to play in the Masters.

April 13, 1978: Reggie! bars are distributed to the 44,667 fans attending the New York Yankees home opener against Chicago. When Reggie Jackson homers in his first trip to the plate, the fans throw thousands of Reggie bars onto the field in tribute.

April 13, 1984: Pete Rose doubles off Jerry Koosman to become the first player in National League history to amass 4,000 hits.

April 13, 1986: Forty-six-year-old Jack Nicklaus shoots a 30 on the back nine and a 65 in the final round to become the oldest golfer to win the Masters.

APRIL 14

April 14, 1910: William Howard Taft begins the presidential tradition of throwing out the first ball on opening day in Washington. Taft watches as Walter Johnson of the Washington Senators pitches a one-hit shutout of the Philadelphia A's, 3–0.

April 14, 1917: Chicago pitcher Eddie Cicotte pitches a no-hitter against St. Louis as the White Sox blank the Browns, 11–0.

April 14, 1941: Baseball great Pete Rose is born in Cincinnati, Ohio.

April 14, 1960: The Montreal Canadiens complete a sweep of the Toronto Maple Leafs with a 4–0 victory, becoming the first team to win five consecutive Stanley Cups.

April 14, 1968: Roberto de Vicenzo loses the Masters because he signs an incorrect scorecard. De Vicenzo finishes the tournament tied with Bob Goalby. His playing partner, Tommy Aaron, incorrectly credits de Vicenzo with a 4 on the 17th hole instead of a 3. De Vicenzo does not catch the mistake and signs the incorrect scorecard. Under PGA rules, he is required to accept the score, and Goalby is declared the winner.

APRIL 15

April 15, 1895: Josephine Blatt sets a women's weightlifting record by lifting 3,564 pounds with hip and harness.

April 15, 1909: New York Giants pitcher Red Ames pitches a no-hitter for nine and one-third innings, only to lose in the 13th inning to Brooklyn, 3–0.

April 15, 1915: Rube Marquard pitches a no-hitter as the New York Giants shut out the Brooklyn Dodgers, 2–0.

April 15, 1947: In his major league debut, baseball's first black player, Brooklyn's Jackie Robinson, goes hitless in three at bats versus Boston.

April 15, 1952: The Detroit Red Wings defeat the Montreal Canadiens to win the Stanley Cup in four straight games. Detroit's Jerry Cusimano throws an octopus on the ice before the game. For the next 15 years, Cusimano will repeat the prank during the playoffs for good luck.

April 15, 1985: "Marvelous" Marvin Hagler knocks out Thomas Hearns in the third round to retain his middleweight championship.

April 15, 1987: Milwaukee's Juan Nieves pitches a no-hitter as the Brewers defeat the Baltimore Orioles, 7–0.

APRIL 16

April 16, 1939: The Boston Bruins defeat the Toronto Maple Leafs four games to one in the first best-of-seven Stanley Cup playoff finals. Previously, the championship series had been the best of five.

April 16, 1940: Twenty-one-year-old Bob Feller pitches a no-hitter on opening day as the Cleveland Indians blank the Chicago White Sox, 1–0.

April 16, 1947: Basketball superstar Kareem Abdul-Jabbar is born.

April 16, 1952: Sugar Ray Robinson comes off the canvas to knock out Rocky Graziano in the third round of their fight in Chicago.

April 16, 1961: The Chicago Black Hawks, led by Bobby Hull and Stan Mikita, defeat Detroit, 5–1, to win the Stanley Cup in six games.

April 16, 1972: Making only his fourth major league start, Chicago's Burt Hooton pitches a no-hitter as the Cubs shut out the Phillies, 4–0.

April 16, 1978: St. Louis pitcher Bob Forsch no-hits the Philadelphia Phillies, 4–0.

April 16, 1983: San Diego first baseman Steve Garvey sets a National League record by playing in his 1,118th consecutive game.

APRIL 17

April 17, 1920: The American Professional Football Association is founded. Two years later, the name will be changed to the National Football League.

April 17, 1947: Jackie Robinson legs out a bunt single for his first major league base hit.

April 17, 1953: New York's Mickey Mantle belts a 565-foot home run off Chuck Stobbs of Washington. The impact nearly tears the cover off the ball, which is found in a backyard one block from the stadium.

April 17, 1955: The Detroit Red Wings win their 15th consecutive hockey game.

April 17, 1969: In only his fourth major league start, Montreal's Bill Stoneman pitches a no-hitter as the Expos defeat Philadelphia, 7–0.

April 17, 1976: Philadelphia's Mike Schmidt hits four home runs in a game against the Chicago Cubs played at Wrigley Field. The Phillies overcome a 13–2 deficit to win, 18–16.

APRIL 18

April 18, 1898: Ronald McDonald wins the second Boston Marathon.

April 18, 1923: New York defeats Boston, 4–1, in the first game played in Yankee Stadium.

April 18, 1945: In his major league debut, one-armed outfielder Pete Gray of the St. Louis Browns goes one for four against Detroit.

April 18, 1962: The Boston Celtics defeat the Los Angeles Lakers, 110–107, in overtime in the seventh game for their fifth consecutive NBA championship.

April 18, 1966: Bill Russell is named coach of the Boston Celtics. Russell is the first black coach in NBA history.

April 18, 1966: The Los Angeles Dodgers defeat the Houston Astros, 6–3, in the Astrodome. The game is played on Astroturf, the first time a major league baseball game is played on an artificial surface.

April 18, 1981: Rochester and Pawtucket of the International League play 32 innings before the game is suspended. The game is resumed on June 23, with Pawtucket winning, 3–2, in 33 innings.

April 18, 1987: Mike Schmidt hits his 500th career home run to give the Philadelphia Phils an 8–6 victory over the Pittsburgh Pirates.

APRIL 19

April 19, 1897: John McDermott wins the first Boston Marathon.

April 19, 1960: White Sox owner Bill Veeck unveils his famed exploding scoreboard at Chicago's Comiskey Park. The game also marks the first time that players' names appear on the backs of their uniforms.

April 19, 1966: Roberta Gibb Bignay becomes the first woman to run in the Boston Marathon.

April 19, 1980: The World Cow-Chip Throwing Championship is held in Beaver, Oklahoma, the self-proclaimed cow-chip capital of the world. Derall Schultz of Melvern, Kansas, wins the event with a heave of 162 feet.

April 19, 1987: The Milwaukee Brewers score five runs in the ninth inning to defeat Texas, 6–4, for their 12th consecutive victory since the start of the season.

April 19, 1987: Pat LaFontaine scores a goal in the fourth overtime to give the New York Islanders a 3–2 victory over Washington in a National Hockey League game that lasts six and a half hours.

APRIL 20

April 20, 1910: Cleveland's Addie Joss pitches a no-hitter against Chicago, winning, 1–0.

April 20, 1912: The Boston Red Sox defeat the New York Yankees, 7–6, in the first game ever played in Fenway Park. Also on this day, Detroit defeats Cleveland, 6–5, in the first game ever played in Tiger Stadium.

April 20, 1916: The Chicago Cubs defeat the Cincinnati Reds, 7–6, in the first game ever played at Wrigley Field.

April 20, 1939: Ted Williams of the Boston Red Sox makes his major league debut. Williams collects his first hit, a double, but New York wins, 2–0.

April 20, 1949: Jockey Bill Shoemaker wins his first race at Golden Gate Racecourse.

April 20, 1985: Carlos Lopes of Portugal sets a world record by winning the Rotterdam Marathon in a time of 2 hours, 7 minutes, and 11 seconds.

April 20, 1986: Chicago's Michael Jordan sets a single-game playoff record with 63 points, but his Bulls lose to the Boston Celtics, 135–131.

APRIL 21

April 21, 1898: Philadelphia pitcher Bill Duggleby hits a grand slam home run in his first major league at bat, the only player to this day ever to accomplish the feat.

April 21, 1944: The Chicago Cardinals and Pittsburgh Steelers of the National Football League announce that they will merge for one season. Despite pooling their talent, Card-Pitt's—or "Carpets," as they are derisively known—lose all of their games.

April 21, 1951: Rochester defeats New York, 79–75, in the seventh game of the NBA championship series.

April 21, 1961: The Boston Celtics defeat the St. Louis Hawks to win the NBA championship in five games.

April 21, 1980: Unknown Rosie Ruiz is the first woman to cross the finish line in the Boston Marathon. Immediately her victory is challenged by other runners who claim that they never saw Ruiz on the course during the race. Ruiz will be disqualified and Jacqueline Gareau named the winner.

April 21, 1985: Ingrid Kristiansen sets a women's world record, winning the London Marathon in a time of 2 hours, 21 minutes, and 6 seconds.

APRIL 22

April 22, 1876: Boston defeats Philadelphia, 6–5, in the first game in National League history. The winning pitcher is Joe Borden, who is rewarded with a then unheard of $2,000-a-year salary. When he fails to live up to expectations, Borden is forced to moonlight as a groundskeeper to earn his pay.

April 22, 1898: Both Jim Hughes of Baltimore and Ted Breitenstein of Cincinnati pitch no-hitters. Pitching in only his second major league game, Hughes no-hits Washington, 9–0. Breitenstein blanks Pittsburgh by the score of 11 to 0.

April 22, 1954: The modern era of professional basketball begins as the NBA adopts the 24-second clock.

April 22, 1959: The Chicago White Sox score 11 runs in the seventh inning of a game against Kansas City on only one base hit.

The Sox take advantage of ten walks, three errors, and a hit batsman in beating the Athletics, 20–6.

April 22, 1970: Tom Seaver strikes out 19 batters as the New York Mets defeat the San Diego Padres, 2–1. Seaver sets another major league record when he strikes out the last ten batters in a row.

APRIL 23

April 23, 1946: Brooklyn pitcher Ed Head, in his first game since returning from the war, pitches a no-hitter as the Dodgers shut out the Boston Braves, 5–0.

April 23, 1950: Minneapolis defeats Syracuse, 110–95, to win the NBA championship in six games.

April 23, 1954: Milwaukee's Hank Aaron hits his first major league home run, off Vic Raschi of the Cardinals.

April 23, 1955: The Chicago White Sox hit seven home runs as they pulverize the Kansas City Athletics, 29–6.

April 23, 1962: Race driver Stirling Moss suffers a near-fatal accident when his Lotus race car crashes in Greenwood, England.

April 23, 1964: Houston's Ken Johnson pitches a no-hitter against Cincinnati but loses, 1–0, on the ninth-inning error by second baseman Nellie Fox.

April 23, 1977: Czech mate! Chess master Vlastimil Hort of Czechoslovakia plays 201 simultaneous games in an exhibition in Iceland and loses only ten.

APRIL 24

April 24, 1901: Chicago defeats Cleveland, 8–2, in the first game in American League history.

April 24, 1906: For the first and last time, dueling pistols is an Olympic event. Leon Moreaux of France wins the 20-meter gold medal and Konstantinos Skarlatos of Greece wins the 25-meter gold.

April 24, 1917: New York's George Mogridge pitches a no-hitter as the Yankees defeat the Boston Red Sox, 2–1.

April 24, 1962: Los Angeles pitcher Sandy Koufax strikes out 18 batters as the Dodgers defeat the Chicago Cubs, 10–2.

April 24, 1963: The Boston Celtics defeat the Los Angeles Lakers, 112–109, in game six of the NBA finals to claim their fifth consecutive title. Guard Bob Cousy plays his last game with the Celtics.

April 24, 1967: Philadelphia defeats San Francisco, 125–122, to win the NBA championship in six games. Philadelphia was one of the greatest teams in NBA history, finishing the regular season with a 68–13 record.

APRIL 25

April 25, 1901: Cleveland's Erve Beck hits the first home run in American League history.

April 25, 1933: New York pitcher Russ Van Atta collects four hits and shuts out the Washington Senators, 16–0, in his debut.

April 25, 1950: The Boston Celtics sign Chuck Cooper, an All-American forward from Duquesne University. Cooper becomes the first black to play in the National Basketball Association.

April 25, 1952: The Minneapolis Lakers defeat New York, 82–65, in the seventh game of the NBA championship series.

April 25, 1964: The Toronto Maple Leafs defeat the Detroit Red Wings in the seventh game of the NHL finals to win their third consecutive Stanley Cup.

April 25, 1965: The Boston Celtics defeat the Los Angeles Lakers, 129–96, in game five of the NBA finals to clinch their seventh consecutive championship.

April 25, 1976: Chicago center fielder Rick Monday becomes a national hero when he rescues an American flag from two people who are attempting to burn it in the outfield of Dodger Stadium.

APRIL 26

April 26, 1851: A rare quadruple dead heat occurs as The Defaulter, Squire of Malton, Reindeer, and Pulcherrima cross the finish line together in the Omnibus Stakes at the Hoo, England.

April 26, 1931: New York first baseman Lou Gehrig hits an apparent home run but is called out after passing teammate Lyn Lary on the base paths. The baserunning blunder costs Gehrig the home run crown, as he and Babe Ruth finish the season tied for the American League lead.

April 26, 1959: Cincinnati pitcher Willard Schmidt has the dubious distinction of becoming the first major league player to be hit by a pitch twice in the same inning. Schmidt is forced to leave the game the next inning when he is struck on the hand by a line drive off the bat of Milwaukee's Johnny Logan. It is a rough day for pitchers, as a record 14 hurlers trudge to the mound in a game won by Cincinnati, 11–10.

April 26, 1964: The Boston Celtics defeat the San Francisco Warriors in game five for their sixth consecutive NBA crown.

April 26, 1975: Jimmy Connors defeats John Newcombe, 6–3, 4–6, 6–2, 6–4, in the Caesar Palace Challenge to win the $500,000 first prize.

APRIL 27

April 27, 1943: Female jockey Judy Johnson rides Lone Gallant to a tenth-place finish in a steeplechase race at Pimlico Racetrack in Baltimore, Maryland. Twenty-six years later, Diana Crump will become the first female jockey to ride in a thoroughbred race in America.

April 27, 1944: Boston Braves pitcher Jim Tobin pitches a no-hitter against the Brooklyn Dodgers. In his previous start, Tobin had pitched a one-hitter.

April 27, 1968: Baltimore's Tom Phoebus pitches a no-hitter against the Boston Red Sox.

April 27, 1968: Jimmy Ellis wins a 15-round decision over Jerry Quarry to claim the vacant heavyweight boxing title.

April 27, 1973: Steve Busby pitches a no-hitter as Kansas City blanks Detroit, 3–0.

April 27, 1983: Houston's Nolan Ryan fans Montreal's Brad Mills to break Walter Johnson's career strikeout mark of 3,508.

APRIL 28

April 28, 1961: Forty-year-old Warren Spahn pitches the second no-hitter of his career. Spahn strikes out nine Giants as Milwaukee wins, 1–0.

April 28, 1966: The Boston Celtics defeat the Los Angeles Lakers, 95–93, in the seventh game of the NBA finals to win their eighth consecutive championship.

April 28, 1967: Heavyweight boxing champion Muhammad Ali is stripped of his title for refusing military induction. Ali will be inactive for three and a half years but will eventually regain the title.

April 28, 1985: World Boxing Association heavyweight champion Greg Page has his championship belt stolen from his hotel room the night before his title defense against Tony Tubbs in Buffalo, New York. The following evening, Page loses the belt for good when Tubbs wins a decision to become the new champion.

April 28, 1988: The Minnesota Twins beat Baltimore, 4–2, to run their losing streak to 21 games, a record for the start of a season.

APRIL 29

April 29, 1892: Philadelphia's Charlie Reilly becomes the first pinch hitter in baseball history.

April 29, 1931: Wes Farrell of the Cleveland Indians pitches a no-hitter against St. Louis. Farrell also bats in four runs as the Indians beat the Browns, 9–0.

April 29, 1933: In a real baseball rarity, Washington catcher Luke Sewell is credited with two putouts on the same play. Both Lou Gehrig and Dixie Walker of the Yankees attempt to score on a base hit by Tony Lazzeri, and both are cut down at the plate on a throw from Goose Goslin.

April 29, 1961: *Wide World of Sports*, hosted by Jim McKay, debuts on ABC with coverage of the Penn and Drake relays from Philadelphia and Des Moines. Originally intended as a twenty-week summer replacement series, *Wide World of Sports* is still going strong.

April 29, 1981: Philadelphia southpaw Steve Carlton records his 3,000th career strikeout in a 6–2 victory over Montreal.

April 29, 1986: Boston's Roger Clemens sets a major league record by striking out 20 batters in a nine-inning game against Seattle.

APRIL 30

April 30, 1922: Making only his third major league start, Chicago's Charlie Robertson pitches a perfect game against the Detroit Tigers.

April 30, 1939: Lou Gehrig, baseball's "Iron Horse," plays in his 2,130th consecutive game, a still-standing major league record.

April 30, 1940: Brooklyn's Tex Carleton pitches a no-hitter against the Cincinnati Reds.

April 30, 1946: Cleveland's Bob Feller pitches his second no-hitter. Feller strikes out 11 in a 1–0 victory over New York.

April 30, 1961: Willie Mays of the San Francisco Giants hits four home runs in a game against Milwaukee.

April 30, 1967: Baltimore's Steve Barber and Stu Miller combine to pitch a no-hitter but lose the game to Detroit, 2–1.

April 30, 1969: Jim Maloney pitches the third no-hitter of his career as Cincinnati blanks Houston, 10–0.

April 30, 1971: The Milwaukee Bucks, led by Kareem Abdul-Jabbar and Oscar Robertson, complete a four-game sweep of Baltimore to win the NBA championship.

MAY 1

May 1, 1884: Catcher Moses Fleetwood Walker makes his debut with Toledo of the American Association, then a major league. Walker becomes the first black player in the majors, predating Jackie Robinson by 63 years.

May 1, 1901: Herb McFarland hits the first grand slam in American League history as the Chicago White Sox defeat Detroit, 19–9.

May 1, 1906: Philadelphia's Johnny Lush pitches a no-hitter and strikes out 11 as the Phillies defeat Brooklyn, 6–0.

May 1, 1920: The Braves and Dodgers play to a 1–1 tie in 26 innings, the greatest number of innings played in a single game in major league history. Both starting pitchers, Joe Oeschger of Boston and Leon Cadore of Brooklyn, go the distance.

May 1, 1948: Citation catches stablemate Coaltown and draws off to a three-and-a-half-length victory in the Kentucky Derby.

May 1, 1962: Bo Belinsky of the Los Angeles Angels pitches a no-hitter against Baltimore in only his fourth major league start.

May 1, 1969: Houston's Don Wilson strikes out 13 and pitches a no-hitter against Cincinnati.

May 1, 1971: Canonero II storms out of the pack to win the Kentucky Derby.

MAY 2

May 2, 1876: Chicago's Ross Barnes hits the first home run in National League history.

May 2, 1917: Cincinnati's Fred Toney and Chicago's Hippo Vaughn combine to pitch the only double no-hitter in baseball history. Vaughn gives up two hits in the tenth inning as Cincinnati wins, 1–0.

May 2, 1939: Lou Gehrig pulls himself out of the Yankee lineup for the first time since 1925. Gehrig will never play another game. Gehrig's replacement, Babe Dahlgren, hits a home run as New York blasts Detroit, 22–2.

May 2, 1953: Long shot Dark Star hangs on to defeat favored Native Dancer by a head in the Kentucky Derby.

May 2, 1964: Northern Dancer wins the Kentucky Derby.

May 2, 1968: The Boston Celtics defeat the Los Angeles Lakers to win the NBA championship in six games.

May 2, 1978: The Portland Trail Blazers defeat Los Angeles, 105–101, to win the NBA championship in four straight games.

May 2, 1987: Alysheba, winner of only one race prior to the Derby, catches Bet Twice in the final furlong to win the Kentucky Derby.

MAY 3

May 3, 1936: Joe DiMaggio of the New York Yankees makes his major league debut against the St. Louis Browns. The Yankee Clipper has three hits in leading New York to a 14–5 romp over the Browns.

May 3, 1941: Whirlaway wins the Kentucky Derby by eight lengths.

May 3, 1958: Tim Tam wins the Kentucky Derby while co-favorite Silky Sullivan finishes 12th.

May 3, 1959: Detroit's Charlie Maxwell hits four consecutive home runs during a doubleheader against the New York Yankees.

May 3, 1969: Unbeaten Majestic Prince wins the Kentucky Derby.

May 3, 1975: Track announcer Chic Anderson mistakenly

calls Prince Thou Art the winner of the Kentucky Derby. Actually, Prince Thou Art is never in contention, finishing sixth, over 12 lengths behind the real winner, Foolish Pleasure.

May 3, 1980: Genuine Risk becomes only the second filly to win the Kentucky Derby.

May 3, 1986: Fifty-four-year-old jockey Bill Shoemaker rides 17-to-1 long shot Ferdinand to victory in the Kentucky Derby.

MAY 4

May 4, 1957: Iron Liege wins the Kentucky Derby by a nose. It appears that Gallant Man is going to win the race when jockey Bill Shoemaker misjudges the finish line. The Derby field is the strongest ever, with Round Table and Bold Ruler finishing third and fourth, respectively.

May 4, 1963: Milwaukee pitcher Bob Shaw sets a record he'd rather forget when he is called for five balks in one game.

May 4, 1965: San Francisco's Willie Mays hits his 512th home run, breaking Mel Ott's National League record.

May 4, 1968: Dancer's Image wins the Kentucky Derby but is disqualified after an illegal drug is found in his system.

May 4, 1974: Cannonade, ridden by Angel Cordero, wins the 100th running of the Kentucky Derby.

May 4, 1984: Dave Kingman hits a towering pop fly that never comes down. The ball gets caught in the ceiling of the Metrodome, and Kingman is credited with a ground-rule double.

May 4, 1985: Spend a Buck leads from start to finish to win the Kentucky Derby by five lengths.

MAY 5

May 5, 1904: Boston's Cy Young pitches a perfect game, defeating the Philadelphia A's by the score of 3 to 0.

May 5, 1917: Ernie Koob of the St. Louis Browns pitches a no-hitter against the Chicago White Sox, winning by the score of 1 to 0.

May 5, 1925: Ty Cobb announces before the Tigers' game with St. Louis that he is swinging for the fences to prove that he can be a home run hitter like Babe Ruth if he puts his mind to it. Cobb proves his point by hitting three home runs in the game.

May 5, 1938: Wayne Lemaster is charged with a loss, despite not allowing a runner to reach base. Lemaster leaves the game with a sore arm with a three-and-one count on leadoff batter Stan Hack. Hack walks and later scores as Chicago routs Philadelphia, 21–2.

May 5, 1969: The Boston Celtics edge the Los Angeles Lakers, 108–106, in the seventh game of the NBA championship series.

May 5, 1973: Superhorse Secretariat wins the Kentucky Derby. Secretariat's time of 1:59⅖ breaks the track record.

May 5, 1979: Spectacular Bid wins the Kentucky Derby.

MAY 6

May 6, 1892: For the only time in major league baseball history, a game is called because of the sun. The game between Boston and Cincinnati is halted in the fourteenth inning with the score tied 0–0 when the setting sun makes it impossible for the batters to see.

May 6, 1915: Babe Ruth of the Boston Red Sox hits his first major league home run, off New York's Jack Warhop.

May 6, 1917: St. Louis pitcher Bob Groom no-hits the Chicago White Sox, 3–0.

May 6, 1933: Broker's Tip and Head Play engage in the most controversial stretch duel in Kentucky Derby history. Jockeys Don Meade and Herb Fisher resort to such dirty tactics as whipping each other and grabbing saddle cloths. Broker's Tip wins by a head.

May 6, 1951: Pittsburgh's Cliff Chambers pitches a no-hitter as the Pirates beat the Braves, 3–0.

May 6, 1953: Bobo Holloman of the St. Louis Browns pitches a no-hitter against Philadelphia in his first major league start.

May 6, 1954: Roger Bannister becomes the first man to run a sub-four-minute mile when he is timed in 3:59.4.

May 6, 1970: Yuchiro Miura of Japan skis down Mt. Everest.

May 6, 1978: Affirmed holds off Alydar to win the Kentucky Derby.

May 6, 1982: The Ancient Mariner, Gaylord Perry, wins his 300th game.

MAY 7

May 7, 1922: Giants pitcher Jesse Barnes pitches a no-hitter against Philadelphia.

May 7, 1925: Pittsburgh shortstop Glenn Wright completes an unassisted triple play against the St. Louis Cardinals.

May 7, 1955: Swaps, ridden by Bill Shoemaker, defeats Nashua, ridden by Eddie Arcaro, by one and a half lengths in the Kentucky Derby.

May 7, 1957: Indians pitching sensation Herb Score is struck in the face by a line drive off the bat of the Yankees' Gil McDougald.

May 7, 1972: The Los Angeles Lakers defeat the New York Knicks to win the NBA championship in five games.

May 7, 1977: Seattle Slew wins the Kentucky Derby.

May 7, 1979: Jeff Sutton and Ricky Tolston, amateur tennis players, begin a match in Kinston, North Carolina, that lasts 105 hours.

May 7, 1988: With a front-running victory, Winning Colors becomes only the third filly to win the Kentucky Derby.

MAY 8

May 8, 1878: Providence outfielder Paul Hines turns in baseball's first triple play.

May 8, 1907: Jeff Pfeffer of the Boston Braves pitches a no-hitter against the Cincinnati Reds.

May 8, 1915: Favored Regret becomes the first filly to win the Kentucky Derby.

May 8, 1929: New York's Carl Hubbell pitches a no-hitter as the Giants blank Pittsburgh, 11–0.

May 8, 1936: Jockey Ralph Neves is declared dead after a fall at Bay Meadows Racetrack. While on the embalming table, Neves unexpectedly revives and rushes back to the racetrack, where fans are mourning his untimely death. His wife, unaware that the reports of his death were highly exaggerated, faints at the sight of the jockey.

May 8, 1968: Oakland's Catfish Hunter pitches a perfect game as the A's defeat the Minnesota Twins, 4–0.

May 8, 1970: The New York Knicks defeat the Los Angeles Lakers in the seventh game of the NBA finals.

MAY 9

May 9, 1901: Cleveland's Earl Moore pitches nine innings of no-hit baseball but loses in the tenth inning to Chicago by the score of 4 to 2.

May 9, 1918: Boston pitcher Babe Ruth has five hits but loses to Washington, 4–3. Ruth will soon give up pitching and become the greatest slugger in baseball history.

May 9, 1930: Gallant Fox wins the Preakness Stakes. In those days, the Preakness was scheduled before the Kentucky Derby. Gallant Fox will win the Derby a week later.

May 9, 1961: Baltimore first baseman Jim Gentile hits two grand slam home runs as the Orioles defeat Minnesota, 13–5.

May 9, 1973: For the second time in his career, this against Philadelphia ace Steve Carlton, Cincinnati catcher Johnny Bench hits three home runs in a game.

May 9, 1984: The Chicago White Sox defeat the Milwaukee Brewers, 7–6, in 25 innings, the longest game with respect to innings played in American League history.

MAY 10

May 10, 1884: Washington catcher Alexander Gardner literally lets the game slip through his fingers. Gardner allows 12 passed balls as Washington loses to New York by the score of 11 to 3.

May 10, 1909: Winchester's Fred Toney pitches a 17-inning no-hitter against Lexington in the Blue Grass League, winning 1–0 and striking out 19.

May 10, 1913: Donerail, a 91-to-1 long shot, wins the Kentucky Derby.

May 10, 1947: Veteran track announcer Clem McCarthy calls the wrong winner in the Preakness. McCarthy's view is blocked on the far turn by spectators standing in the infield and he gets his horses mixed. As a result, McCarthy calls Jet Pilot the winner when it is actually Faultless.

May 10, 1970: Led by Phil Esposito and Bobby Orr, the

Boston Bruins complete a four-game sweep of the St. Louis Blues in the Stanley Cup finals.

May 10, 1973: The New York Knicks defeat the Los Angeles Lakers, 102–93, to win the NBA championship in five games.

May 10, 1981: Montreal's Charlie Lea pitches a no-hitter as the Expos shut out the San Francisco Giants, 4–0.

MAY 11

May 11, 1918: Exterminator, the longest price on the board at 29 to 1, wins the Kentucky Derby. He will go on to become a great champion, winning 50 races during his long career.

May 11, 1919: Cincinnati's Hod Eller pitches a no-hitter against the St. Louis Cardinals.

May 11, 1963: Los Angeles's Sandy Koufax pitches the second of his four career no-hitters, shutting out San Francisco, 8–0.

May 11, 1968: The Montreal Canadiens complete a four-game sweep of the St. Louis Blues to win the Stanley Cup.

May 11, 1972: The Boston Bruins defeat the New York Rangers to win the Stanley Cup in six games.

May 11, 1977: Atlanta Braves owner Ted Turner, his team in the midst of a 16-game losing streak, assumes the role of manager. With Turner in the dugout, the Braves continue their losing ways, dropping a 2–1 decision to Pittsburgh. The next day, National League President Chub Feeney rules that no team stockholder can manage his own team, and Turner's career as manager is over after one game.

MAY 12

May 12, 1910: Philadelphia's Chief Bender pitches a no-hitter against Cleveland.

May 12, 1955: Sad Sam Jones pitches a no-hitter as Chicago defeats Pittsburgh, 4–0.

May 12, 1956: Brooklyn's Carl Erskine pitches a no-hitter, the second of his career, as the Dodgers defeat the Giants, 3–0.

May 12, 1970: Ernie Banks, "Mr. Cub," hits his 500th career home run, against the Atlanta Braves.

May 12, 1974: The Boston Celtics defeat the Milwaukee Bucks, 102–87 in the seventh game of the NBA finals.

May 12, 1979: Tracy Austin defeats Chris Evert, 6–4, 2–6, 7–6, in the semifinals of the Italian Open to snap Evert's 125-match winning streak on clay, which dated back to August 12, 1973.

May 12, 1984: Joe Lucius of Tiffin, Ohio, scores a hole-in-one on the 15th hole of the Mohawk Golf Course, the 13th time he has aced that particular hole.

MAY 13

May 13, 1942: Boston Braves pitcher Jim Tobin belts three home runs in a game against Chicago.

May 13, 1952: ''Rocket'' Ron Necciai strikes out 27 batters in a nine-inning no-hitter against Welch in the Class D Appalachian League. Called up by the Pittsburgh Pirates later in the season, Necciai will be unable to duplicate his minor league success, winning only one game in the majors.

May 13, 1958: Stan Musial of the St. Louis Cardinals collects his 3,000th major league hit.

May 13, 1967: An octagonal boxing ring is tested in the West Orange Armory, in New Jersey. The purpose of the experiment is to see if the octagonal ring will prevent boxers from being trapped in the corners, where serious injuries often occur.

May 13, 1973: Aging tennis hustler Bobby Riggs surprises women's tennis champion Margaret Smith Court in straight sets in their Mother's Day match in Ramona, California.

May 13, 1983: Reggie Jackson becomes the first player to strike out 2,000 times in a career.

MAY 14

May 14, 1874: Harvard defeats McGill University of Canada, 3 goals to 0, in the first football game where admission is charged.

May 14, 1894: A fire breaks out beneath the right-field bleachers during a game between Baltimore and Boston. The fire spreads quickly, destroying over 170 adjoining buildings in Boston, before the blaze can be brought under control. Amazingly, no lives are lost.

May 14, 1914: Chicago's Jim Scott pitches nine innings of no-hit ball before losing to Washington, 1–0, in ten innings.

April 6, 1985: American Randy Dickison breaks the world record in the high dive with a leap of 174 feet, 8 inches at Hong Kong's Ocean Park. The record isn't the only thing Dickison breaks, as he suffers a leg fracture.

April 6, 1987: Sugar Ray Leonard wins a 12-round decision over "Marvelous" Marvin Hagler to claim the world middleweight title.

APRIL 7

April 7, 1935: At the Masters golf tournament, Gene Sarazen sinks a 220-yard four-wood shot on the 15th hole for a double eagle. The miracle shot enables Sarazen to tie Craig Wood for the lead, necessitating an 18-hole playoff that Sarazen will win by five shots.

April 7, 1951: Ben Hogan wins the Masters golf tournament.

April 7, 1956: The Philadelphia Warriors defeat Fort Wayne, 99–88, to win the NBA championship four games to one.

April 7, 1963: Jack Nicklaus wins the Masters golf tournament.

April 7, 1968: In Hockenheim, West Germany, former world driving champion Jim Clark of Scotland is killed instantly when his race car leaves the course at 175 miles per hour and strikes a tree.

April 7, 1979: Houston's Ken Forsch no-hits Atlanta, 6–0, making Forsch and his brother, Bob, the first brother combination to pitch no-hitters. Bob had pitched a no-hitter on April 16, 1978.

April 7, 1984: Detroit's Jack Morris pitches a no-hitter against the Chicago White Sox. The Tigers win by the score of 4 to 0.

APRIL 8

April 8, 1940: Boston Celtics great John Havlicek is born in Martin's Ferry, Ohio.

April 8, 1943: The Detroit Red Wings complete a four-game sweep of the Boston Bruins to win the Stanley Cup.

April 8, 1946: Hall of Fame pitcher Jim "Catfish" Hunter is born.

April 8, 1954: All-star catcher Gary Carter is born in Culver City, California.

April 8, 1974: Hank Aaron of the Atlanta Braves hits the 715th home run of his career, off Al Downing of the Los Angeles

May 14, 1967: Mickey Mantle of the New York Yankees hits his 500th career home run in a game against the Baltimore Orioles.

May 14, 1977: Kansas City's Jim Colborn pitches a no-hitter against the Texas Rangers.

May 14, 1977: The Montreal Canadiens complete a four-game sweep of the Boston Bruins to win the Stanley Cup.

May 14, 1981: The Boston Celtics defeat Houston, 102–91, in game six to win their 14th NBA championship.

MAY 15

May 15, 1862: The first baseball park, the Union Grounds in Brooklyn, is opened.

May 15, 1919: The 13th proves to be an unlucky inning for Brooklyn Dodgers pitcher Al Mamaux. Mamaux is pitching a shutout for 12 innings when Cincinnati erupts for ten runs to win, 10–0.

May 15, 1944: Cincinnati's Clyde Shoun pitches a no-hitter as the Reds shut out Boston, 1–0.

May 15, 1952: Detroit's Virgil Trucks pitches a no-hitter against the Washington Senators.

May 15, 1960: Chicago's Don Cardwell pitches a no-hitter against the St. Louis Cardinals.

May 15, 1973: California's Nolan Ryan pitches the first of his record five career no-hitters, a 3–0 victory over Kansas City.

May 15, 1981: Cleveland's Len Barker pitches a perfect game as the Indians defeat the Toronto Blue Jays, 3–0.

May 15, 1982: Sixteen-year-old jockey Jack Kaenel rides Aloma's Ruler to victory in the Preakness.

MAY 16

May 16, 1869: The Cincinnati Red Stockings, baseball's first all-professional team, play their first game, defeating Antioch, 41–7.

May 16, 1883: Buffalo catcher Jack Rowe commits seven errors in a game against Providence.

May 16, 1933: Washington's Cecil Travis becomes the first player to collect five hits in his first major league game.

May 16, 1939: The Cleveland Indians defeat the Philadelphia A's, 8–3, in the first night game in American League history.

May 16, 1954: Boston's Ted Williams returns to the lineup for the first time since he broke his collarbone in March. Williams responds by collecting eight hits in a doubleheader against Detroit.

May 16, 1957: Mickey Mantle, Billy Martin, Hank Bauer, Whitey Ford, Yogi Berra, and Johnny Kucks of the New York Yankees are involved in a brawl at the Copacabana nightclub in New York. The donnybrook starts when the players come to the defense of entertainer Sammy Davis, Jr.

May 16, 1980: The Los Angeles Lakers defeat the Philadelphia 76ers, 123–107, to win the NBA championship in six games.

MAY 17

May 17, 1875: Aristides wins the first running of the Kentucky Derby. Only $495 is wagered on the race, and Aristides' winning share of the purse is a mere $2,850.

May 17, 1924: Black Gold wins the Kentucky Derby.

May 17, 1963: Houston's Don Nottebart pitches a no-hitter against Philadelphia.

May 17, 1970: Atlanta's Hank Aaron collects his 3,000th career base hit.

May 17, 1975: Master Derby is sent off at odds of 23 to 1 in the Preakness. The handsome chestnut colt wins by a length to become the biggest long-shot winner in the history of the Preakness.

May 17, 1979: The wind is blowing out at Wrigley Field as the Philadelphia Phillies defeat the Chicago Cubs, 23–22.

May 17, 1983: The New York Islanders complete a four-game sweep of the Edmonton Oilers for their fourth consecutive Stanley Cup.

MAY 18

May 18, 1882: Louisville's ambidextrous pitcher Tony Mullane throws both left- and right-handed in a game against Philadelphia.

May 18, 1897: Bill Joyce of the New York Giants sets a major league record by hitting four triples in a game against Pittsburgh.

May 18, 1950: St. Louis third baseman Tommy Glaviano makes errors on three consecutive ground balls.

May 18, 1957: Speedy Bold Ruler wins the Preakness.

May 18, 1958: Carroll Hardy, a lifetime .225 batter, pinch hits for future home run king Roger Maris. Hardy hits a home run.

May 18, 1968: Washington's Frank Howard hits his tenth home run over a six-game period.

May 18, 1972: John Sebastian makes 63 consecutive free throws while blindfolded during an exhibition in Park Ridge, Illinois.

May 18, 1974: Little Current, brilliantly ridden by Miguel Rivera, wins the Preakness by seven lengths.

May 18, 1985: In the Preakness, Tank's Prospect closes with a furious rush to defeat odds-on favorite Chief's Crown by a head.

MAY 19

May 19, 1929: Two people are crushed to death following a stampede at Yankee Stadium caused by a sudden rainstorm.

May 19, 1973: Secretariat makes a bold move down the backstretch to win the Preakness Stakes in near record time. Although two clockers time the race in a record 1:53⅖s, the official time is 1:55. As a result, this is the only race in the Triple Crown that Secretariat does not break the stakes record.

May 19, 1974: The Philadelphia Flyers defeat the Boston Bruins to win the Stanley Cup in six games.

May 19, 1984: Wayne Gretzky scores two first-period goals as the Edmonton Oilers defeat the New York Islanders, 5–2, to win the Stanley Cup in five games.

May 19, 1984: Gate Dancer, trained by Jack Van Berg, wins the Preakness Stakes in a track record time of 1:53⅗. Gate Dancer wears large purple earmuffs to shield the crowd noise.

MAY 20

May 20, 1960: A game between the Chicago Cubs and Milwaukee Braves in Milwaukee's County Stadium is called in the fifth inning because a dense fog makes it impossible to see.

May 20, 1961: Kentucky Derby winner Carry Back wins the Preakness Stakes.

May 20, 1964: Heavyweight Buster Mathis defeats Joe Frazier to qualify for the United States Olympic boxing team. Prior to the Olympics, Mathis is injured and Frazier replaces him on the team. Frazier will go on to win the gold medal.

May 20, 1967: Damascus, a disappointing third in the Kentucky Derby, returns to form to win the Preakness Stakes.

May 20, 1970: Golfer Bill Burke shoots a round of 57 on the Normandie Golf Course in St. Louis, Missouri.

May 20, 1978: Affirmed once again holds off late-running Alydar to win the Preakness.

MAY 21

May 21, 1930: After hitting three home runs in a game against the Philadelphia A's, New York's Babe Ruth elects to bat right-handed in his final trip to the plate. The one-time-only experiment in switch-hitting fails as the Babe is struck out by Jack Quinn.

May 21, 1952: The Brooklyn Dodgers score 15 runs in the first inning of a game against Cincinnati, as 19 consecutive batters reach base. The Dodgers bomb the Reds, 19–1.

May 21, 1960: The ill-fated Bally Ache wins the Preakness.

May 21, 1963: Cincinnati pitcher Jim Maloney strikes out eight batters in a row and 16 overall as the Reds shut out the Milwaukee Braves, 2–0.

May 21, 1977: Unbeaten Seattle Slew wins the Preakness Stakes in Baltimore, Maryland.

May 21, 1981: The New York Islanders defeat the Minnesota North Stars, 5–1, in game five of the NHL finals to win their second consecutive Stanley Cup.

MAY 22

May 22, 1883: Chicago's Billy Sunday strikes out four times in his major league debut. Years later, Sunday will see the light and quit baseball to become an evangelist. Over the next two decades, he will convert millions of followers, using baseball terminology in his sermons and mesmerizing his audiences with his famous "slide for souls."

May 22, 1911: Boston Braves pitcher Cliff Curtis sets a major league record by losing his 23rd game in a row.

May 22, 1930: The New York Yankees belt 14 home runs as

the Bronx Bombers sweep the Philadelphia A's by the scores of 10 to 1 and 20 to 13.

May 22, 1936: A black gelding named Rushaway, ridden by Johnny Longden, wins the Illinois Derby at Aurora Racetrack near Chicago. Immediately after the race the horse is vanned to Latonia Racecourse in Kentucky where the next day he will win the one-and-a-quarter-mile Latonia Derby by six lengths.

MAY 23

May 23, 1876: Boston's Joe Borden pitches the first no-hitter in National League history. It isn't found in the record books, because the official scorer counted two bases on balls issued by Borden as base hits.

May 23, 1883: The Snorkey Baseball Club of Philadelphia defeats the Hoppers, 34–11, in one of the strangest baseball games on record. The Snorkeys are one-armed players, while the Hoppers are all one-legged players. Most of the players are employees of the Reading Railroad who lost limbs in accidents while working on the railroad.

May 23, 1901: The Cleveland Indians stage one of the greatest comebacks in baseball history when they score nine runs after two are out in the ninth inning to defeat Washington, 14–13.

May 23, 1922: Light heavyweight boxer Harry Greb wins a 15-round decision over Gene Tunney, handing the future heavyweight champ his only loss as a professional. Greb, who lost an eye during World War I, would sometimes remove his artificial eye during a match to startle his opponent.

MAY 24

May 24, 1883: Heavyweight boxing champion John L. Sullivan is the winning pitcher as the New York Metropolitans defeat a team of major leaguers, 20–15, in an exhibition game at New York's Polo Grounds.

May 24, 1935: Cincinnati defeats Philadelphia, 2–1, in the first night game in major league baseball history.

May 24, 1936: New York's Tony Lazzeri hits two grand slam home runs and sets an American League record with 11 runs batted in as the Yankees crush Philadelphia, 25–2.

May 24, 1981: Bobby Unser crosses the finish line first in the Indianapolis 500. After viewing films, officials penalize Unser one lap for passing under the yellow flag and name Mario Andretti the winner. Months later, the decision will once again be reversed and Unser will become the official winner.

May 24, 1986: The Montreal Canadiens defeat Calgary, 4–3, in game five to win their 23rd Stanley Cup.

May 24, 1987: Forty-seven-year-old Al Unser wins his fourth Indianapolis 500.

MAY 25

May 25, 1899: Louisville pitcher Deacon Phillippe pitches a no-hitter against the New York Giants.

May 25, 1900: Seventy-year-old Sir Eyre Massey Shaw of Great Britain becomes the oldest gold medalist in Olympic history when he wins the 2-3-ton-class yachting race.

May 25, 1935: In one of the greatest sporting feats of all time, Jesse Owens sets five world records and equals another in the Big Ten Conference track and field meet. Owens accomplishes all this in just 45 minutes.

May 25, 1935: Boston's Babe Ruth hits three home runs in a game against the Pittsburgh Pirates. They are the last home runs Ruth will ever hit.

May 25, 1951: New York Giants rookie Willie Mays goes hitless in five trips to the plate in his major league debut.

May 25, 1965: Heavyweight champion Muhammad Ali knocks out Sonny Liston in the first round of their return fight in Lewiston, Maine.

May 25, 1975: Golden State defeats Washington, 96–95, to win the NBA title in four straight games.

MAY 26

May 26, 1930: Cleveland's Joe Sewell is struck out twice by Chicago's Pat Caraway. Sewell, the hardest man to strike out in baseball history, will not strike out again the rest of the season.

May 26, 1956: Johnny Klippstein, Hersh Freeman, and Joe Black combine to pitch nine and two-thirds innings of hitless baseball against Milwaukee. However, the Reds lose to the Braves, 2–1, in 11 innings.

May 26, 1959: Pittsburgh's Harvey Haddix pitches 12 perfect innings against Milwaukee, only to lose, 1–0, in the 13th inning.

May 26, 1975: Playing in the Surrey Tennis Championships, Keith Glass of Great Britain and Anthony Fawcett of Rhodesia play the longest game in tennis history. The game has 80 points and lasts 31 minutes.

May 26, 1985: Danny Sullivan recovers from a spin on the 120th lap and wins the Indianapolis 500 by 2.4 seconds over Mario Andretti.

May 26, 1988: The Edmonton Oilers defeat the Boston Bruins, 6–3, to win the Stanley Cup in four straight games.

MAY 27

May 27, 1873: Survivor wins the first Preakness Stakes.

May 27, 1928: Aerial golf makes its debut at the Old Westbury Golf Club in New York. Two teams compete, one member in an airplane and the other on the ground. A ball is dropped from the airplane as close to the hole as possible and the golfer on the ground putts out. The team of M. M. Merrill and William Hammond win the match 3 up.

May 27, 1937: New York pitcher Carl Hubbell wins a record 24th consecutive game by defeating Cincinnati, 3–2.

May 27, 1975: The Philadelphia Flyers, known as the "Broad Street Bullies," defeat the Buffalo Sabres to win the Stanley Cup in six games.

May 27, 1981: Third baseman Lenny Randle gets down on his hands and knees to blow a slow roller down the third-base line foul. The umpire is not impressed with his efforts and awards the batter first base.

May 27, 1985: Kentucky Derby winner Spend a Buck holds off Creme Fraiche to win the Jersey Derby. The victory is worth 2.6 million dollars, the largest payday in racing history.

MAY 28

May 28, 1917: Boxer Freddie Welsh is counted out while still on his feet during a bout with Benny Leonard. Welsh, out on his feet, is leaning on the ropes when the referee, seeing his helpless condition, begins the count. At the count of ten, Welsh collapses unconscious to the floor.

May 28, 1951: Willie Mays of the New York Giants gets his first major league base hit, a home run off Boston's Warren Spahn. It is Mays's only hit in his first 26 at bats.

May 28, 1955: Nashua, second to Swaps in the Kentucky Derby, wins the Preakness.

May 28, 1956: Pittsburgh's Dale Long hits a home run off Brooklyn's Carl Erskine to become the first player to hit home runs in eight consecutive games.

May 28, 1980: Both Dwayne Murphy and Wayne Gross of the Oakland A's steal home in the first inning of a 6–3 win over Kansas City.

MAY 29

May 29, 1973: Gordon Johncock wins the rain-shortened Indianapolis 500, a race marred by horrible crashes and two fatalities.

May 29, 1977: A. J. Foyt wins the Indianapolis 500 for a record fourth time. Janet Guthrie becomes the first woman to drive in the racing classic.

May 29, 1977: Sue Press becomes the first woman golfer to hit consecutive holes-in-one when she aces the 13th and 14th holes of the Chatswood Golf Course in Sydney, Australia.

May 29, 1983: Tom Sneva discards his bridesmaid image by winning the Indianapolis 500. Late in the race, Al Unser, Sr., is leading, with Sneva in second place. Unser's son, Al, Jr., tries running interference for his dad, and it appears Sneva may be unable to get by. Finally, Sneva is able to pass both Unsers and pull away to take the checkered flag.

May 29, 1987: In college baseball, Oklahoma State's Robin Ventura singles during the Cowboys' 8–3 victory over Arizona State to extend his NCAA record hitting streak to 57 games.

MAY 30

May 30, 1894: After going nothing for six in the first game of a doubleheader, Boston's Bobby Lowe hits four home runs off

Cincinnati's Icebox Chamberlain as Boston wins the nightcap, 20–11.

May 30, 1911: Ray Harroun wins the first Indianapolis 500, with an average speed of 74.59 miles per hour.

May 30, 1912: Ralph De Palma is leading the Indianapolis 500 on the final lap when a connecting rod on his Mercedes snaps. De Palma pushes his car across the finish line but is disqualified and placed 11th. Joe Dawson is the official winner.

May 30, 1913: Drinking and driving don't mix, but don't tell race-car driver Jules Goux. The dapper Frenchman drinks champagne during pit stops on his way to winning the Indianapolis 500.

May 30, 1925: Peter DePaolo, driving a Duesenberg, becomes the first driver to average over 100 miles per hour in the Indianapolis 500.

May 30, 1977: Cleveland pitcher Dennis Eckersley pitches a no-hitter against the California Angels.

MAY 31

May 31, 1914: Chicago's Joe Benz pitches a no-hitter as the White Sox defeat Cleveland, 6–1.

May 31, 1920: Gaston Chevrolet wins the Indianapolis 500. Ironically, he drives a Monroe and not a Chevrolet to victory.

May 31, 1927: Detroit first baseman Johnny Neun makes an unassisted triple play against Cleveland.

May 31, 1937: The Brooklyn Dodgers defeat the New York Giants, 10–3, to snap pitcher Carl Hubbell's 24-game winning streak.

May 31, 1965: World driving champion Jim Clark of Scotland becomes the first foreigner in 49 years to win the Indianapolis 500.

May 31, 1967: A. J. Foyt wins the Indianapolis 500 when leader Parnelli Jones, driving a turbine car, breaks down with three laps remaining.

May 31, 1975: Fred Newman, an amateur basketball player, makes 12,874 baskets in one day during a basketball exhibition in San Jose, California.

May 31, 1983: The Philadelphia 76ers defeat the Los Angeles Lakers, 115–108, to win the NBA championship in four straight games.

JUNE 1

June 1, 1893: Boston pitcher Harry Staley aids his own cause by driving in nine runs in a 15–4 win over Louisville.

June 1, 1937: Chicago's Bill Dietrich pitches a no-hitter as the White Sox blank St. Louis, 8–0.

June 1, 1939: Heavyweight Lou Nova knocks out former champ Max Baer in the 11th round in the first boxing match televised in the U.S.

June 1, 1946: Assault wins the Belmont Stakes to capture the Triple Crown.

June 1, 1952: Middleweight Peter Muller decks referee Max Pippow during a match against Hans Stretz in Cologne. When another referee enters the ring, Muller proceeds to throw him out onto the concrete floor.

June 1, 1967: Dragon Blood, a 10,000-to-1 long shot ridden by Lester Piggott, wins the Primio Naviglio in Milan, Italy.

June 1, 1975: Nolan Ryan pitches his fourth career no-hitter, blanking Baltimore, 1–0.

June 1, 1979: The Seattle Supersonics defeat Washington, 97–93, to win the NBA championship series in five games.

JUNE 2

June 2, 1893: The first night game in baseball history takes place between two amateur teams in Fort Wayne, Indiana. Fort Wayne defeats Quincy by the score of 19 to 11. It will be another 42 years before a night game will be played in the major leagues.

June 2, 1941: Lou Gehrig dies from amyotrophic lateral sclerosis at the age of 37.

June 2, 1951: Tarboro scores 24 runs in one inning in a Class D minor league game against Wilson. The first 25 batters reach base in the fifth inning as Tarboro rolls to a 31–4 victory.

June 2, 1974: Golfer Robert Taylor aces the same hole for the third consecutive day on a course in Hunstanton, Norfolk, England.

June 2, 1985: Nancy Lopez wins the LPGA golf tournament by eight strokes.

JUNE 3

June 3, 1851: The New York Knickerbockers become the first baseball team to wear uniforms. The Knickerbockers wear blue trousers, white shirts, and straw hats as they defeat the Washington Club of Yorkville, 21–11.

June 3, 1888: The *San Francisco Examiner* publishes Ernest Thayer's poem "Casey at the Bat." The inspiration for the poem may have been Dan Casey or his brother Dennis, both major leaguers.

June 3, 1918: Boston's Dutch Leonard pitches a no-hitter as the Red Sox defeat the Detroit Tigers, 5–0.

June 3, 1932: New York first baseman Lou Gehrig hits four home runs as the Yankees defeat Philadelphia, 20–13.

June 3, 1956: Chicago's Nellie Fox earns the dubious distinction of becoming the only player ever to be hit by a pitch twice in the same at bat. Fox is plunked on the backside by Baltimore pitcher Johnny Schmitz but the home plate umpire rules that Fox had not attempted to get out of the way of the pitch. On the next pitch Fox is hit in the same spot and awarded first base.

June 3, 1971: Chicago's Ken Holtzman pitches a no-hitter as the Cubs shut out the Reds, 1–0.

June 3, 1984: Patty Sheehan wins the LPGA golf tournament by ten strokes.

JUNE 4

June 4, 1927: In Worcester, Massachusetts, the United States defeats Great Britain in the first Ryder Cup golf match.

June 4, 1956: The Soviet Union defeats Switzerland, 153–25, in the most lopsided international basketball game on record.

June 4, 1964: Los Angeles's Sandy Koufax pitches his third career no-hitter as he defeats Philadelphia, 3–0.

June 4, 1968: Don Drysdale sets a major league record by pitching his sixth consecutive shutout as Los Angeles defeats Pittsburgh, 5–0.

June 4, 1974: The Cleveland Indians' 10¢ beer night promotion backfires. In the ninth inning, with the score tied 5–5, drunken fans start coming onto the field. When order cannot be restored, the game is forfeited to Texas.

June 4, 1976: In one of the greatest games in NBA history, the Boston Celtics defeat the Phoenix Suns, 128–126, in three overtimes in the fifth game of their championship series.

June 4, 1987: The 122-race winning streak of Edwin Moses comes to an end when American Danny Harris defeats him by .13 of a second in a 400-meter hurdle race at the Madrid International Meet.

JUNE 5

June 5, 1937: War Admiral wins the Belmont Stakes to complete his Triple Crown sweep.

June 5, 1943: Count Fleet wins the Belmont Stakes by 25 lengths to annex the Triple Crown.

June 5, 1964: Seventeen-year-old Jim Ryun becomes the first high school student to run a sub-four-minute mile when he runs 3:59 in Los Angeles.

June 5, 1975: Richard Dewey bowls 1,472 games over a 114-hour period. Alternating both hands, Dewey averages 126.

June 5, 1977: Portland defeats Philadelphia, 109–107, to win the NBA championship series in six games.

June 5, 1982: On a sloppy track, Conquistador Cielo wins the Belmont Stakes by 14 ½ lengths. The son of Mr. Prospector is later syndicated for a record 36 million dollars.

JUNE 6

June 6, 1892: Benjamin Harrison becomes the first incumbent President to attend a major league baseball game, as he watches Cincinnati defeat Washington, 7–4.

June 6, 1919: In his first race at Belmont Park, Man o' War, considered by many experts to be the greatest thoroughbred of all time, wins by six lengths. The winner's share of the purse is a meager $500.

June 6, 1946: The Basketball Association of America, forerunner of the National Basketball Association, is formed in New York.

June 6, 1976: The Boston Celtics defeat the Phoenix Suns to win the NBA championship in six games.

June 6, 1987: Bet Twice wins the Belmont Stakes by 14

lengths as Kentucky Derby and Preakness winner Alysheba finishes fourth.

June 6, 1988: In a stunning upset, Iran Barkley knocks out Thomas Hearns in the third round to win the middleweight championship.

JUNE 7

June 7, 1808: Honest Harry, Miss Decoy, Beningbrough, and Peteria are involved in the first quadruple dead heat in racing history.

June 7, 1884: Providence's Charlie Sweeney strikes out 19 batters in a 2–1 win over Boston.

June 7, 1906: The Chicago Cubs score 11 runs in the first inning off Christy Mathewson and Joe McGinnity on their way to a 19–0 victory over the New York Giants.

June 7, 1930: Gallant Fox completes his Triple Crown by winning the Belmont Stakes.

June 7, 1941: As expected, Whirlaway wins the Belmont Stakes and the Triple Crown.

June 7, 1978: The Washington Bullets defeat Seattle in the seventh game of the NBA finals.

June 7, 1980: Temperance Hill, a 53-to-1 long shot, wins the Belmont Stakes.

June 7, 1986: Danzig Connection wins the Belmont Stakes, giving trainer Woody Stephens his fifth Belmont in a row.

JUNE 8

June 8, 1917: New York Giants manager John McGraw punches baseball's only singing umpire, Lord Byron.

June 8, 1920: Cincinnati Reds outfielder Edd Roush is ejected for taking a nap in the outfield during a break in play.

June 8, 1933: Philadelphia's Jimmie Foxx hits three home runs off New York's Lefty Gomez to give him four consecutive home runs over two games.

June 8, 1935: Omaha wins the Belmont Stakes and the Triple Crown.

June 8, 1968: Los Angeles pitcher Don Drysdale stretches his record consecutive-inning scoreless streak to 58 before Philadelphia's Howie Bedell finally drives in a run with a sacrifice fly. Ironically, it is Bedell's only RBI of the season and one of only three in his entire career.

June 8, 1977: California's Nolan Ryan strikes out 19 batters as the Angels defeat the Toronto Blue Jays, 2–1.

June 8, 1982: The Los Angeles Lakers defeat the Philadelphia 76ers, 114–104, to win the NBA championship in six games.

June 8, 1986: The Boston Celtics defeat the Houston Rockets, 114–97, in game six to win their 16th NBA title.

JUNE 9

June 9, 1899: Jim Jeffries knocks out Bob Fitzsimmons in the 11th round to win the world heavyweight title.

June 9, 1945: Hoop Jr. wins the Kentucky Derby by six lengths.

June 9, 1966: The Minnesota Twins tie a major league record by hitting five home runs in one inning.

June 9, 1973: Secretariat wins the Belmont Stakes by 31 lengths to become the first horse to win the Triple Crown in 25 years.

June 9, 1976: Rev. Harold Snider has three holes-in-one in a single round on the Ironwood Golf Course in Phoenix, Arizona.

June 9, 1978: Larry Holmes finishes strongly to win a close 15-round decision over Ken Norton to become the heavyweight champion.

June 9, 1979: California's Nolan Ryan strikes out 19 batters as the Angels defeat the Detroit Tigers, 9–1.

June 9, 1984: Martina Navratilova defeats Chris Evert, 6–3, 6–1, to win the French Open and tennis's Grand Slam.

June 9, 1985: The Los Angeles Lakers defeat the Boston Celtics, 111–100, to win the NBA championship in six games.

JUNE 10

June 10, 1890: Two legs of racing's Triple Crown, the Preakness and the Belmont Stakes, are run on the same day at the same racetrack. Montague wins the Preakness and Burlington wins the Belmont Stakes at Morris Park in New York.

June 10, 1892: Wilbert Robinson goes seven for seven and bats in 11 runs as Baltimore defeats St. Louis, 25–4.

June 10, 1944: Cincinnati's Joe Nuxhall becomes the youngest player in major league history. The 15-year-old high school student pitches two-thirds of an inning and gives up five runs as the St. Louis Cardinals defeat Cincinnati, 18–0.

June 10, 1944: In horse racing, a rare triple dead heat takes place in the Carter Handicap.

June 10, 1959: Cleveland slugger Rocky Colavito hits four consecutive home runs in a game against Baltimore.

June 10, 1966: Cleveland's Sonny Siebert pitches a no-hitter against Washington.

June 10, 1977: Golfer Al Geiberger sets a PGA tournament record when he shoots a round of 59 in the Danny Thomas Open.

June 10, 1978: Affirmed defeats Alydar by a nose in the Belmont Stakes to win the Triple Crown.

JUNE 11

June 11, 1895: Frenchman Emile Lavassor wins the first original automobile race in history. His Panhard-Lavassor, equipped with a three-and-a-half horsepower engine, averages 15 miles per hour.

June 11, 1904: Chicago's Bob Wicker holds the New York Giants without a hit until Sam Mertes singles with one out in the tenth inning. Chicago defeats New York, 1–0, in 12 innings.

June 11, 1938: Johnny Vander Meer of the Cincinnati Reds pitches the first of his two consecutive no-hitters, mastering the Boston Braves, 3–0.

June 11, 1955: At LeMans, 81 spectators are killed when the car driven by Pierre Levegh sails into the crowd after colliding with another car.

June 11, 1977: Seattle Slew wins the Belmont Stakes by four lengths over Run Dusty Run to become the first undefeated horse to win the Triple Crown.

June 11, 1982: Heavyweight champion Larry Holmes knocks out challenger Gerry Cooney in the 13th round to retain his title.

June 11, 1988: Risen Star, a son of Secretariat, wins the Belmont Stakes by 14 lengths.

JUNE 12

June 12, 1880: Worcester's John Lee Richmond pitches the first perfect game in major league history, defeating Cleveland, 1–0.

June 12, 1920: Man o' War wins the Belmont Stakes by 20 lengths in track-record time.

June 12, 1930: When Jack Sharkey is disqualified for a low blow in the fourth round, German Max Schmeling becomes the only boxer to win the heavyweight title on a foul.

June 12, 1948: Citation wins the Belmont Stakes to become the fourth horse of the decade to win the Triple Crown.

June 12, 1954: Milwaukee's Jim Wilson pitches a no-hitter against the Philadelphia Phillies.

June 12, 1957: In an unmatched feat of strength, Olympic weight lifter Paul Anderson lifts a lead-filled safe weighing 6,270 pounds.

June 12, 1970: Pittsburgh's Dock Ellis pitches a no-hitter as the Pirates blank the San Diego Padres, 2–0.

June 12, 1984: The Boston Celtics defeat the Los Angeles Lakers, 111–102, to win their 15th NBA championship.

JUNE 13

June 13, 1905: New York's Christy Mathewson pitches a no-hitter, outdueling Mordecai "Three Finger" Brown of the Chicago Cubs, 1–0.

June 13, 1935: James J. "Cinderella Man" Braddock confounds the experts by winning a 15-round decision over Max Baer to capture the heavyweight title.

June 13, 1948: Babe Ruth is honored at Yankee Stadium on Old-Timers' Day. Ruth is suffering from cancer and can barely speak. Two month later, Ruth will be dead.

June 13, 1953: Native Dancer wins the Belmont Stakes.

June 13, 1953: Ben Hogan wins the U.S. Open for the fourth time, defeating runner-up Sam Sneed by six shots.

June 13, 1982: Jan Stephenson wins the LPGA golf tournament.

June 13, 1987: Sachio Kinugasa, a 40-year-old third baseman for the Hiroshima Carp, plays in his 2,131st consecutive game, breaking Lou Gehrig's durability record. Kinugasa has not missed a game since October 18, 1970.

JUNE 14

June 14, 1870: Baseball's first professional team, the Cincinnati Red Stockings, lose for the first time in 130 games. The Atlantics defeat Cincinnati, 8–7.

June 14, 1876: Boston and St. Louis combine to make 40 errors in a game won by St. Louis, 17–6.

June 14, 1894: Mike Leonard knocks out Jack Cushing in the sixth round of their fight, the first sporting event ever to be filmed.

June 14, 1934: Max Baer floors champion Primo Carnera 11 times before knocking him out in the 11th round to win the heavyweight boxing title.

June 14, 1949: Philadelphia first baseman Eddie Waitkus is shot by a deranged teenage girl in a room at the Edgewater Beach Hotel in Chicago. The incident provides the inspiration for a scene in the movie *The Natural*.

June 14, 1965: Cincinnati's Jim Maloney pitches a ten-inning no-hitter, only to lose, 1–0, in 11 innings to the New York Mets.

June 14, 1974: California's Nolan Ryan strikes out 19 Boston Red Sox.

June 14, 1987: The Los Angeles Lakers defeat the Boston Celtics, 106–93, to win the NBA championship in six games.

JUNE 15

June 15, 1902: Nig Clarke of Corsicana sets a minor league record when he hits eight home runs in a 51–3 victory over Texarkana.

June 15, 1938: Cincinnati's Johnny Vander Meer becomes the only player in baseball history to pitch no-hitters in two consecutive games. Vander Meer no-hits the Brooklyn Dodgers, 6–0.

June 15, 1951: On the comeback trail, Joe Louis knocks out Lee Savold in the sixth round in the first closed-circuit boxing match.

June 15, 1963: San Francisco's Juan Marichal pitches a no-hitter as the Giants defeat Houston, 1–0.

June 15, 1974: Despite shooting seven over par for the tournament, Hale Irwin wins the U.S. Open at tough Winged Foot Golf Course.

June 15, 1976: A game between the Houston Astros and Pittsburgh Pirates is rained out in the Astrodome when a torrential downpour in Houston floods the streets, preventing the fans from reaching the stadium.

June 15, 1984: Thomas Hearns knocks down Roberto Duran three times before knocking him out in the second round.

JUNE 16

June 16, 1890: Madison Square Garden, the world's most famous sports arena, is opened in New York City.

June 16, 1916: Boston's Tom Hughes pitches a no-hitter as the Braves defeat the Pittsburgh Pirates, 2–0.

June 16, 1946: Golfer Byron Nelson loses the U.S. Open when he is penalized after his caddy accidentally kicks the golf ball.

June 16, 1949: Jake LaMotta stops Marcel Cerdan in the tenth round to win the world middleweight championship.

June 16, 1953: Satchel Paige outpitches Whitey Ford as the St. Louis Browns defeat the New York Yankees, 3–1. Going into the game, the Yankees had won 18 games in a row while the Browns had lost 14 in a row.

June 16, 1971: Against Washington, Oakland's Mike Epstein hits his fourth consecutive home run in a two-game period.

June 16, 1978: Cincinnati's Tom Seaver pitches a no-hitter as the Reds blank the St. Louis Cardinals, 4–0.

June 16, 1984: Edwin Moses wins his 100th consecutive 400-meter hurdle race in a qualifying heat for the U.S. Olympic Trials.

JUNE 17

June 17, 1880: Providence's Monte Ward pitches a perfect game.

June 17, 1886: Two-year-old Tremont wins the six-furlong Paddock Stakes, his fifth stakes victory in 12 days.

June 17, 1912: Wishing Ring wins a race at Latonia Racetrack for the largest payoff in American racing history. Wishing Ring pays $1,885.50 to win for a $2 ticket. Only four tickets are sold on Wishing Ring; even her owner bets on another horse.

June 17, 1915: Chicago's Zip Zabel pitches 18⅓ innings, the longest relief stint in baseball history, in a 4–3 victory over Brooklyn.

June 17, 1943: Boston's Joe Cronin becomes the first player to have pinch-hit home runs in both games of a doubleheader.

June 17, 1960: Boston's Ted Williams hits his 500th career home run.

June 17, 1962: ''Marvelous'' Marv Throneberry of the New York Mets hits an apparent triple against the Chicago Cubs but is called out for forgetting to touch first base and second base.

June 17, 1973: Johnny Miller fires a 63 in the final round to give him a thrilling come-from-behind victory in the U.S. Open.

JUNE 18

June 18, 1941: Heavyweight champion Joe Louis knocks out former light heavyweight champion Billy Conn in the 13th round.

June 18, 1947: Cincinnati's Ewell Blackwell pitches a no-hitter as the Reds blank the Boston Braves, 6–0.

June 18, 1953: The Boston Red Sox score 17 runs in the seventh inning to defeat the Detroit Tigers by the score of 23 to 3. Gene Stephens becomes the only player to have three hits in an inning, and catcher Sammy White sets another record by scoring three runs in one inning.

June 18, 1960: Arnold Palmer shoots a 65 to come from seven shots behind in the final round to win the U.S. Open.

June 18, 1963: Cassius Clay comes off the canvas to stop Henry Cooper of Great Britain in the fifth round of their match in London. After the fight, Clay quips that the reason he went down at the end of the fourth round was that he wanted to get a better look at Elizabeth Taylor, who was seated at ringside.

June 18, 1967: Houston's Don Wilson pitches a no-hitter and strikes out 15 as the Astros defeat the Atlanta Braves, 2–0.

JUNE 19

June 19, 1846: The New York Nine defeat the New York Knickerbockers, 23–1, at Elysian Fields in Hoboken, New Jersey, in the first baseball game using the modern rules devised by Alexander Cartwright.

June 19, 1867: Ruthless wins the first Belmont Stakes.

June 19, 1889: Washington outfielder Dummy Hoy throws out three base runners in one inning. Despite being deaf, Hoy played 14 years in the majors.

June 19, 1936: Former heavyweight champion Max Schmeling knocks out Joe Louis in the 12th round.

June 19, 1952: Brooklyn's Carl Erskine pitches a no-hitter as the Dodgers defeat the Chicago Cubs, 5–0.

June 19, 1966: Arnold Palmer blows a seven-shot lead with nine holes to play in the U.S. Open. Palmer loses to Billy Casper in an 18-hole playoff.

June 19, 1974: Kansas City's Steve Busby pitches his second no-hitter as the Royals beat the Milwaukee Brewers, 2–0.

June 19, 1985: Angelo Spagnola of Fayette City, Pennsylvania, is named the worst avid golfer in America by *Golf Digest*. Spagnola earns the dubious distinction by shooting a horrendous round of 257 in a playoff with America's four worst golfers. The lowlight of his round is a 66 on the 17th hole.

JUNE 20

June 20, 1912: Josh Devore steals four bases in the ninth inning as the New York Giants defeat the Boston Braves, 21–12.

June 20, 1960: Floyd Patterson knocks out Ingemar Johansson in the fifth round to become the first boxer to regain the heavyweight championship.

June 20, 1964: Golfer Ken Venturi overcomes heat exhaustion and 100-degree temperatures to win the U.S. Open.

June 20, 1967: Boxer Muhammad Ali is convicted of draft evasion and sentenced to five years in prison. Eventually, the decision will be overturned.

June 20, 1968: Jim Hines becomes the first sprinter to break

10 seconds in the 100-meter dash when he is timed in 9.9 seconds at the AAU track and field championships in Sacramento, California.

June 20, 1976: Twenty-two-year-old golfer Jerry Pate wins the U.S. Open.

June 20, 1980: Roberto Duran wins a 15-round decision over Sugar Ray Leonard to capture the WBC welterweight championship.

June 20, 1982: Tom Watson chips in from off the green on the 17th hole and goes on to defeat Jack Nicklaus in the U.S. Open.

JUNE 21

June 21, 1901: In his major league debut, Cincinnati pitcher Doc Parker gives up 21 runs and 26 hits against Brooklyn.

June 21, 1910: Brooklyn rookie Jack Dalton collects five hits off the great Christy Mathewson in only his second major league game.

June 21, 1916: Boston's Rube Foster pitches a no-hitter against the New York Yankees.

June 21, 1932: Challenger Jack Sharkey wins a controversial 15-round split decision over Max Schmeling to win the heavyweight title, prompting Schmeling's manager, Joe Jacobs, to utter the immortal words, "We wuz robbed!"

June 21, 1938: Boston's Pinky Higgins has eight consecutive base hits in a doubleheader against Chicago to run his consecutive-hit streak to 12.

June 21, 1964: Philadelphia's Jim Bunning pitches a perfect game as the Phillies defeat the New York Mets, 6–0.

June 21, 1970: Light-hitting shortstop Cesar Gutierrez of the Detroit Tigers has seven hits in seven at bats in a game against the Cleveland Indians.

June 21, 1988: The Los Angeles Lakers defeat the Detroit Pistons, 108–105, in the seventh game of the NBA championship series.

JUNE 22

June 22, 1889: The Louisville Colonels set a major league record for futility when they lose their 26th game in a row. With manager Chicken Wolf at the helm, the Colonels will suffer through a dismal 27–111 season.

June 22, 1891: Brooklyn's Tom Lovett pitches a no-hitter against the New York Giants.

June 22, 1937: Joe Louis knocks out champion James J. Braddock in the eighth round to win the heavyweight title.

June 22, 1938: Joe Louis knocks out Max Schmeling in the first round to avenge an earlier loss to the German.

June 22, 1947: Cincinnati pitcher Ewell "The Whip" Blackwell comes within two outs of pitching back-to-back no-hitters.

June 22, 1949: Ezzard Charles wins a 15-round decision over Jersey Joe Walcott to claim the heavyweight title vacated by Joe Louis.

June 22, 1976: Carlos Palomino knocks out John Strachey in the 12th round to win the WBC welterweight title.

JUNE 23

June 23, 1917: Even though he didn't start the game, Boston pitcher Ernie Shore is credited with pitching a perfect game. Babe Ruth starts the game but is ejected after arguing a ball-four call to Washington's leadoff batter, Eddie Morgan. Without the benefit of warming up, Shore enters the game. Morgan is thrown out attempting to steal second and Shore proceeds to retire the next 26 batters in order.

June 23, 1956: Kansas City sportswriter Dick Wade uses a stopwatch to determine how much action takes place during a typical major league baseball game. During a game between the Kansas City A's and the Washington Senators, the ball is in play only 9 minutes and 55 seconds of the 2 hours and 38 minutes of playing time.

June 23, 1963: Jimmy Piersall celebrates hitting his 100th major league home run by running around the bases backward.

June 23, 1971: Philadelphia's Rick Wise pitches a no-hitter and hits two home runs as the Phillies defeat Cincinnati, 4–0.

June 23, 1973: Philadelphia pitcher Ken Brett hits a home run, in the fourth consecutive start he has done so.

JUNE 24

June 24, 1882: Richard Higham becomes the only umpire in major league history to be suspended for life. It was discovered that he had informed gamblers on how to bet on games he was umpiring.

June 24, 1922: The National Football League is born. Formerly, the league had been called the American Football Association. Curly Lambeau pays $50 for the franchise rights to the Green Bay Packers, which had been founded by Lambeau's employer, the Indian Packing Company.

June 24, 1962: The New York Yankees defeat Detroit, 9–7, in a 22-inning marathon that lasts seven hours. Jack Reed wins the game with a two-run homer, the only home run of his major league career. Detroit's Rocky Colavito has seven hits in a losing cause.

June 24, 1968: Detroit's Jim Northrup hits two grand slam home runs in a 14–3 victory over Cleveland.

June 24, 1970: Bobby Murcer of the New York Yankees hits two grand slam home runs in a doubleheader against Cleveland.

JUNE 25

June 25, 1881: Chicago's George Gore sets a major league record when he steals seven bases in one game.

June 25, 1928: Third baseman Fred Lindstrom has nine hits as the New York Giants sweep a doubleheader from Philadelphia by the scores of 12 to 4 and 8 to 2.

June 25, 1930: "Slapsie" Maxie Rosenbloom wins a 15-round decision over Jimmy Slattery to claim the world light heavyweight championship.

June 25, 1952: Middleweight champ Sugar Ray Robinson cannot answer the bell for the 14th round in his fight with light heavyweight champion Joey Maxim. Ahead on points, Robinson is unable to continue because of the oppressive 104-degree heat in Yankee Stadium. It will be the only time in 201 pro fights that he fails to go the distance.

June 25, 1968: Bobby Bonds of the San Francisco Giants becomes only the second player in major league history to hit a grand slam home run in his first game.

June 25, 1977: Amateur basketball player Ted St. Martin breaks his own record when he makes 2,036 consecutive free throws.

JUNE 26

June 26, 1916: In a game against the Chicago White Sox, the Cleveland Indians become the first major league baseball team to wear numbers on their uniforms. Unlike today's uniforms, the numbers are on the sleeves instead of the back. At New York's Polo Grounds, three fans are arrested for petty larceny for keeping baseballs hit into the stands.

June 26, 1944: Over 50,000 fans pack the Polo Grounds to witness a unique exhibition game featuring all three New York baseball teams. The teams rotate with one team sitting out the inning. The final score is the Brooklyn Dodgers 5, New York Yankees 1, New York Giants 0.

June 26, 1959: Ingemar Johansson knocks down Floyd Patterson seven times in the third round to win the world heavyweight boxing championship.

June 26, 1962: Detroit's Earl Wilson pitches a no-hitter and hits a home run as the Tigers defeat Los Angeles, 2–0.

June 26, 1970: Baltimore slugger Frank Robinson hits grand slam home runs in the fifth and sixth innings of a 12–2 victory over Washington.

June 26, 1972: Roberto Duran wins the world lightweight boxing title by stopping Ken Buchanan of Scotland in the 13th round.

JUNE 27

June 27, 1884: Larry Corcoran of the Chicago Cubs pitches a no-hitter against Providence.

June 27, 1893: John Berry, riding a horse named Poison, wins a 1,000-mile horse race that began in Chardon, Nebraska, two weeks earlier.

June 27, 1930: Forty-five-year-old Jack Quinn of the Philadelphia Athletics becomes the oldest player ever to hit a home run in a major league game. The mighty Quinn, a pitcher, won 247 games during his lengthy career.

June 27, 1972: It's a bad night for the Quarry brothers in Las Vegas. Muhammad Ali knocks out Jerry Quarry in the seventh round of their heavyweight bout, and light heavyweight champion

Bob Foster knocks out Mike Quarry in the fourth round of their title fight.

June 27, 1975: Golfers Lee Trevino, Jerry Heard, and Bobby Nichols are struck by lightning during the second round of the Western Open.

June 27, 1980: Jerry Reuss of the Los Angeles Dodgers pitches a no-hitter against the San Francisco Giants.

June 27, 1988: Mike Tyson knocks out Michael Spinks in the first round to retain his heavyweight boxing title.

JUNE 28

June 28, 1907: The Washington Senators steal a record 13 bases off New York catcher Branch Rickey en route to a 16–5 victory. (Forty years later, Rickey will gain fame as the Brooklyn Dodgers executive who signs Jackie Robinson, the first black to play in the major leagues.)

June 28, 1910: Chicago shortstop Joe Tinker steals home twice as the Cubs rout Cincinnati, 11–1.

June 28, 1939: The New York Yankees live up to their nickname of the "Bronx Bombers" as they belt 13 home runs during a 23–2, 10–0 doubleheader sweep of the Philadelphia Athletics.

June 28, 1939: Heavyweight champion Joe Louis comes off the canvas to knock out "Two Ton" Tony Galento in the fourth round of their title fight.

June 28, 1957: Baseball commissioner Ford Frick removes three Cincinnati Reds from the starting all-star lineup after fans in Cincinnati stuff the ballot box. Frick adds St. Louis first baseman Stan Musial, New York outfielder Willie Mays, and Milwaukee outfielder Henry Aaron to the starting team.

JUNE 29

June 29, 1897: Chicago smashes Louisville, 36–7, setting a record for runs scored in a major league baseball game.

June 29, 1933: Primo Carnera knocks out Jack Sharkey in the sixth round to win the world heavyweight championship.

June 29, 1950: The Boston Red Sox defeat the Philadelphia Athletics, 22–14, in the highest-scoring game in American League history.

June 29, 1950: In one of sports' greatest upsets, the United States defeats Great Britain, 1–0, to win the world soccer championship in Rio de Janeiro.

June 29, 1957: Golfer Betsy Rawls wins the U.S. Open after leader Jacqueline Pung is disqualified for signing an incorrect scorecard.

June 29, 1984: Pete Rose sets a major league record by playing in his 3,309th game.

June 29, 1987: The American League overcomes an 11–0 deficit and goes on to defeat the National League, 24–11, in the annual Old-Timers' Game. Thirteen home runs are hit in the game, including three by former Detroit slugger Willie Horton.

JUNE 30

June 30, 1908: Forty-one-year-old Cy Young pitches his third career no-hitter and has three hits as Boston blanks New York, 8–0.

June 30, 1929: Bobby Jones wins the United States Open by an incredible 23 shots at the famed Winged Foot Golf Course in Mamaroneck, New York.

June 30, 1948: Bob Lemon of the Cleveland Indians pitches a no-hitter against the Detroit Tigers.

June 30, 1962: Sandy Koufax pitches the first of his four career no-hitters as the Los Angeles Dodgers defeat the New York Mets, 5–0.

June 30, 1978: First baseman Willie McCovey hits the 500th home run of his career, off pitcher Jamie Easterly of the Atlanta Braves.

June 30, 1984: The Los Angeles Express defeat the Michigan Panthers, 27–21, in the longest professional football game on record. Mel Gray scores the winning touchdown on a 24-yard run in the third overtime period of the USFL playoff game.

JULY 1

July 1, 1859: Amherst defeats Williams, 66–32, in the first college baseball game ever played. In those days, there were 13 players to a side, and the first team to score 65 runs was declared the winner.

July 1, 1920: Walter Johnson pitches a no-hitter as Washington defeats Boston, 1–0.

July 1, 1938: Don Budge defeats Wilfred Austin for his second consecutive Wimbledon title.

July 1, 1951: Bob Feller pitches his third career no-hitter as the Cleveland Indians defeat the Detroit Tigers, 2–1.

July 1, 1961: Olympic gold medalist Carl Lewis is born in Willingboro, New Jersey.

July 1, 1973: Eighty-three tennis players boycott Wimbledon in support of suspended player Nikki Pilic.

July 1, 1982: Fifty-two-year-old Glenn Allison bowls a perfect 900 series at the aptly named La Habra 300 Bowl.

JULY 2

July 2, 1903: Hall of Fame baseball player Ed Delahanty is killed under mysterious circumstances at Niagara Falls. Delahanty becomes drunk on a train and is put off by the conductor at Fort Erie, Ontario. Apparently, Delahanty attempted to chase the train across the International Bridge and fell to his death. His body was swept over Niagara Falls.

July 2, 1921: Heavyweight champion Jack Dempsey knocks out Georges Carpentier in the fourth round before 80,000 spectators at Boyle's Thirty Acres.

July 2, 1937: American Don Budge defeats Baron Gottfried von Cramm of Germany to win the Wimbledon tennis championship.

July 2, 1963: San Francisco's Willie Mays hits a home run in the 16th inning to break up a scoreless pitching duel between Juan Marichal of the Giants and Warren Spahn of the Milwaukee Braves.

July 2, 1971: Nineteen-year-old Evonne Goolagong defeats Margaret Court, 6–4, 6–1, to win her first Wimbledon title.

July 2, 1975: Baltimore's Don Baylor hits three home runs in a game against the Detroit Tigers to give him four consecutive home runs.

July 2, 1988: Steffi Graf defeats Martina Navratilova, 5–7, 6–2, 6–1, to end Navratilova's six-year reign as Wimbledon champion.

JULY 3

July 3, 1905: Marvin Hart knocks out Jack Root in the 12th round to win the world heavyweight boxing title.

July 3, 1912: New York's Rube Marquard defeats Brooklyn, 2–1, for his 19th consecutive win, a major league record for one season.

July 3, 1954: Forty-year-old Babe Didrikson Zaharias wins the U.S. Open by a record 12 shots. Zaharias is making a miraculous comeback from cancer surgery.

July 3, 1954: Maureen Connolly wins her third Wimbledon championship.

July 3, 1966: Atlanta pitcher Tony Cloninger hits two grand slam home runs in a 17–3 victory over the San Francisco Giants.

July 3, 1968: Cleveland's Luis Tiant strikes out 19 batters as the Indians defeat the Minnesota Twins, 1–0, in ten innings.

July 3, 1970: California's Clyde Wright pitches a no-hitter against the Oakland A's.

July 3, 1983: John McEnroe defeats Chris Lewis to win his second Wimbledon championship. Lewis, ranked only number 99 in the world, is a surprise finalist.

JULY 4

July 4, 1880: Many people lose money betting on horses, but George Warren actually loses a 20-million-dollar bet that he can outrun one. Warren, a miner, bets George Atkins that he can outrace a horse over 100 yards. Warren bets his share in a mine while Atkins wagers his horse. The horse wins, and the share in the mine eventually nets Atkins 20 millions dollars.

July 4, 1908: Hooks Wiltse of the New York Giants pitches a ten-inning no-hitter against the Philadelphia Phillies.

July 4, 1910: Jack Johnson stops Jim Jeffries in the 15th round of their heavyweight championship fight in Reno, Nevada. Jeffries, "The Great White Hope," had come out of retirement for the fight.

July 4, 1912: Detroit's George Mullin pitches a no-hitter against the St. Louis Browns.

July 4, 1919: Jack Dempsey knocks out champion Jess Willard in the third round to win the world heavyweight title. Dempsey knocks down the 6-foot-6-inch Willard seven times in the first round alone.

July 4, 1983: Dave Righetti pitches a no-hitter as the New York Yankees shut out the Boston Red Sox, 4–0.

JULY 5

July 5, 1946: When asked why the New York Giants, managed by Mel Ott, were in the National League cellar, Brooklyn manager Leo Durocher utters the immortal words, "Nice guys finish last."

July 5, 1947: Outfielder Larry Doby of the Cleveland Indians becomes the first black to play in the American League.

July 5, 1975: Arthur Ashe defeats Jimmy Connors to win the Wimbledon singles title.

July 5, 1980: Bjorn Borg wins his fifth consecutive Wimbledon crown with a dramatic, 1–6, 7–5, 6–3, 6–7, 8–6, victory over John McEnroe. The highlight of the match is the fourth-set tiebreaker, which is won by McEnroe 18 points to 16.

July 5, 1980: Niatross, generally considered to be the greatest harness horse in racing history, suffers his first loss when he inexplicably flips over the rail while leading a race at Saratoga.

July 5, 1987: The headlines read, "Cash is better than a Czech," as Australian Pat Cash upsets Ivan Lendl of Czechoslovakia, 7–6, 6–2, 7–5, to win the men's singles title at Wimbledon.

JULY 6

July 6, 1933: The American League defeats the National League, 4–2, in the first all-star game.

July 6, 1935: Helen Wills Moody wins her seventh Wimbledon title.

July 6, 1957: Althea Gibson defeats Darlene Hard to become the first black tennis player to win Wimbledon.

July 6, 1962: Mickey Mantle of the New York Yankees hits a pair of home runs to run his consecutive-home-run streak to four.

July 6, 1975: Ruffian breaks down during a match race with Foolish Pleasure.

July 6, 1983: The American League makes up for years of frustration by beating the National League, 13–3, in the 50th-anniversary all-star game.

July 6, 1985: Kathy Jordan and Elizabeth Smylie defeat Martina Navratilova and Pam Shriver, 5–7, 6–3, 6–4, to win the Wimbledon doubles title. The loss snaps a 109-match winning streak of Navratilova and Shriver.

July 6, 1986: Atlanta's Bob Horner hits four home runs in an 11–8 loss to Montreal.

JULY 7

July 7, 1924: Harold Abrahams of Great Britain wins the Olympic 100-meter-dash gold medal in Paris. Abraham's story will be recounted in the 1981 Academy Award–winning film *Chariots of Fire*.

July 7, 1937: Dizzy Dean suffers a broken toe when he is hit by a line drive off the bat of Earl Averill during the all-star game. When he returns to action, Dean favors the toe and hurts his arm trying to change his motion.

July 7, 1939: Young Bobby Riggs is the toast of Wimbledon as he wins the singles, doubles, and mixed-doubles championships.

July 7, 1964: Johnny Callison hits a three-run home run in the ninth inning as the National League defeats the American League, 7–4.

July 7, 1977: Billie Jean King wins her 20th Wimbledon title as she teams with Martina Navratilova to win the ladies' doubles.

July 7, 1979: Philadelphia third baseman Mike Schmidt hits his fourth round-tripper in a row over a two-day period.

July 7, 1985: Seventeen-year-old Boris Becker of West Germany defeats Kevin Curren, 6–3, 6–7, 7–6, 6–4, to become the first unseeded player ever to win Wimbledon.

JULY 8

July 8, 1889: John L. Sullivan knocks out Jake Kilrain in the 75th round to retain his bare-knuckle world heavyweight title in Richburg, Mississippi. After the fight, Sullivan is arrested, because boxing is illegal in Mississippi.

July 8, 1898: Philadelphia's Red Donahue pitches a no-hitter against Boston.

July 8, 1909: Grand Rapids of the Central League defeats Zanesville, 11–10, in the first minor league night game. It will be another 26 years before the first major league night game is played.

July 8, 1941: Ted Williams hits a three-run home run with two out in the ninth inning to give the American League a dramatic 7–5 victory over the National League in the all-star game.

July 8, 1962: St. Louis's Stan "The Man" Musial hits his fourth consecutive home run over a two-game span.

July 8, 1976: Golfer Fuzzy Zoeller shoots eight birdies in a row while firing a round of 63 in the Quad City Open.

July 8, 1984: John McEnroe overpowers Jimmy Connors, 6–1, 6–1, 6–2, in the finals at Wimbledon.

JULY 9

July 9, 1932: New York outfielder Ben Chapman hits two inside-the-park home runs as the Yankees defeat the Detroit Tigers, 14–9.

July 9, 1946: Ted Williams has four hits, scores four runs, and bats in five as the American League defeats the National League, 12–0, in the all-star game. In the eighth inning, Williams hits a Rip Sewell blooper pitch for a home run, a feat no one else had ever accomplished.

July 9, 1969: With one out in the ninth inning, Chicago's Jim Qualls spoils Ted Seaver's bid for a perfect game with a single.

July 9, 1971: Oakland A's pitchers strike out a record 26 batters in a 20-inning 1–0 victory over the California Angels.

July 9, 1976: Houston's Larry Dierker pitches a no-hitter as the Astros defeat the Montreal Expos, 6–0.

July 9, 1984: A record crowd of 67,596 watch as the United States Olympic basketball team defeats the NBA all-stars, 97–82, in the Hoosier Dome.

July 9, 1985: Famed artist Andy Warhol announces that he is working on a limited edition of silk-screen prints to commemorate Pete Rose's feat of passing Ty Cobb to become baseball's all-time hit leader.

JULY 10

July 10, 1928: Washington's Milt Gaston pitches a 14-hit shutout against the Cleveland Indians.

July 10, 1932: The Cleveland Indians collect 33 hits but lose to the Philadelphia A's, 18–17, in 18 innings. Cleveland's Johnny Burnett sets a major league record with nine hits in the game. The winning pitcher is Eddie Rommel, who gives up 29 hits and 14 runs in 17 innings of relief.

July 10, 1934: Carl Hubbell strikes out Babe Ruth, Lou Gehrig, Jimmie Foxx, Al Simmons, and Joe Cronin in succession at the all-star game. However, the American League wins the game, 9–7.

July 10, 1936: Philadelphia's Chuck Klein hits four home runs as the Phillies defeat the Pittsburgh Pirates, 9–6.

July 10, 1947: Cleveland's Don Black pitches a no-hitter against the Philadelphia A's.

July 10, 1964: Tony "Champagne" Lema wins the British Open at St. Andrews, Scotland.

July 10, 1971: Lee Trevino wins the British Open for his third national title in 19 days. Earlier, he had won the U.S. Open and Canadian Open.

JULY 11

July 11, 1924: Eric Liddell, who will later be memorialized in the film *Chariots of Fire*, wins the 400-meter race at the Paris Olympics.

July 11, 1929: Golfer Wanda Morgan shoots a round of 60, including a 29 on the back line, at the Birchington Golf Club in England.

July 11, 1950: Red Schoendienst hits a home run in the 14th inning to give the National League a 4–3 win in the all-star game.

July 11, 1961: Pitcher Stu Miller is blown off the mound by a gust of wind during the all-star game played at Candlestick Park in San Francisco.

July 11, 1967: Tony Perez hits a home run off Catfish Hunter in the 15th inning to give the National League a 2–1 victory in the all-star game.

July 11, 1971: Philadelphia's Deron Johnson hits four home runs in a row.

July 11, 1982: John McEnroe outlasts Mats Wilander, 9–7, 6–2, 15–17, 3–6, 8–6, in a Davis Cup tennis match that lasts 6 hours and 39 minutes.

July 11, 1983: Eighty-seven-year-old Ruth Needham of Escanaba, Michigan, scores a hole-in-one on the third hole of the Escanaba Country Club.

July 11, 1985: Nolan Ryan of the Houston Astros fans out New York's Danny Heep for his 4,000th career strikeout.

JULY 12

July 12, 1900: Cincinnati's Noodles Hahn pitches a no-hitter.

July 12, 1928: The first televised tennis match takes place on the roof of the Bell Telephone Laboratories in New York City. The image is projected onto a two-and-a-half-inch television screen.

July 12, 1930: Bobby Jones becomes the first golfer to break par in the U.S. Open. For Jones, it's his fourth U.S. Open title.

July 12, 1931: The term "doubleheader" takes on a double meaning as the St. Louis Cardinals and Chicago Cubs combine for 32 doubles in a twin bill played in St. Louis. Twenty-three doubles are hit in the second game alone.

July 12, 1951: Allie Reynolds of the New York Yankees pitches a no-hitter against the Cleveland Indians. Reynolds outduels Bob Feller, 1–0.

July 12, 1955: The National League wins the all-star game, 6–5, on a 12th-inning home run by Stan Musial.

July 12, 1979: Disco Demolition Night at Chicago's Comiskey Park results in a forfeit. Fans are offered 98¢ admission to the ballpark if they bring a disco record to burn between games of a doubleheader between Chicago and Detroit. When the fans refuse to leave the field, the second game is forfeited to Detroit.

JULY 13

July 13, 1896: Philadelphia's Ed Delahanty hits four inside-the-park home runs in a game against Chicago.

July 13, 1897: Exactly one year after his four-home-run

game, Ed Delahanty goes eight for eight in a doubleheader against Louisville.

July 13, 1943: The American League defeats the National League, 5–3, in the first all-star game played at night.

July 13, 1961: Cleveland's Willie Kirkland ties a major league record with his fourth consecutive home run.

July 13, 1963: Cleveland's Early Wynn lives up to his name by winning his 300th career game, a 7–4 victory over Kansas City. It proves to be Wynn's last win in the major leagues.

July 13, 1971: The American League wins the all-star game, 6–4, marking the only time the AL wins the midsummer classic between 1962 and 1983. The highlight of the game is a tape-measure home run by Reggie Jackson that strikes a light tower on the right-field roof of Tiger Stadium.

July 13, 1973: Hal Breeden of the Montreal Expos becomes the first player in National League history to hit pinch-hit home runs in both games of a doubleheader.

July 13, 1980: Amy Alcott wins the U.S. Open by nine shots.

JULY 14

July 14, 1912: In the 13th round of their title fight, light-weight boxing champion Ad Wolgast and challenger Joe Rivers simultaneously knock each other down. Wolgast's handpicked referee, Joe Welsh, shocks ringsiders by helping the champion to his feet while counting out his unlucky opponent.

July 14, 1946: Fifty-three-year-old Tazio Nuvolari wins the Albi Grand Prix to become the oldest driver ever to win a Grand Prix race.

July 14, 1951: Citation wins the Hollywood Gold Cup to become the first thoroughbred to go over a million dollars in career earnings. Marta wins the Molly Pitcher Handicap at Monmouth Park. CBS telecasts the race, marking the first time that a sporting event is televised in color.

July 14, 1956: Mel Parnell of the Boston Red Sox pitches a no-hitter.

July 14, 1967: Houston's Eddie Mathews hits his 500th home run.

July 14, 1968: Hank Aaron of the Atlanta Braves hits his 500th home run.

July 14, 1970: Pete Rose bowls over catcher Ray Fosse to score the winning run in the 12th inning and give the National League a 5–4 victory over the American League in the all-star game.

JULY 15

July 15, 1876: George "Grin" Bradley pitches the first official no-hitter in National League history as St. Louis defeats Hartford, 2–0.

July 15, 1901: Christy Mathewson pitches a no-hitter as the New York Giants defeat St. Louis, 5–0.

July 15, 1912: Jim Thorpe wins the gold medal in the decathlon, accumulating nearly 800 points more than his closest competitor.

July 15, 1922: Only a month after winning the PGA tournament, Gene Sarazen wins the U.S. Open in Glencoe, Illinois.

July 15, 1952: Detroit first baseman Walt Dropo collects his 12th consecutive base hit to tie the major league record set by Pinky Higgins in 1938.

July 15, 1973: Nolan Ryan pitches a no-hitter and strikes out 17 batters as the California Angels blank Detroit, 6–0. It is Ryan's second no-hitter in two months.

July 15, 1986: Harness driver Bill Haughton dies of head injuries suffered ten days earlier in an accident at Yonkers Raceway.

JULY 16

July 16, 1853: The first two-column baseball box score appears in the *New York Clipper*. It shows that the Knickerbockers defeated Gotham, 21–12, but it's hardly news, as the game was played 11 days earlier.

July 16, 1941: Joe DiMaggio, the "Yankee Clipper," has three hits against Cleveland to extend his hitting streak to 56 games.

July 16, 1947: Rocky Graziano knocks out champion Tony Zale in the sixth round to win the world middleweight boxing title. Eight years later, Hollywood will make a film of Graziano's life titled *Somebody Up There Likes Me*, starring a then little-known young actor named Paul Newman.

July 16, 1974: Nate Colbert, Willie McCovey, and Dave Winfield hit consecutive home runs in the bottom of the ninth inning to give the San Diego Padres a 5–4 victory over the Philadelphia Phillies.

JULY 17

July 17, 1914: New York Giants outfielder Red Murray is struck by lightning as he runs the base paths. Murray is not seriously injured.

July 17, 1924: Jesse Haines pitches a no-hitter as the St. Louis Cardinals defeat the Boston Braves, 5–0.

July 17, 1941: Joe DiMaggio's 56-game hitting streak is stopped by Cleveland pitchers Al Smith and Jim Bagby.

July 17, 1961: Ty Cobb, whose .367 lifetime batting average is the highest in baseball history, dies in Atlanta, Georgia, at the age of 74. In other baseball news, Commissioner Ford Frick rules that New York Yankees outfielder Roger Maris must break Babe Ruth's single-season home run record of 60 in 154 games or less for the record to appear in the record books without an asterisk. Maris will break the record, but it takes him eight additional games.

July 17, 1974: St. Louis pitcher Bob Gibson strikes out Cincinnati's Cesar Geronimo for his 3,000th career strikeout. Geronimo will also become Nolan Ryan's 3,000th strikeout victim.

JULY 18

July 18, 1924: Swimmer Johnny Weissmuller wins the 400-meter freestyle gold medal at the Paris Olympics.

July 18, 1948: Chicago's Pat Seerey hits four home runs as the White Sox defeat Philadelphia, 12–11.

July 18, 1951: Thirty-seven-year-old Jersey Joe Walcott becomes the oldest fighter ever to win the heavyweight title when he knocks out champion Ezzard Charles in the seventh round.

July 18, 1961: St. Louis first baseman Bill White has 14 base hits in back-to-back doubleheaders against the Chicago Cubs over a two-day period.

July 18, 1970: San Francisco's Willie Mays strokes his 3,000th base hit.

July 18, 1976: Romanian gymnast Nadia Comaneci receives

the first perfect score of 10 in Olympic history. Before the Montreal Games are over, the 14-year-old will receive seven perfect marks of 10.

July 18, 1982: Seventy-five-year-old Luke Appling hits a home run off Warren Spain in the annual Old-Timers' Baseball Game.

July 18, 1987: Don Mattingly of the New York Yankees ties a major league record by homering in his eighth consecutive game.

JULY 19

July 19, 1877: Two hundred spectators pay one shilling apiece to attend the first Wimbledon tennis championships. Because there are no bleachers, spectators sit in carriages to watch the tennis match. Spencer Gore defeats William Marshall, 6–1, 6–2, 6–4, to win the men's title, while Maude Watson wins the women's division. Unimpressed by the first Wimbledon, the men's champion is quoted as saying, ''Lawn tennis is a bit boring. It will never catch on.'' In fact, the Wimbledon Club had been formed to play croquet, not tennis.

July 19, 1900: Frenchman Michel Theato wins the Olympic marathon in Paris, run in blistering 102-degree heat. Arthur Newton of the United States crosses the finish line believing he is the winner, only to discover that Theato finished the race an hour earlier. Rumors circulate that the French runners may have used shortcuts or ridden in carriages for a portion of the 26-mile distance, and Theato is not declared the official winner until 12 years later.

July 19, 1909: In a game against Boston, Cleveland shortstop Neal Ball pulls off baseball's first unassisted triple play.

July 19, 1974: Dick Bosman pitches a no-hitter as Cleveland defeats Oakland, 4–0.

JULY 20

July 20, 1859: For the first time, spectators are charged admission to attend a baseball game. Five hundred fans pay 50¢ apiece to watch a team from New York defeat a club from Brooklyn, 22–18.

July 20, 1906: Mal Eason pitches a no-hitter as Philadelphia defeats Brooklyn, 2–0.

July 20, 1924: Johnny Weissmuller wins the Olympic gold medal in the 100-meter freestyle at Paris.

July 20, 1954: Tennis champion Maureen Connolly is seriously injured in a freak horse-truck accident. The horse Connolly is riding rears, pinning her leg against a cement truck. Connolly's right leg is shattered, ending her meteoric tennis career at the age of 19.

July 20, 1958: Detroit's Jim Bunning pitches a no-hitter and fans 12 as the Tigers defeat Boston, 3–0.

July 20, 1970: Los Angeles pitcher Bill Singer throws a no-hitter as the Dodgers defeat Philadelphia, 5–0.

July 20, 1976: Milwaukee's Henry Aaron hits his 755th and final career home run, off pitcher Dick Drago of the California Angels.

JULY 21

July 21, 1963: Jack Nicklaus wins the PGA golf tournament in Dallas, Texas.

July 21, 1970: San Diego manager Preston Gomez removes pitcher Clay Kirby in the ninth inning of a game against New York, despite the fact that Kirby has held the Mets hitless. The strategy backfires as the Padres lose both the no-hitter and the game.

July 21, 1973: Atlanta's Henry Aaron hits home run number 700, off Ken Brett of the Philadelphia Phillies.

July 21, 1975: Joe Torre of the New York Mets grounds into four double plays in a game against the Pittsburgh Pirates.

July 21, 1981: Patrick Young pockets 13,437 balls in 24 hours during an exhibition of pool at the Lord Stanley-Plaistow Hotel in London.

July 21, 1985: Ten-year-old gelding John Henry is retired from racing with record earnings of $6,597,947.

July 21, 1987: Lady's Secret wins an allowance race at Monmouth Park to break All Along's money-earning record for a filly or mare.

JULY 22

July 22, 1876: Cal McVey has six hits as Chicago destroys Louisville, 30–7. Louisville pitcher Johnny Ryan uncorks ten wild pitches in his first and last game in the major leagues.

July 22, 1905: Weldon Henley pitches a no-hitter as the Philadelphia A's defeat St. Louis, 6–0.

July 22, 1926: Babe Ruth catches a baseball dropped from an airplane flying above Mitchell Field, New York.

July 22, 1952: American Bob Richards wins the gold medal in the pole vault at the Helsinki Summer Olympics.

July 22, 1963: In a virtual instant replay of their first fight, heavyweight champion Sonny Liston knocks out Floyd Patterson in the first round.

July 22, 1976: East German Kornelia Ender wins the 200-meter freestyle to become the first female swimmer to win four gold medals in an Olympic Games.

July 22, 1984: Kathy Whitworth wins the Rochester Open for her 85th tournament victory, passing Sam Snead as golf's winningest player.

JULY 23

July 23, 1922: Ray Grimes of the Chicago Cubs sets a major league record by batting in a run for the 17th consecutive game.

July 23, 1944: Bill Nicholson of the Chicago Cubs hits four consecutive home runs in a doubleheader against the New York Giants.

July 23, 1960: Golfer Betsy Rawls wins the U.S. Open for a record fourth time in Worcester, Massachusetts.

July 23, 1964: Bert Campaneris of the Kansas City Athletics hits two home runs in his first major league game, off Minnesota pitcher Jim Kaat.

July 23, 1969: Willie McCovey hits two home runs to lead the National League to a 9–3 victory over the American League in the all-star game.

July 23, 1976: A torrential downpour halts the college all-star game, with the Pittsburgh Steelers leading the all-stars, 24–0. Sagging attendance will result in the series' being discontinued.

July 23, 1985: The British Bloodstock Agency of England pays a record $13.1 million for a colt sired by Nijinsky II at the Keeneland selected thoroughbred yearling sales.

JULY 24

July 24, 1882: Cleveland outfielder Dave Rowe tries his hand at pitching, with disastrous results. Rowe gives up a record 35 runs as Chicago buries Cleveland, 35–4.

July 24, 1908: American marathoner John Hayes is awarded the gold medal at the Olympics in London when Italian Dorando Pietri is disqualified after being helped across the finish line.

July 24, 1983: With two out in the ninth inning, Kansas City third baseman George Brett hits a two-run home run off New York's Goose Gossage. Yankees manager Billy Martin protests that Brett has pine tar on his bat more than the allowable 18 inches from the handle. The umpires agree, calling Brett out and ending the game with the Yankees apparently having won, 4–3. The Royals protest the game, and the American League President Lee MacPhail will rule that Brett's home run counts and the game should be resumed. When the game is resumed, weeks later, the Royals hold on to win, 5–4.

July 24, 1985: The Republicans defeat the Democrats, 9–3, in the annual congressional baseball game in Washington, D.C. The GOP leads the series, 17–6.

July 24, 1987: Boris Becker of West Germany defeats John McEnroe, 4–6, 15–13, 8–10, 6–2, 6–2, in a Davis Cup match that lasts 6 hours and 38 minutes.

JULY 25

July 25, 1883: Hoss Radbourn pitches a no-hitter as Providence shuts out Cleveland, 8–0.

July 25, 1908: While carrying a Bible in his left hand for inspiration, American Forrest Smithson wins the 110-meter hurdles at the London Olympics.

July 25, 1913: Washington fireballer Walter Johnson strikes out St. Louis pitcher Carl Weilman six consecutive times. Johnson strikes out 16 batters in 11⅓ innings of relief.

July 25, 1937: Washington's Mel Almada sets a major league record by scoring nine runs in a doubleheader against St. Louis.

July 25, 1941: Boston's Lefty Grove wins his 300th game, a 10–6 verdict over Cleveland. It proves to be Grove's last major league win.

July 25, 1969: Pancho Gonzalez defeats Charlie Pasarell, 22–24, 1–6, 16–14, 6–3, 11–9, in the longest match in Wimbledon history.

July 25, 1976: In a busy day at the Montreal Olympics, Edwin Moses wins the 400-meter hurdles, Mac Wilkins wins the discus, and Cuban Alberto Juantorena wins the 800-meter race.

JULY 26

July 26, 1920: At the Olympic Games in Antwerp, Belgium, seventy-two-year-old Oscar Swahn of Sweden wins a silver medal in shooting, making him the oldest medalist in Olympic history.

July 26, 1935: Joe DiMaggio has a 66-game hitting streak snapped in the minor leagues. On the major league level, New York's Jesse Hill hits a line drive off Washington pitcher Ed Linke's head. The ball ricochets to catcher Jack Redmond, who throws the ball to second base to complete an unusual double play.

July 26, 1952: Bob Mathias repeats as Olympic decathlon champion.

July 26, 1956: Figure skater Dorothy Hamill, winner of the 1976 Olympic gold medal at Innsbruck, is born in Chicago.

July 26, 1980: It's a good day for the British as Steve Ovett and Sebastian Coe run one-two in the 800-meter race and Daley Thompson wins the decathlon at the Moscow Olympics.

July 26, 1983: Richard DeWitt and Richard Bowling engage in a Ping-Pong rally that lasts 10 hours and 9 minutes at the YWCA at New Haven, Connecticut.

JULY 27

July 27, 1885: John Clarkson pitches a no-hitter as Chicago defeats Providence, 6–0.

July 27, 1938: Detroit's Hank Greenberg hits four consecutive home runs over a two-game period against Washington.

July 27, 1946: Boston's Rudy York hits two grand slam home runs and bats in 10 runs in a 13–6 victory over St. Louis.

July 27, 1952: Emil Zatopek of Czechoslovakia wins the

Olympic marathon to become the only man to sweep the 5,000 meters, 10,000 meters, and the marathon.

July 27, 1983: Pete Rose passes Ty Cobb to become baseball's all-time singles leader.

July 27, 1985: Steve Cram of Great Britain sets a world record for a mile when he is timed at 3:46.3 seconds in Oslo, Norway.

July 27, 1985: Lee Elder sets a seniors tour record when he shoots a round of 61.

July 27, 1986: Greg LeMond becomes the first American to win the Tour de France bicycle race.

JULY 28

July 28, 1943: Basketball star and U.S. senator Bill Bradley is born in Capital City, Missouri.

July 28, 1970: California Angels catcher Tom Egan permits five passed balls in a game.

July 28, 1971: Brooks Robinson, a 16-time Gold Glove winner at third base, makes three errors in a game against Oakland, the only time he will ever do so. However, Baltimore wins the game on a three-run homer by Frank Robinson.

July 28, 1974: Charles Lamb, the thoroughbred handicapper for the *Baltimore News American*, picks ten winners out of ten races at Delaware Park.

July 28, 1976: Chicago's Blue Moon Odom and Francisco Barrios combine to pitch a no-hitter against Oakland. Odom is removed from the game after walking nine batters in five innings. It proves to be Odom's last major league victory.

July 28, 1978: Boston's Fred Lynn hits two doubles, two triples, and a home run in a game.

JULY 29

July 29, 1911: Smokey Joe Wood pitches a no-hitter and strikes out 12 as Boston defeats St. Louis, 5–0.

July 29, 1928: Paavo Nurmi of Finland wins the 10,000-meter race at the Amsterdam Olympics for his ninth gold medal.

July 29, 1968: George Culver pitches a no-hitter as the Cincinnati Reds defeat the Philadelphia Phillies, 6–1.

July 31, 1932: Babe Didrikson, perhaps the greatest all-around female athlete of all time, wins a gold medal in the javelin at the Los Angeles Olympics.

July 31, 1935: Kitty Burke becomes the only woman ever to bat in the major leagues. In the late innings of a game at Cincinnati's Crosley Field, the capacity crowd begins overflowing onto the playing field. Burke boldly strides up to the plate, where Cincinnati's Babe Herman is ready to bat against St. Louis's Daffy Dean. She grabs the bat from Herman's hands, signals Dean to throw her a pitch, and Dean obliges.

July 31, 1954: Milwaukee first baseman Joe Adcock hits four home runs and a double against Brooklyn. The 18 total bases establishes a major league record.

July 31, 1978: Cincinnati's Pete Rose ties Wee Willie Keeler's National League record by hitting safely in his 44th consecutive game.

AUGUST 1

August 1, 1881: In Newport, Rhode Island, the first national tennis championship is held. Richard Sears defeats W. E. Glyn in the men's finals.

August 1, 1906: Brooklyn pitcher Harry McIntyre holds Pittsburgh hitless for 10⅔ innings before losing, 1–0, in 13 innings.

August 1, 1945: Mel Ott of the New York Giants becomes the first National League player to hit 500 home runs.

August 1, 1962: Bill Monbouquette pitches a no-hitter as Boston defeats Chicago, 1–0.

August 1, 1970: Pittsburgh's Willie Stargell has five extra-base hits as the Pirates defeat the Atlanta Braves, 20–10.

August 1, 1972: Nate Colbert hits five home runs and bats in 13 as the San Diego Padres sweep a doubleheader from the Atlanta Braves.

August 1, 1978: Atlanta pitchers Larry McWilliams and Gene Garber hold Pete Rose hitless, snapping his 44-game hitting streak.

August 1, 1986: Minnesota's Bert Blyleven has a career-high 15 strikeouts to reach the 3,000 mark, as the Twins overwhelm Oakland, 10–1.

AUGUST 2

August 2, 1864: Saratoga Racetrack opens in upstate New York. Only eight races are run during the four-day meet. In fact, only 26 horses are stabled on the grounds.

August 2, 1932: Stella Walsh wins the 100-meter dash at the Los Angeles Olympics. When Walsh died in 1980, it was discovered that she was really a man.

August 2, 1938: Dandelion-colored baseballs are used in a doubleheader between Brooklyn and St. Louis to determine if they are easier to see than the traditional white baseballs. The yellow baseballs are used in the first game and the white ones are used in the nightcap.

August 2, 1952: Middleweight Floyd Patterson knocks out Vasile Tita of Romania in the first round to win the Olympic gold medal. The same day, Swedish heavyweight Ingemar Johansson is disqualified for refusing to mix it up with his American opponent, Edward Sanders. Years later, Patterson and Johansson will engage in three memorable heavyweight championship fights.

August 2, 1980: Cuban heavyweight Teofilo Stevenson wins his third consecutive Olympic gold medal.

AUGUST 3

August 3, 1894: Philadelphia's Billy Hamilton steals seven bases in one game.

August 3, 1914: In one inning, New York catcher Les Nunamaker throws out three Detroit base runners attempting to steal.

August 3, 1932: French discus thrower Jules Noel loses a gold medal when officials, momentarily watching another event, miss his winning throw. Given another chance, Noel cannot repeat his earlier effort and finishes fourth.

August 3, 1936: With Adolf Hitler looking on, American Jesse Owens wins the 100-meter gold medal at the Berlin Olympics.

August 3, 1949: The NBA is formed by the merger of the National Basketball League and the Basketball Association of America.

August 3, 1960: The Detroit Tigers trade manager Jimmy

Dykes in exchange for Chicago Indians manager Joe Gordon.

August 3, 1984: American Mary Lou Retton scores a perfect 10 in the vault to edge out Romania's Ecaterina Szabo for the gold medal in the Olympic gymnastic all-around championship.

AUGUST 4

August 4, 1884: Buffalo's Pud Galvin pitches a no-hitter.

August 4, 1936: Six-foot-tall American sprinter Helen Stephens wins the 100-meter dash. According to reports, Adolf Hitler makes a pass at her after the race, but she rebuffs his advances.

August 4, 1945: In his only major league appearance, Bert Shepard of the Washington Senators, who lost part of a leg during World War II, pitches 5⅓ innings of three-hit ball against the Boston Red Sox.

August 4, 1945: Golfer Byron Nelson wins the Canadian Open for his 11th straight tour victory.

August 4, 1982: After hitting a single off Chicago's Ferguson Jenkins in an afternoon game, Mets outfielder Joel Youngblood is informed that he has been traded to Montreal. Youngblood arrives in Philadelphia in time for an evening game, where he singles off the Phillies' Steve Carlton.

August 4, 1985: Tom Seaver of the Chicago White Sox defeats New York, 4–1, for his 300th major league win. In Anaheim, Rod Carew of the California Angels gets his 3,000th hit in a 6–5 victory over Minnesota.

AUGUST 5

August 5, 1921: Harold Arlin of KDKA in Pittsburgh broadcasts the first major league baseball game on radio.

August 5, 1936: Jesse Owens wins the 200-meter dash at the Berlin Olympics, narrowly defeating Mack Robinson, older brother of Jackie Robinson.

August 5, 1967: The Denver Broncos defeat the Detroit Lions, 13–7, marking the first time an American Football League team had defeated a National Football League opponent.

August 5, 1973: Phil Niekro pitches a no-hitter as the Atlanta Braves defeat the San Diego Padres, 9–0.

August 5, 1984: American Joan Benoit wins the first Olympic women's marathon. Edwin Moses wins the 400-meter hurdles, his 90th consecutive victory in a final heat.

August 5, 1985: Amateur golfer Jim Cobb scores three holes-in-one over a 30-hour period. The odds against this happening are 8,404,101,101 to 1.

August 5, 1986: Philadelphia's Steve Carlton strikes out Eric Davis for his 4,000th career strikeout, but the Reds win the game, 11–6.

AUGUST 6

August 6, 1890: Cleveland rookie pitcher Cy Young defeats Chicago, 6–1, for the first of his 511 major league wins.

August 6, 1892: Jack Stivetts pitches a no-hitter as Boston beats Brooklyn, 11–0.

August 6, 1926: Gertrude Ederle sets a record when she swims the English Channel in 14 hours and 39 minutes.

August 6, 1948: Seventeen-year-old Bob Mathias wins the decathlon at the London Summer Olympics. Four years later, he will repeat as Olympic decathlon champion.

August 6, 1952: Forty-six-year-old Satchel Paige of the St. Louis Browns pitches a 12-inning shutout against the Detroit Tigers.

August 6, 1972: Gary Player wins the PGA golf tournament.

August 6, 1978: Golfer John Mahaffey wins the PGA tournament in a sudden-death playoff.

AUGUST 7

August 7, 1899: Vic Willis pitches a no-hitter as Boston defeats Washington, 7–1.

August 7, 1906: The New York Giants forfeit a game to Chicago when manager John McGraw refuses to allow umpire James Johnston into the ballpark.

August 7, 1932: Babe Didrikson is denied the Olympic gold medal in the high jump when it is ruled that her jumping style is illegal. After the Olympics, Didrikson's jumping style is legalized.

August 7, 1954: In a race billed as the "Mile of the Century," Roger Bannister defeats rival John Landy in a time of 3:58.8 at the British Empire Games in Vancouver, Canada.

August 7, 1956: Over 57,000 fans, the largest crowd in minor league history, turn out in Miami to see 50-year-old Satchel Paige pitch.

August 7, 1972: A minor league baseball game in Midland, Texas, is postponed because of a grasshopper attack.

August 7, 1972: Former number-one heavyweight boxing contender Eddie Machen falls to his death while sleepwalking in his San Francisco apartment.

AUGUST 8

August 8, 1903: A portion of the grandstand at the Baker Bowl in Philadelphia collapses, killing 12 fans. Fans had crowded along the back bleacher wall to watch a fight in the street below causing the stands to collapse.

August 8, 1906: Oh, what a relief it is! Starting pitcher Jack Taylor is relieved for the first time since June 20, 1901. During the streak, Taylor pitched 203 consecutive complete games.

August 8, 1920: Detroit's Howard Ehmke pitches the shortest game in American League history, defeating the New York Yankees in just 1 hour and 13 minutes.

August 8, 1931: Bobby Burke pitches a no-hitter as Washington blanks Boston, 5–0.

August 8, 1976: In a 5–2 victory over Kansas City, the Chicago White Sox make major league history by wearing shorts.

August 8, 1984: Carl Lewis wins the gold medal in the Olympic 200-meter dash. Englishman Daley Thompson wins the decathlon for the second consecutive time.

AUGUST 9

August 9, 1942: The Chicago Cubs defeat the Cincinnati Reds, 10–8, in 18 innings as a major league record 44 runners are left on base.

August 8, 1976: John Candelaria pitches a no-hitter as Pittsburgh defeats Los Angeles, 2–0.

August 9, 1981: Gary Carter hits two home runs and Mike Schmidt connects for the game winner as the National League scores a come-from-behind 5–4 victory over the American League in the all-star game, the senior circuit's tenth consecutive win in the midsummer classic.

August 9, 1984: Evander Holyfield, an American boxer in the 178-pound class, is disqualified for allegedly knocking down New Zealand's Kevin Barry on the break. At the awards ceremony, gold medal winner Anton Josipovic of Yugoslavia graciously invites Holyfield to join him atop the winner's stand.

August 9, 1985: Actor Paul Newman qualifies for the pole position for the Nissan Trans-Am Road Race in Lime Rock, Connecticut. Newman sets a course record when he averages 102.595 miles per hour.

AUGUST 10

August 10, 1888: New York pitcher Tim Keefe defeats Pittsburgh, 2–1, for his 19th consecutive win.

August 10, 1929: Pitcher Grover Cleveland Alexander wins his 373rd game, tying him with Christy Mathewson for the all-time National League record.

August 10, 1932: Swimmer Buster Crabbe wins the 400-meter freestyle gold medal at the Los Angeles Olympics. Crabbe later gains greater fame in the movies portraying Buck Rogers and Flash Gordon.

August 10, 1971: Harmon Killebrew of the Minnesota Twins hits the 500th home run of his major league career, off Baltimore's Mike Cuellar.

August 10, 1981: Pete Rose breaks Stan Musial's National League record by collecting base hit number 3,631, off St. Louis pitcher Mark Littell.

August 10, 1984: Favorite Mary Decker is tripped by South African rival Zola Budd in the finals of the 3,000-meter run at the Los Angeles Olympic Games. Romania's Maricica Puica wins the race.

August 10, 1985: Tom Selleck hits a home run and is the winning pitcher as a team of Hollywood stars defeat the Los Angeles media, 5–4, in a game played at Dodger Stadium.

AUGUST 11

August 11, 1908: Boston's Tom Tuckey pitches a no-hitter in his first major league start, downing the St. Louis Cardinals, 2–0.

August 11, 1928: Swimmer Johnny Weissmuller repeats as the Olympic 100-meter freestyle gold medalist.

August 11, 1929: New York's Babe Ruth becomes the first player to amass 500 career home runs.

August 11, 1950: Vern Bickford pitches a no-hitter as the Boston Braves defeat the Brooklyn Dodgers, 7–0.

August 11, 1961: Warren Spahn chalks up his 300th major league victory as the Milwaukee Braves defeat the Chicago Cubs, 2–1.

August 11, 1984: Carl Lewis wins his fourth gold medal as part of the 4 × 100-meter relay team. The American boxing team wins nine gold medals and freestyle wrestlers take home seven gold medals.

August 11, 1986: Simon Le Bon, lead singer for the rock group Duran Duran, nearly drowns when his yacht capsizes during the Fastnet Race off the coast of England.

August 11, 1986: Bob Tway holes a miracle bunker shot on the final hole to edge Greg Norman for the PGA title.

AUGUST 12

August 12, 1936: Thirteen-year-old Marjorie Gestring of the United States wins the springboard diving competition at the Berlin Olympics to become the youngest gold medalist in Olympic history. Over 100,000 fans, the largest crowd ever for a baseball game, watch an exhibition game at Berlin's Olympic Stadium. Unfortunately, few of them understand the rules and often cheer at the wrong time.

August 12, 1974: Nolan Ryan strikes out 19 batters as California defeats Boston, 4–2.

August 12, 1978: New England wide receiver Darryl Stingley is paralyzed after being tackled by Oakland defensive back Jack Tatum during a preseason game.

August 12, 1982: Featherweight boxing champion Salvador Sanchez is killed when his sports car collides with a truck in Mexico.

August 12, 1984: Diver Greg Louganis wins the 10-meter platform diving competition at the Los Angeles Olympics, his second gold medal of the Games. The United States will win a record 83 gold medals at the Games.

AUGUST 13

August 13, 1919: In the Sanford Memorial Stakes, a horse named Upset pulls off the greatest upset in thoroughbred racing history when he hands the mighty Man o' War his only defeat.

August 13, 1947: Willard Brown of the St. Louis Browns becomes the first black player to hit a home run in the American League, an inside-the-park version against the Detroit Tigers.

August 13, 1969: Jim Palmer pitches a no-hitter as the Baltimore Orioles defeat the Oakland A's, 8–0.

August 13, 1979: Lou Brock of the St. Louis Cardinals collects his 3,000th major league hit, off Chicago Cubs pitcher Dennis Lamp.

August 13, 1985: Terry Forster, the overweight Atlanta Braves relief pitcher whom comedian David Letterman described as a "fat tub of goo," films a music video for his song "Fat Is In." Forster sums up his philosophy by saying, "The waist is a terrible thing to mind."

AUGUST 14

August 14, 1936: In a low-scoring contest played outdoors on a sand court, the United States Olympic basketball team defeats Canada, 19–8, to win the first Olympic basketball gold medal. Olympic officials had tried to ban all players over 6 feet 3 inches tall, but changed their minds at the last minute.

August 14, 1958: Cleveland's Vic Power steals home twice in a 10–9 win over Detroit. Power had only one other stolen base all season.

August 14, 1959: Earvin "Magic" Johnson is born in East Lansing, Michigan.

August 14, 1966: Cincinnati's Art Shamsky ties a major league record with his fourth consecutive home run.

August 14, 1971: Bob Gibson pitches a no-hitter and strikes out ten as the St. Louis Cardinals defeat the Pittsburgh Pirates, 11–0.

August 14, 1986: Kenny Walker, the first-round draft choice of the New York Knicks, outruns pacer Pugwash in a photo finish in a 1/16-mile race at Monticello Raceway.

AUGUST 15

August 15, 1886: Louisville pitcher Guy Hecker hits three home runs, two doubles, and a single, and scores seven runs in a 22–5 victory over Baltimore. Hecker will become the only pitcher in baseball history to win a batting title.

August 15, 1926: Brooklyn's daffy slugger Babe Herman doubles into a double play. With the bases loaded, Herman hits a drive off the right-field wall. Due to a mixup on the base paths, three Dodgers end up standing on third base. Herman is called out for passing a base runner, and teammate Chick Fewster is tagged out after leaving the bag in confusion.

August 15, 1941: The Washington Senators find yet another way to lose a baseball game. The Senators are leading Boston, 6–3, in the eighth inning when the rains come. After the grounds crew take their time covering the field, the umpires rule that they did so intentionally and declare the game a forfeit.

August 15, 1970: Patricia Palinkas becomes the first woman to play in a professional football game. The 122-pounder is the holder for the Orlando Panthers in an Atlantic Coast League game against the Bridgeport Jets. Orlando wins the game, 26–7.

AUGUST 16

August 16, 1893: Bill Hawke pitches a no-hitter as Baltimore defeats Washington, 6–0.

August 16, 1920: Cleveland shortstop Ray Chapman is hit in the temple by a pitch thrown by the Yankees' Carl Mays. Chapman dies the next day.

August 16, 1920: American Charles Paddock wins the gold medal in the 100-meter dash at the Antwerp Olympics.

August 16, 1921: Molla Mallory upsets Suzanne Lenglen in the second round of the U.S. Open tennis tournament. Mallory wins the first set and is leading 3–2 in the second when Lenglen forfeits due to illness. It is the only time Lenglen loses a match from 1919 until her retirement in 1926.

August 16, 1930: Jim Dandy, a 100-to-1 long shot, defeats

Triple Crown winner Gallant Fox by six lengths to win the Travers Stakes at Saratoga Racetrack.

August 16, 1954: The first issue of *Sports Illustrated* is published.

AUGUST 17

August 17, 1882: Providence's John Montgomery Ward pitches an 18-inning shutout.

August 17, 1894: Philadelphia's Sam Thompson hits for the cycle in a 29–4 trouncing of Louisville. Louisville pitcher Jack Wadsworth yields a major-league record 36 base hits.

August 17, 1904: Boston pitcher Jesse Tannehill pitches a no-hitter as the Red Sox defeat the Chicago White Sox, 6–0.

August 17, 1938: Henry Armstrong wins the lightweight title from Lou Ambers on a 15-round decision to become the only boxer in history to hold three titles simultaneously. Earlier, Armstrong had won the featherweight and welterweight titles.

August 17, 1980: Al Oliver hits four home runs as the Texas Rangers sweep a doubleheader from Detroit, 9–3 and 12–6. Oliver's 21 total bases establishes an American League record.

AUGUST 18

August 18, 1941: A record crowd of 135,132 watch Tony Zale knock out Billy Prior in the ninth round of a fight held in Milwaukee.

August 18, 1956: The Cincinnati Reds hit eight home runs as they defeat the Milwaukee Braves, 13–4.

August 18, 1960: Lew Burdette pitches a no-hitter as the Milwaukee Braves defeat the Philadelphia Phillies, 1–0.

August 18, 1962: In one of the most exciting races in thoroughbred history, Jaipur defeats Ridan by a nose in the Travers Stakes.

August 18, 1965: Milwaukee's Henry Aaron has a home run taken away when St. Louis catcher Bob Uecker points out to the umpire that Aaron is standing partially out of the batter's box when he hits it.

August 18, 1967: Boston Red Sox slugger Tony Conigliaro is beaned by California pitcher Jack Hamilton. Conigliaro suffers retina damage and eventually, at the age of 26, is forced to retire.

August 18, 1983: The famous "pine tar game" between the Kansas City Royals and the New York Yankees is resumed. Both sides are retired without a runner reaching base as the Royals defeat the Yankees, 5–4.

AUGUST 19

August 19, 1931: Jockey Bill Shoemaker is born in Fabens, Texas. Shoemaker is born premature and is not expected to live. His grandmother places the tiny "Shoe" in a shoe box and uses an oven as a makeshift incubator.

August 19, 1951: St. Louis Browns owner Bill Veeck sends 3-foot-seven-inch midget Eddie Gaedel to the plate in a game against the Detroit Tigers. Detroit pitcher Bob Cain walks Gaedel on four pitches.

August 19, 1962: Golfer Homero Blancas shoots a 55 in the first round of the Premier Invitation Tournament.

August 19, 1965: Cincinnati's Jim Maloney pitches his second extra-inning no-hitter of the season as the Reds defeat the Chicago Cubs, 1–0.

August 19, 1967: At the U.S. Indoor tennis tournament, Mark Cox and Robert Wilson defeat Charles Pasarell and Ron Holmburg, 26–24, 17–19, 30–28, in a marathon match that lasts 6 hours and 23 minutes. The same day in Newport, Rhode Island, Dick Leach and Dick Dell outlast Tom Mozur and Lenny Schloss, 3–6, 49–47, 22–20.

August 19, 1969: Ken Holtzman pitches a no-hitter without striking out a single batter as the Chicago Cubs defeat the Atlanta Braves, 3–0.

AUGUST 20

August 20, 1880: Pud Galvin pitches a no-hitter as Buffalo defeats Worcester, 1–0.

August 20, 1952: Bradford's Frank Etchberger and Batavia's Jim Mitchell pitch the only double no-hitter in minor league history. Bradford wins the game, 1–0, on an error in the eighth inning.

August 20, 1957: Bob Keegan pitches a no-hitter as the Chicago White Sox blank Washington, 6–0.

August 20, 1964: New York's Phil Linz is fined $200 for playing a harmonica on the team bus after the Yankees had just dropped a four-game series to the Chicago White Sox.

August 20, 1974: Second baseman Dave Lopes has three home runs, five hits, and five stolen bases in leading the Los Angeles Dodgers to an 18–8 victory over the Chicago Cubs. Elsewhere, California's Nolan Ryan strikes out 19 batters, but his Angels lose to the Detroit Tigers, 1–0, in 11 innings.

AUGUST 21

August 21, 1864: A horse named Kentucky wins the first Travers Stakes at Saratoga Racetrack.

August 21, 1883: Providence beats Philadelphia, 28–0, in the worst rout in major league history.

August 21, 1887: Philadelphia pitcher Dan Casey strikes out in the ninth inning of a game against New York, perhaps providing the inspiration for the famous poem "Casey at the Bat."

August 21, 1898: Walter Thornton pitches a no-hitter as Chicago defeats Brooklyn, 2–0.

August 21, 1920: American Patrick McDonald wins the gold medal in the 56-pound weight throw at the Antwerp Olympics. The 42-year-old McDonald is the oldest track and field athlete ever to win an Olympic gold medal.

August 21, 1926: Ted Lyons pitches a no-hitter as the Chicago White Sox defeat the Boston Red Sox, 6–0.

August 21, 1931: New York's Babe Ruth hits the 600th major league home run of his career, off St. Louis pitcher George Blaeholder.

AUGUST 22

August 22, 1886: The term "dogging it" takes on new meaning in a game between Cincinnati and Louisville. The score is tied, 3–3, in the 11th inning when Louisville batter Chicken Wolf hits a ball into the gap. As Cincinnati outfielder Abner Powell tries to retrieve the ball, he wakes up a sleeping dog lying near the fence. The adage "let sleeping dogs lie" is never more appropriate as the mongrel grabs Powell's trouser leg. By the time Powell shakes him off, Wolf has circled the bases with the winning run.

August 22, 1892: Ben Sanders pitches a no-hitter as Louisville defeats Baltimore, 6–2.

August 22, 1957: Heavyweight champion Floyd Patterson comes off the canvas to knock out Pete Rademacher in the sixth round. Rademacher is fighting his first professional fight after winning the Olympic gold medal in 1956.

August 22, 1965: San Francisco pitcher Juan Marichal hits Los Angeles catcher John Roseboro over the head with his bat. Marichal is angered when Roseboro returns a pitch from Sandy Koufax too close to Marichal's ear. Marichal is suspended for nine days and fined $1,750.

AUGUST 23

August 23, 1912: Walter Johnson wins his 16th consecutive game as Washington defeats Detroit, 8–1.

August 23, 1926: Molla Mallory defeats Elizabeth Ryan for her seventh U.S. Open tennis title.

August 23, 1931: Lefty Grove's 16-game winning streak is snapped when outfielder Jim Moore misjudges a fly ball, giving St. Louis a 1–0 victory over Philadelphia.

August 23, 1936: Seventeen-year-old Bob Feller of the Cleveland Indians strikes out 15 batters in his first major league start.

August 23, 1961: The San Francisco Giants hit five home runs and score 12 runs in the ninth inning on their way to a 14–0 victory over the Cincinnati Reds.

August 23, 1985: Martina Navratilova and Pam Shriver defeat 67-year-old Bobby Riggs and Vitas Gerulaitis, 6–2, 6–3, 6–4, in their $500,000 exhibition match in Atlantic City. The match results from Gerulaitis's comment that Navratilova, the women's number-one player, could not beat the 100th-best male tennis player.

AUGUST 24

August 24, 1884: In a game versus Boston, New York's Mickey Welch strikes out the first nine batters he faces.

August 24, 1946: Eternal Reward lives up to his name by winning the American Derby at odds of 102 to 1.

August 24, 1951: Baseball fans are notorious second-guessers, so St. Louis Browns owner Bill Veeck decides to give them the opportunity to first-guess. Veeck equips over a thousand fans with "Yes" and "No" placards, which they flash whenever they are asked a question about what strategy to use. The ploy works, as the Browns defeat the Philadelphia A's, 5–3.

August 24, 1968: Superhorse Dr. Fager carries 134 pounds as he wins the Washington Park Handicap at Arlington Park in a world-record time of 1:32⅕ for the mile.

August 24, 1975: Ed Halicki pitches a no-hitter as the San Francisco Giants defeat the New York Mets, 6–0. The same day, Los Angeles second baseman Dave Lopes sets a major league record by stealing his 38th consecutive base.

AUGUST 25

August 25, 1922: The Chicago Cubs defeat the Philadelphia Phillies, 26–23, in the highest-scoring game in major league history.

August 25, 1952: Detroit's Virgil Trucks pitches his second no-hitter of the year as the Tigers defeat the New York Yankees, 1–0. Incredibly, Trucks's record for the year is a dismal 5–19.

August 25, 1967: Dean Chance pitches a no-hitter as the Minnesota Twins defeat the Cleveland Indians, 2–1.

August 25, 1973: Allan Abbott sets a world record by pedaling a bicycle 140.5 miles per hour on the Bonneville Salt Flats in Utah. Abbott achieves the incredible speed by slipstreaming behind a windshield mounted on a 1955 Chevy.

August 25, 1985: Teleprompter, a 14-to-1 long shot owned by Lord Derby, leads all the way to win the Arlington Million. That the race is run at all is a miracle, considering that the grandstand at Arlington Park burned to the ground on July 31. Only around-the-clock construction of temporary grandstands permitted the race to be run.

AUGUST 26

August 26, 1890: W. S. Franklin of New York announces his intention to form a women's professional baseball league. His requirements for players include that they not be over 20 years old and possess good looks and a good figure.

August 26, 1916: "Bullet" Joe Bush pitches a no-hitter as the Philadelphia A's defeat the Cleveland Indians, 5–0.

August 26, 1939: New York station W2XBS broadcasts the first major league baseball game on television. The game between the Brooklyn Dodgers and Cincinnati Reds is played at Ebbets Field.

August 26, 1947: Brooklyn's Don Bankhead becomes the first black pitcher to play in the major leagues. Bankhead also hits a home run in his first major league at bat.

August 26, 1960: American swimmer Lance Larson and Australian John Devitt finish together in the 100-meter freestyle at the Rome Olympics. Most observers believe Larson is the winner, and Devitt even congratulates the American after the race. Nearly everyone is shocked when Devitt is declared the winner.

August 26, 1962: Jack Kralick pitches a no-hitter as the Minnesota Twins defeat the Kansas City Athletics, 1–0.

AUGUST 27

August 27, 1873: Lipman Pike, baseball's first professional player and one of the fastest base runners of his day, outruns a trotter in a 100-yard dash. Pike finishes four yards ahead of the standardbred.

August 27, 1887: Mike "King" Kelly has six hits in leading Boston to a 29–14 drubbing of Pittsburgh. Kelly was baseball's highest-paid player, earning the princely sum of $5,000 a year.

August 27, 1911: Ed Walsh pitches a no-hitter as Chicago defeats Boston, 5–0.

August 27, 1938: Monte Pearson pitches a no-hitter as the New York Yankees trounce the Cleveland Indians, 13–0.

August 27, 1977: Toby Harrah and Bump Wills hit back-to-back inside-the-park home runs as the Texas Rangers defeat the New York Yankees, 8–2.

August 27, 1982: Oakland's Rickey Henderson steals his 119th base of the season in a game against Milwaukee to break Lou Brock's single-season stolen base record.

AUGUST 28

August 28, 1887: Star Pointer becomes the first pacer to break the two-minute-mile barrier when he is timed at 1:59¼ at Readville, Massachusetts.

August 28, 1926: Cleveland's Dutch Levsen becomes the last major league pitcher to complete both games of a doubleheader as the Indians sweep Boston by the scores of 6 to 1 and 5 to 1. Oddly, Levsen does not strike out a batter in either game.

August 28, 1955: In NFL football, Los Angeles defeats New York, 23–17, in overtime in a preseason game. The sudden-death rule is employed for the first time.

August 28, 1970: Detroit Tigers ace Denny McLain is suspended for eight days for dousing two sportswriters with ice water.

August 28, 1977: Steve Garvey hits three doubles and two home runs as the Los Angeles Dodgers defeat the St. Louis Cardinals, 11–0.

August 28, 1982: Kirkland, Washington, defeats Taiwan, 6–0, to win the Little League World Series. The star of the game is Cody Webster, who hits a tape-measure home run and pitches a shutout.

AUGUST 29

August 29, 1885: Charlie Ferguson pitches a no-hitter as Philadelphia defeats Providence, 1–0.

August 29, 1889: At Newport, Rhode Island, George Kerr defeats Thomas Pettit, 6–3, 6–1, 6–1, in the first professional tennis match played in the United States.

August 29, 1920: John Kelly, the father of Grace Kelly, wins a gold medal in the single sculls at the Antwerp Olympics. Kelly will win 126 races in a row and three Olympic gold medals during his rowing career.

August 29, 1972: Jim Barr of the San Francisco Giants retires the first 20 St. Louis Cardinals he faces to extend his streak of consecutive batters retired to 41.

August 29, 1977: Lou Brock of the St. Louis Cardinals steals his 893rd base to break the all-time record set by Ty Cobb.

August 29, 1977: Middleweight boxing champion Carlos Monzon announces his retirement. Monzon had not lost a fight in 13 years.

AUGUST 30

August 30, 1884: Jack "The Nonpareil" Dempsey knocks out George Fulljames in the 22nd round to win the middleweight title, the first boxing match in which gloves are used.

August 30, 1904: American Thomas Hicks wins the marathon at the St. Louis Olympics. Another American, Fred Lorz, finishes 15 minutes ahead of Hicks but is disqualified when it is discovered that he rode in an automobile for 11 of the 26 miles.

August 30, 1910: New York's Tommy Hughes holds the Red Sox hitless for nine innings but runs out of gas in the 11th inning as Boston wins, 5–0.

August 30, 1912: Earl Hamilton pitches a no-hitter as St. Louis defeats Detroit, 5–1.

August 30, 1916: Dutch Leonard pitches a no-hitter as Boston defeats the St. Louis Browns, 4–0.

August 30, 1941: Lon Warneke pitches a no-hitter as the St. Louis Cardinals defeat the Cincinnati Reds, 2–0.

August 30, 1978: Sadaharu Oh of the Yomiuri Giants hits his 800th career home run.

AUGUST 31

August 31, 1895: Jeanette, Pennsylvania, defeats Latrobe, Pennsylvania, 12–0, in the first professional football game. Latrobe quarterback John Brallier is paid $10 for the game.

August 31, 1915: Jimmy Lavender pitches a no-hitter as the New York Giants defeat the Chicago Cubs, 2–0.

August 31, 1950: First baseman Gil Hodges smashes four home runs as the Brooklyn Dodgers defeat the Boston Braves, 19–3.

August 31, 1955: Nashua avenges his loss in the Kentucky Derby, defeating Swaps by six and a half lengths in their celebrated match race in Chicago.

August 31, 1981: John Henry wins the first running of the Arlington Million by a nose over long shot The Bart.

August 31, 1984: Pinklon Thomas wins a 15-round decision over Tim Witherspoon to claim the WBC world heavyweight title.

August 31, 1985: The Longest-Hole golf tournament, a 37-mile hole across the South Nevada Desert from State Line, Nevada, to Las Vegas is inaugurated. The par-400 hole takes the average player three days to complete.

SEPTEMBER 1

September 1, 1890: The Brooklyn Dodgers defeat the Pittsburgh Pirates, 10–9, 3–2, and 8–4, in a rare baseball tripleheader.

September 1, 1946: Patty Berg wins the first women's U.S. Open golf tournament in Spokane, Washington.

September 1, 1960: Armin Hary of Germany wins the 100-meter dash at the Rome Olympics. Hary's start is so fast that some of the other competitors accuse him of jumping the gun.

September 1, 1972: American swimmer Rick DeMont wins the Olympic gold medal in the 400-meter freestyle, only to be disqualified when it is discovered he has traces of the banned drug ephedrine in his system. DeMont took the medication for his asthma condition, unaware that it contained an illegal drug.

September 1, 1984: Mississippi State clobbers Kentucky State, 86–0, as wide receiver Jerry Rice catches 17 passes for 294 yards. Quarterback Willie Totten completes 37 passes for 536 yards as Mississippi State rolls up 699 yards through the air.

September 1, 1985: Stock-car driver Bill Elliot wins a million-dollar bonus as he finishes first in the Southern 500.

SEPTEMBER 2

September 2, 1880: Two department-store baseball teams play a night game in Nantasket Bay, Massachusetts. Teams from Jordan Marsh & Co. and R. H. White & Co. play to a 16–16 tie.

September 2, 1964: Norman Manley becomes the first golfer to score holes-in-one on consecutive par-four holes. Manley aces the seventh and eighth holes at the Del Valle Country Club course in Saugus, California. At last count, Manley has a record 53 holes-in-one to his credit.

September 2, 1972: American Dave Wottle unleashes a furious stretch kick to win the 800-meter race at the Munich Olympics. Wottle passes two Kenyans in the homestretch and just catches Russian Yevgeny Arzhanov at the tape.

September 2, 1972: Milt Pappas pitches a no-hitter as Chicago defeats St. Louis, 8–0. Pappas barely misses a perfect game when he walks Larry Stahl on a 3–2 pitch with two outs in the ninth inning.

September 2, 1985: The Cannonball and Bellyflopping Diving Contest is held in Gainesville, Florida. Randy "Stump" Williams, the Greg Louganis of bellyflopping, wins the backflip bellyflop and with it the coveted green bathrobe.

SEPTEMBER 3

September 3, 1894: Joe Kelley goes nine for nine in a doubleheader as Baltimore sweeps Cleveland by the scores of 13 to 2 and 16 to 4.

September 3, 1927: Boston's Doc Gautreau steals home twice as the Braves defeat the Brooklyn Dodgers, 4–3.

September 3, 1928: Ty Cobb of the Philadelphia A's collects his 4,191st and final major league base hit.

September 3, 1947: Bill McCahan pitches a no-hitter as Philadelphia blanks Washington, 3–0.

September 3, 1977: Japanese slugger Sadaharu Oh hits his 756th career home run, eclipsing Hank Aaron's all-time professional baseball record.

September 3, 1983: Minor league player Mike Ashman of the Albany Colonie A's becomes the first player to play all ten positions in one game. Ashman plays all nine positions on the field and serves as the designated hitter.

SEPTEMBER 4

September 4, 1906: The New York Highlanders play a doubleheader for the fifth consecutive day. Amazingly, New York wins all ten games.

September 4, 1920: Man o' War wins the Lawrence Realization Stakes by an incredible 100 lengths at Belmont Park.

September 4, 1923: "Sad" Sam Jones pitches a no-hitter as the New York Yankees defeat the Philadelphia A's, 2–0.

September 4, 1949: Marie Robie scores a hole-in-one on a 393-yard par four at the Furnace Brook Golf Course in Wollaston, Massachusetts.

September 4, 1951: Sixteen-year-old tennis sensation Maureen Connolly wins the U.S. Open.

September 4, 1972: Mark Spitz wins his seventh gold medal of the Munich Games as a member of the victorious American 4 × 100-meter relay team.

September 4, 1982: Rick Baker plays a round of golf in only 25 minutes at Queensland, Australia.

SEPTEMBER 5

September 5, 1885: Arbroath defeats Bon Accord, 36–0, in Scotland, the most lopsided soccer match on record.

September 5, 1908: Nap Rucker pitches a no-hitter and strikes out 14 as Brooklyn defeats Boston, 6–0.

September 5, 1918: Babe Ruth pitches a shutout as the Boston Red Sox defeat the Chicago Cubs, 1–0, in the first game of the World Series.

September 5, 1954: Joe Bauman hits three home runs for Roswell of the Longhorn League, giving him 72 homers for the season. Despite setting minor league home run records, Bauman never got the chance to play in the majors.

September 5, 1960: Cassius Clay wins a unanimous decision over Zbigniew Pietrzykowski of Poland to win the Olympic gold medal in the light heavyweight division at the Rome Olympics.

September 5, 1971: Houston's J. R. Richard strikes out 15 batters in his first major league game.

September 5, 1985: Readers of *USA Today* are asked to vote for the sexiest athletes. When the votes are counted, golfer Jan Stephenson is selected as the sexiest female athlete and baseball pitcher Jim Palmer is chosen as the sexiest male.

SEPTEMBER 6

September 6, 1883: Chicago scores 18 runs in the seventh inning of a 26–6 victory over Detroit.

September 6, 1905: Frank Smith pitches a no-hitter as the Chicago White Sox blank the Detroit Tigers, 15–0.

September 6, 1912: Jess Tesreau pitches a no-hitter as the New York Giants defeat Philadelphia, 3–0.

September 6, 1913: Philadelphia second baseman Eddie Collins steals home twice in a game against Boston.

September 6, 1920: WWJ in Detroit carries the first radio broadcast of a prizefight. Jack Dempsey knocks out Billy Miske in the third round.

September 6, 1943: Cincinnati's Woody Williams ties a National League record with ten consecutive base hits. Sixteen-year-old Carl Scheib becomes the youngest player in American League history when he pitches two-thirds of an inning for the Philadelphia Athletics.

September 6, 1974: Evonne Goolagong defeats Chris Evert in the semifinals of the U.S. Open, snapping Evert's 56-match winning streak.

SEPTEMBER 7

September 7, 1892: Gentleman Jim Corbett knocks out champion John L. Sullivan in the 21st round to win the heavyweight boxing title.

September 7, 1896: The first automobile racetrack, a one-mile dirt oval at Narragansett Park in Cranston, Rhode Island, is opened.

September 7, 1923: Boston's Howard Ehmke pitches a no-hitter as the Red Sox defeat the Philadelphia A's, 4–0.

September 7, 1935: Cleveland third baseman Odell Hale uses his head to start a triple play. Boston's Joe Cronin hits a line drive that ricochets off Hale's forehead. The ball deflects to shortstop Bill Knickerbocker, who starts the triple play.

September 7, 1953: Eighteen-year-old Maureen Connolly wins the U.S. Open to become the first woman tennis player to complete the Grand Slam.

September 7, 1970: Jockey Bill Shoemaker wins his 6,033rd race to pass Johnny Longden and become racing's winningest rider.

September 7, 1985: In one of the most exciting tennis matches of all time, Hana Mandlikova of Czechoslovakia wins two tiebreakers to defeat Martina Navratilova, 7–6, 1–6, 7–6, in the final of the U.S. Open.

SEPTEMBER 8

September 8, 1906: The greatest pacer of all time, Dan Patch, sets a world record by pacing a mile in 1:55 at Hamline, Missouri. During his storied career, Dan Patch never lost a final heat.

September 8, 1914: The "Miracle" Braves take over first place with a 5–4 victory over the New York Giants. Boston had been in the cellar on July 18.

September 8, 1950: Sandy Saddler regains the featherweight boxing title when champion Willie Pep is unable to answer the bell for the eighth round.

September 8, 1957: Althea Gibson defeats Louise Brough to become the first black tennis player to win the U.S. Open.

September 8, 1965: Oakland's Bert Campaneris becomes the first major league baseball player to play all nine positions in a game.

September 8, 1969: Rod Laver defeats Tony Roche in the finals of the U.S. Open to become the first tennis player to win two Grand Slams.

September 8, 1972: Jim Ryun falls during a qualifying heat of the Olympic 1,500-meter run. Ryun gets up and continues the race but is unable to qualify for the finals.

SEPTEMBER 9

September 9, 1876: Hartford sweeps Cincinnati, 14–6 and 8–3, in baseball's first doubleheader.

September 9, 1914: George Davis pitches a no-hitter as the Boston Braves defeat the Philadelphia Phillies, 7–0.

September 9, 1945: Dick Fowler pitches a no-hitter as the Philadelphia A's shut out the St. Louis Browns, 1–0.

September 9, 1948: Rex Barney pitches a no-hitter as the Brooklyn Dodgers defeat the New York Giants, 2–0.

September 9, 1965: Sandy Koufax pitches a perfect game, his fourth career no-hitter, as the Los Angeles Dodgers defeat the Chicago Cubs, 1–0. His luckless mound opponent, Bob Hendley, pitches a one-hitter in defeat.

September 9, 1968: Arthur Ashe defeats Tom Okker to become the first black man to win the U.S. Open.

September 9, 1979: Sixteen-year-old Tracy Austin defeats Chris Evert in the women's final of the U.S. Open.

September 9, 1984: John McEnroe defeats Ivan Lendl for his fourth U.S. Open title.

SEPTEMBER 10

September 10, 1881: Troy's Roger Connor hits the first grand slam in National League history in an 8–7 victory over Worcester.

September 10, 1919: Boston's Ray Caldwell pitches a no-hitter as the Red Sox defeat the New York Yankees, 3–0.

September 10, 1960: Mickey Mantle of the New York Yankees hits a tape-measure home run over the right-field stands in Detroit that lands 643 feet from home plate in a nearby lumberyard.

September 10, 1962: Rod Laver defeats Roy Emerson in the final of the U.S. Open to complete his Grand Slam.

September 10, 1963: Stan Musial of the St. Louis Cardinals has two reasons to celebrate when he hits a home run and becomes a grandfather.

September 10, 1967: Joel Horlen pitches a no-hitter as the Chicago White Sox defeat the Detroit Tigers, 6–0.

September 10, 1972: The United States' 62-game winning streak in basketball is snapped by a controversial 51–50 loss to the Soviet Union.

September 10, 1972: Ilie Nastase defeats Arthur Ashe in five sets to win the U.S. Open.

SEPTEMBER 11

September 11, 1888: Pittsburgh's Billy Sunday becomes the first outfielder to turn in an unassisted double play. After his playing days are over, Sunday will become a famous evangelist.

September 11, 1911: Second baseman Eddie Collins steals six bases as the Philadelphia A's defeat the Detroit Tigers, 9–7.

September 11, 1928: Philadelphia outfielder Ty Cobb plays the final game of his illustrious career, against the New York Yankees.

September 11, 1946: The Brooklyn Dodgers and Cincinnati Reds play to a 0–0 tie in 19 innings, the longest scoreless tie in baseball history.

September 11, 1974: The St. Louis Cardinals defeat the New York Mets, 4–3, in 25 innings. The marathon game lasts 7 hours and 4 minutes and ends at 3:13 in the morning.

September 11, 1983: Jimmy Connors defeats Ivan Lendl for his fifth U.S. Open title.

September 11, 1985: Cincinnati's Pete Rose singles off San Diego's Eric Show to become baseball's all-time hit leader. For Rose it is hit number 4,192, breaking Ty Cobb's 57-year-old record.

SEPTEMBER 12

September 12, 1925: Led by "Big Bill" Tilden, the United States wins the Davis Cup for the sixth consecutive year.

September 12, 1930: Jockey Albert Adams wins the first race at Marlborough Racecourse, giving him nine consecutive winners over a three-day period, an American record.

September 12, 1951: Sugar Ray Robinson knocks out Randy Turpin in the tenth round to avenge a loss to Turpin two months earlier and regain the middleweight crown.

September 12, 1962: In a game against Baltimore, Washington pitcher Tom Cheney strikes out a major league record 21 batters.

September 12, 1965: Brant Alyea of the Washington Senators hits a home run on the first pitch made to him in the major leagues.

September 12, 1976: Fifty-three-year-old Minnie Minoso of the Chicago White Sox hits a single off Sid Monge in a game against the California Angels to become the oldest major leaguer to get a hit.

September 12, 1979: Boston's Carl Yastrzemski collects his 3,000th major league hit in a 9–2 victory over the New York Yankees.

SEPTEMBER 13

September 13, 1883: Hugh "One Arm" Daily pitches a no-hitter as Cleveland defeats Philadelphia, 1–0. Daily had lost his left arm in a fireworks accident.

September 13, 1925: Dazzy Vance pitches a no-hitter as the Brooklyn Dodgers defeat the Philadelphia Phillies, 10–1.

September 13, 1936: Seventeen-year-old Bob Feller strikes out 17 batters and pitches a two-hitter as the Cleveland Indians defeat Philadelphia, 5–2.

September 13, 1946: Ted Williams crosses up the "Boudreau Shift" by hitting an inside-the-park home run to left field. The blow provides the only run of the game and clinches the pennant for Boston.

September 13, 1965: Willie Mays hits his 500th career home run as the San Francisco Giants defeat Houston, 5–1.

September 13, 1970: Margaret Court defeats Rosemary Casals in the final of the U.S. Open to complete her Grand Slam.

September 13, 1970: The first New York City Marathon is won by Gary Muhrcke.

September 13, 1971: Frank Robinson blasts his 500th major league home run as Baltimore beats Detroit, 10–5.

SEPTEMBER 14

September 14, 1903: Larry Cheney pitches a 14-hit shutout as Chicago defeats New York, 7–0.

September 14, 1923: Jack Dempsey knocks out Luis Firpo in the second round to retain his heavyweight title. During the wild bout, Firpo knocks Dempsey completely out of the ring. The groggy Dempsey is pushed back into the ring by sportswriters at ringside, probably saving his title.

September 14, 1923: Boston first baseman George Burns turns in an unassisted triple play against Cleveland.

September 14, 1951: Bob Nieman of the St. Louis Browns becomes the only player in major league history to hit a home run in his first two major league at bats, but the Browns lose to Boston, 9–6.

September 14, 1968: Detroit pitcher Denny McLain defeats Oakland, 5–4, for his 30th win of the season.

September 14, 1971: Washington defeats Cleveland, 8–6, in a game in which a record 18 pitchers are used.

September 14, 1987: The Toronto Blue Jays hit a record ten home runs in an 18–3 victory over Baltimore.

SEPTEMBER 15

September 15, 1946: A game between Brooklyn and Chicago at Ebbets Field is called after a swarm of gnats attack both players and spectators. The game is called after five innings, with Brooklyn leading, 2–0.

September 15, 1960: Warren Spahn pitches a no-hitter and strikes out 15 as the Milwaukee Braves blank the Philadelphia Phillies, 4–0.

September 15, 1963: Washington quarterback George Izo throws a 99-yard touchdown pass to Bobby Mitchell in a game against the Cleveland Browns.

September 15, 1966: Kansas City manager Alvin Dark uses seven pitchers as his A's shut out Cleveland, 1–0.

September 15, 1968: Washington quarterback Sonny Jurgensen throws a 99-yard touchdown pass to Gerry Allen in a game against Chicago.

September 15, 1969: St. Louis's Steve Carlton strikes out 19 batters but loses to the New York Mets, 4–3, on a pair of two-run homers by Ron Swoboda.

September 15, 1973: Secretariat defeats stablemate Riva Ridge in the first running of the Marlboro Cup.

September 15, 1978: Muhammad Ali wins a 15-round decision over Leon Spinks to become the first boxer to win the heavyweight title three times.

SEPTEMBER 16

September 16, 1899: The hapless Cleveland Spiders lose their 24th game in a row. The Spiders, managed by an Australian undertaker, lose 40 of their last 41 games.

September 16, 1924: Jim Bottomley bats in a major league record 12 runs as the St. Louis Cardinals defeat Brooklyn, 17–3.

September 16, 1960: Amos Alonzo Stagg retires from college coaching at the age of 98.

September 16, 1965: Dave Morehead pitches a no-hitter as the Boston Red Sox defeat the Cleveland Indians, 2–0.

September 16, 1973: Buffalo's O. J. Simpson rushes for 250 yards in a game against the New England Patriots.

September 16, 1975: Pittsburgh second baseman Rennie Stennett has seven hits as the Pirates blank the Chicago Cubs, 22–0.

September 16, 1978: In the first-ever meeting between two Triple Crown winners, Seattle Slew defeats Affirmed by three lengths in the Marlboro Cup.

September 16, 1981: Sugar Ray Leonard stops Thomas Hearns in the 14th round to win the welterweight title.

SEPTEMBER 17

September 17, 1920: The American Professional Football Association, the forerunner of the National Football League, is founded in Canton, Ohio. The historic meeting is held in a Hupmobile showroom, and most of the owners sit on automobile fenders and running boards. Franchises are awarded to cities for a meager $100.

September 17, 1935: Brooklyn outfielder Len Koenecke is killed attempting the first skyjacking. Enraged by his release from the Dodgers, Koenecke skyjacks a plane over Canada, but in the ensuing struggle he is hit over the head with a fire extinguisher and killed.

September 17, 1938: Don Budge wins the U.S. Open to complete his Grand Slam.

September 17, 1961: Quarterback Fran Tarkenton throws four touchdown passes in his first NFL game, as the Minnesota Vikings defeat Chicago, 37–13.

September 17, 1968: San Francisco's Gaylord Perry pitches a no-hitter and outduels St. Louis's Bob Gibson, 1–0.

September 17, 1984: Reggie Jackson hits his 500th major league home run, off Kansas City's Bud Black.

SEPTEMBER 18

September 18, 1897: Cy Young pitches a no-hitter as Cleveland defeats Cincinnati, 6–0.

September 18, 1903: Chick Fraser pitches a no-hitter as Philadelphia blanks Chicago, 10–0.

September 18, 1908: Cleveland's Bob Rhoads no-hits the Boston Red Sox, 2–0. In 1906, Rhoads had literally saved the

Cleveland franchise from bankruptcy. During an exhibition tour in Texas, the team had run out of money. Rhoads proceeded to win a fortune at the craps table of a local gambling house that he presented to the team to bail them out.

September 18, 1934: Bobo Newsom no-hits Boston for nine innings. However, his St. Louis Browns lose to the Boston Red Sox, 2–1, in ten innings.

September 18, 1963: Dick Nen hits a home run in his first major league game to help the Los Angeles Dodgers to a pennant-clinching 6–5 win.

September 18, 1968: One day after San Francisco's Gaylord Perry no-hits the Cardinals, St. Louis's Ray Washburn returns the favor by no-hitting the Giants, 2–0.

September 18, 1977: Ted Turner skippers *Courageous* to a four-race sweep of Australia in the America's Cup.

SEPTEMBER 19

September 19, 1924: "Big Bill" Tilden wins the U.S. Open for the sixth consecutive year.

September 19, 1965: The Dallas Cowboys defeat the New York Giants, 31–2, in a game played in 97-degree heat in Dallas.

September 19, 1971: Green Bay's Ken Ellis runs back a field goal attempt 100 yards in a game against the New York Giants.

September 19, 1973: Frank Robinson of the California Angels hits a home run in Texas's Arlington Stadium, the 32nd major league park where he has homered. Robinson's home run sparks the Angels to a 9–4 victory over the Texas Rangers.

September 19, 1983: Philadelphia second baseman Joe Morgan celebrates his 40th birthday by going four for five with two home runs in a 7–6 victory over the Chicago Cubs.

September 19, 1986: Joe Cowley pitches a no-hitter as the Chicago White Sox defeat the California Angels, 7–1.

SEPTEMBER 20

September 20, 1882: Larry Corcoran pitches a no-hitter as Chicago defeats Worcester, 5–0.

September 20, 1902: Nixey Callahan pitches a no-hitter as the Chicago White Sox blank Detroit, 3–0.

September 20, 1907: In only his third major league game, Pittsburgh's Nick Maddox no-hits Brooklyn, 2–1.

September 20, 1908: Chicago's Frank Smith pitches a no-hitter as he blanks the Philadelphia A's, 1–0.

September 20, 1913: Twenty-year-old amateur golfer Francis Ouimet wins the U.S. Open.

September 20, 1958: Hoyt Wilhelm pitches a no-hitter as the Baltimore Orioles defeat the New York Yankees, 1–0.

September 20, 1960: Carroll Hardy, a .225 lifetime batter, pinch hits for Ted Williams. Hardy promptly hits into a double play.

September 20, 1969: Pittsburgh's Bob Moose pitches a no-hitter, a 4–0 win over the New York Mets.

September 20, 1973: Billie Jean King defeats 55-year-old tennis hustler Bobby Riggs, 6–4, 6–3, 6–3, in the celebrated "Battle of the Sexes."

SEPTEMBER 21

September 21, 1934: Dizzy Dean pitches a three-hit shutout as the St. Louis Cardinals defeat the Brooklyn Dodgers, 13–0, in the first game of a doubleheader. In the nightcap, Dizzy's brother, Daffy Dean, pitches a no-hitter as the Cardinals win, 3–0.

September 21, 1938: A baseball game between the Boston Bees and the St. Louis Cardinals in Boston is canceled because of a hurricane.

September 21, 1970: Oakland's Vida Blue no-hits Minnesota, 6–0, in only his fourth major league start.

September 21, 1970: The Cleveland Browns defeat the Dallas Cowboys, 31–21, in the first *Monday Night Football* telecast. Howard Cosell, Don Meredith, and Keith Jackson report the action. Frank Gifford will replace Jackson the following year.

September 21, 1980: New York Jets quarterback Richard Todd completes a record 42 passes in a game against the San Francisco 49ers.

September 21, 1985: Michael Spinks wins a close decision over Larry Holmes to become the first light heavyweight champion ever to challenge successfully for the heavyweight title.

SEPTEMBER 22

September 22, 1911: Forty-four-year-old Cy Young earns his 511th and final victory as Boston shuts out Pittsburgh, 1–0.

September 22, 1927: Gene Tunney wins a ten-round decision over Jack Dempsey in the celebrated "long-count fight" in Chicago.

September 22, 1954: Brooklyn Dodgers rookie Karl Spooner strikes out 15 while shutting out the New York Giants, 3–0, in his first major league start. Four days later, Spooner pitches another shutout, striking out 12. Unfortunately, Spooner hurt his arm the following season and was replaced on the roster by another young hard-throwing southpaw. His name was Sandy Koufax.

September 22, 1968: The Minnesota Twins' Cesar Tovar plays all nine positions in a 2–1 victory over the Oakland A's.

September 22, 1969: In a game against the San Diego Padres, San Francisco's Willie Mays hits his 600th career home run.

September 22, 1977: Bert Blyleven pitches a no-hitter as the Texas Rangers defeat the California Angels, 6–0.

SEPTEMBER 23

September 23, 1908: Fred Merkle costs the New York Giants a pennant with a baserunning blunder. Merkle is on first base when Al Bridwell hits an apparent game-winning single against the Chicago Cubs. Merkle, seeing the winning run scoring, doesn't bother to touch second base. Chicago second baseman Johnny Evers alertly tags second base and umpire Hank O'Day rules the play a force out. New York protests, and the game is replayed two weeks later. The Cubs win the game and the pennant.

September 23, 1926: A crowd of 120,757 in Philadelphia watch Gene Tunney decision Jack Dempsey to win the heavyweight title.

September 23, 1952: Rocky Marciano knocks out Jersey Joe Walcott in the 13th round to win the heavyweight title.

September 23, 1983: Steve Carlton wins his 300th game as the Philadelphia Phillies defeat the St. Louis Cardinals, 6–2.

September 23, 1983: South African Gerrie Coetzee knocks

out Michael Dokes in the tenth round to win the WBA heavyweight title.

September 23, 1985: Speaking at a reunion of his Grand Rapids high-school class, former President Gerald Ford says, "I'm a hit man for the PGA."

SEPTEMBER 24

September 24, 1916: Cleveland's Marty Kavanaugh hits the first pinch-hit grand slam home run in American League history. Kavanaugh's hit rolls through a hole in the outfield wall, which under the existing rules is considered a home run.

September 24, 1940: Boston's Jimmie Foxx hits his 500th home run in a 16–8 victory over the Philadelphia A's.

September 24, 1950: Chicago Cardinals quarterback Jim Hardy throws an NFL record eight interceptions in a 45–7 loss to the Philadelphia Eagles. The following week, Hardy will redeem himself by throwing six touchdown passes against the Baltimore Colts.

September 24, 1967: Jim Bakken kicks a record seven field goals as the St. Louis Cardinals defeat the Pittsburgh Steelers, 28–14.

September 24, 1974: Detroit outfielder Al Kaline collects his 3,000th base hit, off Baltimore's Dave McNally.

September 24, 1977: Louisiana State University wide receiver Carlos Carson scores five touchdowns in his first college game. Carson catches five passes, all for touchdowns, in LSU's 77–0 rout of Rice.

SEPTEMBER 25

September 25, 1909: Washington's Bob Groom pitches a two-hitter but loses to Chicago, 2–1, his 19th consecutive defeat.

September 25, 1946: Cleveland Indians owner Bill Veeck offers free admission for a game against the Chicago White Sox. A crowd of 12,800 watch the Indians lose to Chicago, 4–1.

September 25, 1949: In Landover, Maryland, golfer Louise Suggs wins the U.S. Open by 14 shots.

September 25, 1962: Sonny Liston knocks out Floyd Patterson in the first round to win the heavyweight title.

September 25, 1965: Fifty-nine-year-old Satchel Paige of the Kansas City Athletics pitches three shutout innings against the Boston Red Sox. The only hit Paige yields is a double to Boston star Carl Yastrzemski.

September 25, 1974: Sixty-four-year-old golfer Michael Austin hits a record 515-yard drive on the fifth hole of the Winterwood Golf Course during the U.S. National Seniors Open championship. The tremendous drive lands only a yard from the cup but rolls off the green, coming to rest 65 yards beyond the hole.

SEPTEMBER 26

September 26, 1908: Ed Reulbach of the Chicago Cubs pitches shutouts in both games of a doubleheader against Brooklyn.

September 26, 1926: The St. Louis Browns sweep the New York Yankees, 6–1 and 6–2, in the fastest doubleheader on record. The twin bill takes only 2 hours and 7 minutes to play, less than most single games.

September 26, 1961: Roger Maris of the New York Yankees hits his 60th home run of the season to tie Babe Ruth's single-season record.

September 26, 1964: New York pitcher Mel Stottlemyre has five hits and pitches a two-hit shutout as the Yankees defeat the Washington Senators, 7–0.

September 26, 1981: Nolan Ryan becomes the first major leaguer to pitch five no-hitters as the Houston Astros whitewash the Los Angeles Dodgers, 5–0.

September 26, 1983: *Australia II*, captained by John Bertrand, defeats Dennis Conner's *Liberty*, 4–3, to end the United States' 132-year domination of the America's Cup.

September 26, 1983: Bob Forsch pitches a no-hitter as the St. Louis Cardinals defeat the Montreal Expos, 3–1.

SEPTEMBER 27

September 27, 1881: Twelve fans, the smallest crowd in major league baseball history, watch Chicago defeat Troy, 10–8, in a driving rainstorm.

September 27, 1930: Golfer Bobby Jones wins the U.S. Amateur to complete the Grand Slam.

September 27, 1940: Rookie pitcher Floyd Giebell outduels Bob Feller as the Detroit Tigers defeat the Cleveland Indians, 2–0, to clinch the American League pennant. It is Giebell's third and final victory in the majors.

September 27, 1956: Rookie outfielder Bill Sharman of the Brooklyn Dodgers earns the dubious distinction of being ejected from a major league game without ever appearing in one. Umpire Frank Dascoli clears the Dodger bench, including Sharman, after a disputed play at the plate. Sharman later decided to give up baseball, and he became a perennial all-star guard with the Boston Celtics.

September 27, 1963: The Houston Colts live up to their name by playing an all-rookie lineup in a 10–3 loss. The starters, all 21 years old or younger, include such future stars as Joe Morgan, Rusty Staub, and Jimmy Wynn.

September 28, 1941: Boston Red Sox outfielder Ted Williams goes six for eight in a doubleheader on the final day of the season to finish the year with a .406 batting average.

September 28, 1951: Allie Reynolds pitches a no-hitter as the New York Yankees blank the Boston Red Sox, 8–0, to clinch the American League pennant.

September 28, 1960: In his final major league at bat, Ted Williams of the Boston Red Sox hits a home run off Baltimore's Jack Fisher.

SEPTEMBER 28

September 28, 1919: Pitcher Jesse Barnes pitches the New York Giants to a 6–1 victory over Philadelphia in a game lasting only 51 minutes.

September 28, 1938: Chicago catcher Gabby Hartnett hits the famous "homer in the gloamin' " off Pittsburgh's Mace Brown as the Cubs defeat the Pirates, 6–5, to clinch the National League pennant.

September 28, 1974: Nolan Ryan pitches his third no-hitter and strikes out 15 as the California Angels defeat the Minnesota Twins, 4–0.

September 28, 1975: Vida Blue, Glenn Abbott, Paul Lindblad, and Rollie Fingers combine to pitch a no-hitter as the Oakland A's defeat the California Angels, 5–0.

SEPTEMBER 29

September 29, 1892: Mansfield Teachers College and Wyomia Seminary of Kingston, Pennsylvania, play the first night football game.

September 29, 1954: Willie Mays makes an incredible over-the-shoulder catch of Vic Wertz's 440-foot drive in game one of the World Series.

September 29, 1963: Outfielder John Paciorek plays the game of his life in his major league debut with Houston. Paciorek goes three for three, walks twice, scores four runs, and bats in three. The reason it was the game of his life is that it was his first and only major league game.

September 29, 1971: Montreal second baseman Ron Hunt is plunked by Chicago's Milt Pappas, marking the 50th time that season that he had been hit by a pitch.

September 29, 1973: Prove Out upsets superhorse Secretariat in the Woodward Stakes.

September 29, 1976: John "The Count" Montefusco pitches a no-hitter as the San Francisco Giants defeat the Atlanta Braves, 9–0.

September 29, 1983: Oakland's Mike Warren pitches a no-hitter as he defeats the Chicago White Sox, 3–0.

SEPTEMBER 30

September 30, 1916: Boston Braves pitcher Lefty Tyler defeats the New York Giants, snapping New York's record 26-game winning steak. The Giants also had a 17-game winning streak earlier in the season, yet will finish fourth in the standings.

September 30, 1927: Babe Ruth of the New York Yankees hit his 60th home run of the season, off Washington's Tom Zachary.

September 30, 1939: Bill Stern calls the play-by-play of the first televised college football game, between Fordham and Waynesburg.

September 30, 1961: Kansas City relief pitcher Bill Fischer issues his first base on balls after pitching a record 84⅓ innings without walking a batter.

September 30, 1967: Damascus, the 1967 Horse of the Year, wins the Woodward Stakes by ten lengths over a stellar field that includes 1966 Horse of the Year Buckpasser and 1968 Horse of the Year Dr. Fager.

September 30, 1984: California's Mike Witt pitches a perfect game as the Angels defeat the Texas Rangers, 1–0.

OCTOBER 1

October 1, 1903: The Pittsburgh Pirates defeat the Boston Red Sox, 7–3, in the first World Series game. Pirate outfielder Jimmy Sebring hits the first home run in World Series history, off loser Cy Young.

October 1, 1932: In game three of the World Series between the Yankees and the Cubs, New York's Babe Ruth gestures toward the center-field stands, then deposits Charlie Root's next pitch into the center-field bleachers. Ruth's home run breaks a 4–4 tie as the Yankees go on to win, 7–5.

October 1, 1950: Dick Sisler of the Phillies hits a dramatic home run in the tenth inning to clinch the pennant for Philadelphia's "Whiz Kids."

October 1, 1961: On the last day of the season, Roger Maris of the New York Yankees hits his 61st home run of the season to break Babe Ruth's record.

October 1, 1975: Joe Frazier is unable to answer the bell for the 15th round of his fight with Muhammad Ali, the classic "Thrilla in Manila."

October 1, 1977: In his final game, soccer star Pele plays the first half for the New York Cosmos and the second half for his old team, Santos of Brazil.

October 1, 1980: The fabulous Niatross paces a world-record mile in 1:49⅕ at the Red Mile in Lexington, Kentucky.

OCTOBER 2

October 2, 1908: Addie Joss pitches a perfect game as the Cleveland Indians defeat the Chicago White Sox, 1–0.

October 2, 1920: In baseball's last tripleheader, Pittsburgh's Clyde Barnhart becomes the only player ever to have hits in three games in a single day. Cincinnati wins the first two games by the scores of 13 to 4 and 7 to 3, but is trailing Pittsburgh, 6–0, in the third game when it is called.

October 2, 1968: Bob Gibson strikes out a World Series record 17 batters as the St. Louis Cardinals defeat Denny McLain and the Detroit Tigers, 4–0, in game one.

October 2, 1972: Bill Stoneman pitches a no-hitter as the Montreal Expos blank the New York Mets, 2–0.

October 2, 1976: Forego, carrying high weight of 137 pounds, charges down the stretch to defeat Honest Pleasure by a head in the Marlboro Cup.

October 2, 1978: The New York Yankees defeat the Boston Red Sox, 5–4, in the American League Eastern Division playoff to cap their amazing comeback.

October 2, 1980: Heavyweight champion Larry Holmes wins a technical knockout over Muhammad Ali in the 11th round.

OCTOBER 3

October 3, 1920: The Dayton Triangles defeat the Columbus Panhandles, 14–0, and the Rock Island Independents shut out the Muncie Flyers, 45–0, in the first games of the American Professional Football Association, forerunner of the National Football League.

October 3, 1947: New York pitcher Bill Bevens nearly becomes the first player to pitch a no-hitter in the World Series. Bevens is leading 2–1 with two out in the ninth inning when Brooklyn pinch hitter Cookie Lavagetto hits a two-run double to give the Dodgers a 3–2 victory. Neither Bevens nor Lavagetto will play in another game in the major leagues.

October 3, 1951: Bobby Thomson hits the "Shot Heard 'Round the World" in the deciding game of the National League playoff between the New York Giants and the Brooklyn Dodgers. Thomson hits a three-run home run off Ralph Branca with two out in the ninth inning to give the Giants a 5–4 victory over the Dodgers.

October 3, 1964: Floyd Rood hits the final shot in his 13-month quest to hit a golf ball across the United States. Rood uses 3,511 golf balls and takes 114,737 strokes in his 3,397-mile journey.

OCTOBER 4

October 4, 1884: Thirty-one-year-old Brooklyn rookie Sam Kimber pitches ten hitless innings against Toledo.

October 4, 1891: Ted Breitenstein pitches a no-hitter in his first major league start as St. Louis defeats Louisville, 8–0.

October 4, 1895: Horace Rawlings wins the first U.S. Open golf tournament in Newport, Rhode Island.

October 4, 1907: Jimmy Dygert of the Philadelphia A's pitches his third shutout in four days.

October 4, 1941: Bill Hearne of Union College runs back a kickoff 109 yards for a touchdown against Transylvania College.

October 4, 1948: The Cleveland Indians defeat the Boston Red Sox, 8–3, to win the American League pennant in a playoff.

October 4, 1955: The Brooklyn Dodgers, behind the pitching of Johnny Podres, defeat the New York Yankees for their first world championship. Brooklyn outfielder Sandy Amoros makes a game-saving catch of Yogi Berra's fly ball down the left-field line in the sixth inning.

October 4, 1980: The Oklahoma Sooners defeat the Colorado Buffaloes, 82–42, in the highest-scoring game in major college football history.

OCTOBER 5

October 5, 1921: With Grantland Rice at the microphone, WCJ of Newark, New Jersey, broadcasts the first World Series game on radio.

October 5, 1941: With two out in the ninth inning, catcher Mickey Owen's passed ball on a third strike gives the Yankees' Tommy Heinrich new life. The miscue opens the floodgates, as the Yankees rally for four runs in a 7–4 victory in game four of the World Series.

October 5, 1942: The St. Louis Cardinals defeat the New York Yankees, 3–2, to win the World Series in five games.

October 5, 1947: Brooklyn outfielder Al Gionfriddo makes one of the greatest catches in World Series history in game six against the New York Yankees. The Dodgers win the game, 8–6. Gionfriddo will not play in another major league game.

October 5, 1953: The New York Yankees defeat the Brooklyn Dodgers, 4–3, in game six to become the first team to win five consecutive World Series.

October 5, 1967: Jim Lonborg pitches a one-hitter as the Boston Red Sox defeat the St. Louis Cardinals, 5–0, in game two of the World Series.

October 5, 1985: Grambling's Eddie Robinson wins his 324th game, making him the winningest college football coach in history.

OCTOBER 6

October 6, 1880: The Cincinnati Reds are kicked out of the National League for selling beer at the ballpark against league rules.

October 6, 1923: In only his second major league game, Boston Braves shortstop Ernie Padgett turns in an unassisted triple play.

October 6, 1935: Colgate, Amherst, and St. Lawrence play a round-robin football tournament. Each team plays another for two 15-minute quarters. Colgate defeats St. Lawrence, 31–0, Colgate defeats Amherst, 12–0, and St. Lawrence defeats Amherst, 13–0.

October 6, 1936: The New York Yankees defeat the New York Giants, 13–5, to win the World Series in six games.

October 6, 1941: The New York Yankees defeat the Brooklyn Dodgers, 3–1, to win the World Series in five games.

October 6, 1947: The New York Yankees defeat the Brooklyn Dodgers, 5–2, in the seventh game of the World Series.

October 6, 1948: Cleveland's Bob Feller pitches a two-hitter but the Indians lose to the Boston Braves, 1–0, in game one of the World Series. In the eighth inning, the Braves' Phil Masi is apparently picked off second but is called safe. Tommy Holmes singles home Masi with the winning run.

OCTOBER 7

October 7, 1916: Georgia Tech annihilates Cumberland College, 222–0, in the worst rout in college football history.

October 7, 1933: Mel Ott hits a home run in the tenth inning to give the New York Giants a 4–3 victory over the Washington Senators and a win of the World Series in five games.

October 7, 1935: Goose Goslin hits a home run in the ninth inning as the Detroit Tigers defeat the Chicago Cubs, 4–3, to win the World Series.

October 7, 1950: The New York Yankees defeat the Philadelphia Phillies, 5–2, to sweep the World Series in four games.

October 7, 1952: The New York Yankees defeat the Brooklyn Dodgers, 4–2, in the seventh game of the World Series for their fourth world championship in a row.

October 7, 1965: Aided by a 50-mile-per-hour wind at his back, golfer Robert Mitera scores a hole-in-one on the 444-yard tenth hole at the appropriately named Miracle Hill Golf Club in Omaha, Nebraska.

October 7, 1984: Walter Payton rushes for 154 yards as the Chicago Bears defeat the New Orleans Saints, 20–7. Payton breaks Jim Brown's career rushing record of 12,312 yards.

OCTOBER 8

October 8, 1922: The New York Giants defeat the New York Yankees, 5–3, to win the World Series in five games.

October 8, 1927: The New York Yankees defeat the Pittsburgh Pirates, 4–3, to complete a four-game sweep in the World Series.

October 8, 1930: The Philadelphia A's defeat the St. Louis Cardinals, 7–1, to win the World Series in six games.

October 8, 1939: New York's Charlie "King Kong" Keller barrels into Cincinnati catcher Ernie Lombardi on a close play at the plate. The collision knocks Lombardi senseless, and while he lies on the ground a few feet from home plate, Joe DiMaggio circles the bases. "Lombardi's snooze" helps the Yankees to a 7–4 victory and a four-game sweep in the World Series.

October 8, 1940: The Cincinnati Reds defeat the Detroit Tigers, 2–1, in the seventh game of the World Series.

October 8, 1956: Don Larsen pitches the only perfect game in World Series history as the New York Yankees defeat the Brooklyn Dodgers, 2–0.

October 8, 1959: The Los Angeles Dodgers defeat the Chicago White Sox, 9–3, to win the World Series in six games.

OCTOBER 9

October 9, 1919: The Cincinnati Reds defeat the Chicago White Sox, 10–5, to win the World Series. A year later it is learned that Chicago threw the Series, leading to the infamous "Black Sox" scandal.

October 9, 1928: Babe Ruth hits three home runs to lead the New York Yankees to a 7–3 victory over the St. Louis Cardinals and a four-game sweep of the World Series.

October 9, 1934: The St. Louis Cardinals defeat the Detroit Tigers, 11–0, in the seventh game of the World Series.

October 9, 1938: The New York Yankees defeat the Chicago Cubs, 8–3, to complete a four-game sweep of the World Series.

October 9, 1949: The New York Yankees defeat the Brooklyn Dodgers, 10–6, to win the World Series in five games.

October 9, 1958: The New York Yankees defeat the Milwaukee Braves, 6–2, in the seventh game of the World Series.

October 9, 1966: The Baltimore Orioles defeat the Los Angeles Dodgers, 1–0, to sweep the World Series in four games. The anemic-hitting Dodgers were shut out the last three games.

OCTOBER 10

October 10, 1924: The Washington Senators defeat the New York Giants, 4–3, in the seventh game of the World Series.

October 10, 1926: Grover Cleveland Alexander comes out of the bullpen to strike out Tony Lazzeri with the bases loaded and preserve a 3–2 victory for the St. Louis Cardinals over the New York Yankees in the seventh game of the World Series.

October 10, 1931: The St. Louis Cardinals, led by Pepper Martin, defeat the Philadelphia A's, 4–2, to win the World Series in seven games.

October 10, 1937: Pitcher Lefty Gomez knocks in the winning run as the New York Yankees defeat the New York Giants, 4–2, to win the World Series.

October 10, 1945: The Detroit Tigers defeat the Chicago Cubs, 9–3, in the seventh game of the World Series.

October 10, 1956: Johnny Kucks pitches a shutout as the

New York Yankees defeat the Brooklyn Dodgers, 9–0, in the seventh game of the World Series.

October 10, 1957: Lew Burdette wins his third game of the World Series as the Milwaukee Braves defeat the New York Yankees, 5–0, to win the world championship.

October 10, 1968: The Detroit Tigers defeat the St. Louis Cardinals, 4–1, in the seventh game of the World Series.

OCTOBER 11

October 11, 1913: Eddie Plank pitches a two-hitter and the Philadelphia A's defeat Christy Mathewson and the New York Giants, 3–1, to win the World Series in five games.

October 11, 1943: Spud Chandler pitches a ten-hit shutout as the New York Yankees defeat the St. Louis Cardinals, 2–0, to win the World Series in five games.

October 11, 1948: The Cleveland Indians defeat the Boston Braves, 4–3, to win the World Series in six games.

October 11, 1959: National Football League commissioner Bert Bell suffers a fatal heart attack during the final two minutes of a game between the Pittsburgh Steelers and the Philadelphia Eagles. Pete Rozelle will be named the new commissioner.

October 11, 1972: Johnny Bench hits a dramatic ninth-inning home run to help lift the Cincinnati Reds to a 4–3 victory over the Pittsburgh Pirates in the fifth and deciding game of the National League Championship Series. The winning run scores on a wild pitch by Bob Moose.

OCTOBER 12

October 12, 1907: Mordecai "Three Finger" Brown pitches a shutout as the Chicago Cubs defeat the Detroit Tigers, 2–0, to sweep the World Series four games to none with one tie.

October 12, 1916: Ernie Shore pitches a three-hitter as the Boston Red Sox defeat the Brooklyn Dodgers, 4–1, to win the World Series in five games.

October 12, 1920: Stan Coveleski pitches a shutout and wins his third game of the Series as the Cleveland Indians defeat the Brooklyn Dodgers, 3–0, to win the World Series five games to two. From 1919 to 1921 the World Series was a best-of-nine format.

October 12, 1920: Man o' War defeats Triple Crown winner Sir Barton by seven lengths in his final race at Kenilworth Park in Canada.

October 12, 1929: The Chicago Cubs are leading 8–0 in the seventh inning of game four of the World Series when the Philadelphia A's erupt for ten runs en route to a 10–8 victory.

October 12, 1983: In San Diego, California, golfer Scott Palmer plays four consecutive rounds in which he scores a hole-in-one.

OCTOBER 13

October 13, 1903: Big Bill Dinneen pitches a four-hit shut-out as the Boston Red Sox defeat the Pittsburgh Pirates, 3–0, to win baseball's first World Series.

October 13, 1914: The Miracle Braves defeat the Philadelphia A's, 3–1, to sweep the World Series in four games.

October 13, 1915: Harry Hooper hits two home runs, including the game winner, as the Boston Red Sox defeat the Philadelphia Phillies, 5–4, to win the World Series in five games.

October 13, 1921: Art Nehf pitches a four-hit shutout as the New York Giants blank the New York Yankees, 1–0, to win the World Series.

October 13, 1960: Pittsburgh second baseman Bill Mazeroski hits a home run in the bottom of the ninth inning to give the Pirates a dramatic 10–9 victory over the New York Yankees in the seventh game of the World Series.

October 13, 1971: The Pittsburgh Pirates defeat the Baltimore Orioles, 4–3, in the first World Series game played at night.

OCTOBER 14

October 14, 1905: Christy Mathewson pitches his third shut-out of the World Series as the New York Giants defeat the Philadelphia A's, 2–0, to win the World Series in five games.

October 14, 1906: The Chicago White Sox, baseball's "Hitless Wonders," defeat the Chicago Cubs, 8–3, to win the World Series in six games.

October 14, 1908: Orvie Overall pitches a three-hitter as the Chicago Cubs defeat the Detroit Tigers, 2–0, to win the World Series in five games.

July 29, 1975: Eight years before the infamous ''pine tar game,'' Thurman Munson of the New York Yankees has an RBI single against the Minnesota Twins wiped off the books when it is discovered that there is too much pine tar on his bat.

July 29, 1983: Steve Garvey's National League record 1,207-consecutive-game playing streak ends when he dislocates his left thumb in a home-plate collision.

July 29, 1987: The United States Football League is awarded $1 in damages in their antitrust suit against the National Football League. The USFL had sought $1,690,000,000.

JULY 30

July 30, 1908: American George Schuster wins the first around-the-world automobile race. In a scenario that sounds like the movie *The Great Race*, German Hans Koeppen finishes four days ahead of his nearest competition, only to be disqualified when it is learned that he had been transported by train for part of the distance.

July 30, 1959: In his major league debut, San Francisco's Willie McCovey has two triples and two singles against Philadelphia.

July 30, 1968: Washington shortstop Ron Hansen turns in an unassisted triple play against the Cleveland Indians.

July 30, 1973: Jim Bibby pitches a no-hitter and strikes out 13 as the Texas Rangers blank the Oakland A's, 8–0.

July 30, 1976: American Bruce Jenner wins the gold medal in the decathlon at the Montreal Summer Olympics.

July 30, 1982: Chief Noc-A-Homa and his tepee are removed from the left-field bleachers in Atlanta in order to make room for more seats. The Braves, without their mascot, lose 19 of their next 21 games, blowing a 10½-game lead. When the tepee is resurrected, the Braves recover and regain first place.

JULY 31

July 31, 1880: Bullfighting makes a less-than-spectacular debut in New York City. Though boxing gloves are placed on the bulls' horns, all the matadors run at the first sight of the animal charging out of the chute.

July 31, 1891: Amos Rusie pitches a no-hitter as New York defeats Brooklyn, 6–0.

October 14, 1929: The Philadelphia A's score three runs in the ninth inning to defeat the Chicago Cubs, 3–2, to win the World Series in five games.

October 14, 1964: American Billy Mills pulls off one of the greatest upsets in Olympic history when he comes from behind to win the 10,000-meter race at the Tokyo Summer Games.

October 14, 1965: Sandy Koufax pitches a three-hit shutout as the Los Angeles Dodgers defeat the Minnesota Twins in the seventh game of the World Series.

October 14, 1984: Kirk Gibson hits two home runs as the Detroit Tigers defeat the San Diego Padres, 8–4, to win the World Series in five games.

OCTOBER 15

October 15, 1892: Farmboy Bumpus Jones pitches a no-hitter in his first major league game as Cincinnati defeats Pittsburgh, 7–1.

October 15, 1917: The Chicago White Sox defeat the New York Giants, 4–2, to win the World Series in six games.

October 15, 1923: The New York Yankees win their first world championship as they defeat the New York Giants, 6–4, in game six of the World Series.

October 15, 1925: The Pittsburgh Pirates defeat the Washington Senators, 9–7, in the seventh game of the World Series.

October 15, 1946: Enos Slaughter scores from first base on a single as St. Louis defeats Boston, 4–3, in the seventh game of the World Series.

October 15, 1964: The St. Louis Cardinals defeat the New York Yankees, 7–5, in the seventh game of the World Series.

October 15, 1970: The Baltimore Orioles defeat the Cincinnati Reds, 9–3, to win the World Series four games to one.

October 15, 1985: Richard Nixon is selected to arbitrate a dispute between major league baseball and the Major League Umpire Association. Nixon, who instituted wage and price controls during his administration to curb inflation, decides to give the men in blue a 40 percent pay increase.

OCTOBER 16

October 16, 1909: Rookie pitcher Babe Adams wins his third game of the Series as the Pittsburgh Pirates defeat the Detroit Tigers, 8–0, to win the World Series in seven games.

October 16, 1912: New York center fielder Fred Snodgrass muffs an easy fly ball, which results in a two-run rally in the tenth inning as the Boston Red Sox defeat the Giants, 3–2, in the seventh game of the World Series.

October 16, 1962: Second baseman Bobby Richardson catches Willie McCovey's vicious line drive with two out in the ninth and the winning runs in scoring position, as the New York Yankees hold on to defeat the San Francisco Giants in the seventh game of the World Series.

October 16, 1969: The New York Mets defeat the Baltimore Orioles, 5–3, to win the World Series in five games.

October 16, 1973: Aboard Ocean King in a race at Warwick, England, jockey Victor Lawson wins his first race. What makes the achievement remarkable is that Lawson is 67 years old.

October 16, 1983: The Baltimore Orioles defeat the Philadelphia Phillies, 5–0, to win the World Series in five games.

OCTOBER 17

October 17, 1860: Eight golfers compete in the first British Open, at the Prestwick Golf Club in Scotland. Willie Park wins the 36-hole tournament with a score of 174. Three rounds are played on the 12-hole course—all in the same day.

October 17, 1883: The first scoring system is established for the game of football. Under the rules, five points are awarded for a field goal, two points for a touchdown, and one point for a safety.

October 17, 1943: The Chicago Cardinals hold the Detroit Lions to a minus 53 yards rushing, an NFL record for fewest yards gained rushing in a game.

October 17, 1971: The Pittsburgh Pirates defeat the Baltimore Orioles, 2–1, in the seventh game of the World Series.

October 17, 1974: The Oakland A's defeat the Los Angeles Dodgers, 3–2, in game five to win their third consecutive world championship.

October 17, 1978: The New York Yankees defeat the Los Angeles Dodgers, 7–2, to win the World Series in six games.

October 17, 1979: The Pittsburgh Pirates defeat the Baltimore Orioles, 4–1, to win the World Series four games to three.

OCTOBER 18

October 18, 1924: The incomparable Red Grange scores touchdowns of 95, 67, 56, 44, and 15 yards the first five times he touches the ball, as Illinois defeats Michigan, 39–14.

October 18, 1950: Eighty-eight-year-old Connie Mack retires after managing the Philadelphia A's for 50 years.

October 18, 1956: Tennis superstar Martina Navratilova is born in Prague, Czechoslovakia.

October 18, 1960: Despite winning ten pennants in 12 years as manager of the New York Yankees, Casey Stengel is fired. Realizing that his age was a factor in the decision to fire him, Stengel says, "I'll never make the mistake of being seventy again."

October 18, 1968: American Bob Beamon long jumps an incredible 29 feet, 2½ inches to win the gold medal at the Mexico City Olympics.

October 18, 1977: Reggie Jackson, "Mr. October," hits three home runs to power the New York Yankees to an 8–4 victory over the Los Angeles Dodgers to win the World Series in six games. Jackson sets a World Series record with five home runs.

OCTOBER 19

October 19, 1924: Following Notre Dame's 13–7 victory over Army, *New York Herald Tribune* sportswriter Grantland Rice refers to the Fighting Irish backfield of Stuhldreher, Miller, Crowley, and Layden as the "Four Horsemen of the Apocalypse."

October 19, 1964: Tamara Press of the Soviet Union wins the gold medal in the discus at the Tokyo Olympics. The next day, she easily wins the shotput. Press mysteriously disappears from international competition once sex tests are imposed.

October 19, 1968: Bill Toomey, a 29-year-old English teacher from California, wins the Olympic decathlon in Mexico City.

October 19, 1981: Rick Monday hits a home run off Steve Rogers to give the Los Angeles Dodgers a 2–1 victory over the Montreal Expos in the fifth and deciding game of the National League Championship Series.

OCTOBER 20

October 20, 1865: The Philadelphia Athletics baseball team defeats Williamsport, 101–8. To prove that it's no fluke, they demolish Danville, 160–11, in a game later the same day.

October 20, 1888: A group of major league all-stars begin a world tour to promote the game of baseball. Games are scheduled in such exotic locations as Honolulu, Cairo, Sydney, Naples, Rome, Paris, and London. One of the games is played at the foot of Mt. Vesuvius and another is played in the shadow of the Great Pyramid.

October 20, 1931: Former New York Yankees star Mickey Mantle is born in Spavinaw, Oklahoma.

October 20, 1968: Kip Keino of Kenya defeats American Jim Ryun in the 1,500-meter race at the Mexico City Olympics. Using his patented "Fosbury Flop" jumping style, American Richard Fosbury wins the high jump with a leap of 7 feet, 4 inches.

October 20, 1979: John Tate wins a 15-round unanimous decision over South African Gerrie Coetzee to win the vacant WBA heavyweight title.

October 20, 1982: The St. Louis Cardinals defeat the Milwaukee Brewers, 6–3, in the seventh game of the World Series.

OCTOBER 21

October 21, 1877: Right-handed Boston pitcher Tommy Bond and Cincinnati left-hander Bobby Mitchell throw baseballs around a stake to prove that curve balls really curve.

October 21, 1922: King College blows out Lenoir, 206–0, in a college football game played in Bristol, Tennessee.

October 21, 1973: Reggie Jackson hits the game-winning home run as the Oakland A's defeat the New York Mets, 5–2, in game seven of the World Series.

October 21, 1975: Carlton Fisk hits a home run in the bottom of the 12th inning to give the Boston Red Sox a 7–6 victory over the Cincinnati Reds in game six of the World Series, a game often cited as the most exciting in baseball history.

October 21, 1976: Johnny Bench hits two home runs as the Cincinnati Reds defeat the New York Yankees, 7–2, to sweep the World Series in four games.

October 21, 1979: Roy Green of the St. Louis Cardinals runs a kickoff return 106 yards for a touchdown against the Dallas Cowboys.

October 21, 1980: The Philadelphia Phillies defeat the Kansas City Royals, 4–1, to win the World Series in six games.

OCTOBER 22

October 22, 1855: Overreach, Lady Go-Lightly, Gamester, and The Unexpected run a rare quadruple dead heat at Newmarket, England.

October 22, 1921: In college football, Georgetown's John Flavin returns a punt 110 yards for a touchdown against Holy Cross.

October 22, 1950: The high-powered Los Angeles Rams embarrass the Baltimore Colts, 70–27. The following week, the Rams beat the Detroit Lions, 65–17.

October 22, 1961: Erich Barnes of the New York Giants returns an interception 102 yards for a touchdown against the Dallas Cowboys.

October 22, 1972: The Oakland A's defeat the Cincinnati Reds, 3–2, in the seventh game of the World Series.

October 22, 1975: The Cincinnati Reds defeat the Boston Red Sox, 4–3, to win the World Series in seven games.

October 22, 1980: The Philadelphia 76ers edge Detroit, 94–93, the Pistons' 21st consecutive loss, an NBA record.

OCTOBER 23

October 23, 1884: The original New York Mets of the American Association, behind the shutout pitching of Old Hoss Radbourn, defeat Providence of the National League, 6–0, to win an early version of the World Series in three straight games.

October 23, 1910: The Philadelphia A's defeat the Chicago Cubs, 7–2, to win the World Series in five games.

October 23, 1964: Joe Frazier wins a close decision over German Hans Huber to win the gold medal in the heavyweight division at the Tokyo Olympics. Frazier had been defeated by 300-pound Buster Mathis in the Olympic Trials, but got another chance when Mathis broke a knuckle in training. Ironically, Frazier wins the Olympics fighting with a broken right hand.

October 23, 1968: George Foreman stops Russian Ionas Chepulis in the second round to win the Olympic super heavyweight boxing gold medal.

October 23, 1975: Eighteen-year-old Bill Willoughby of the Atlanta Hawks becomes the youngest player in NBA history.

October 23, 1979: Billy Martin makes headlines when he punches a 52-year-old marshmallow salesman named Joseph Cooper.

OCTOBER 24

October 24, 1857: The world's first soccer team, the Sheffield Football Club, is founded in England.

October 24, 1917: Lightweight boxing champion Benny Leonard knocks out challenger Toughey Ramsey in the seventh round, his fourth successful title defense in five days.

October 24, 1965: Despite being held to a minus ten yards rushing and 63 yards total offense, the Green Bay Packers take advantage of five Dallas turnovers and defeat the Cowboys, 13–3.

October 24, 1971: Detroit Lions wide receiver Chuck Hughes collapses and dies of a heart attack during a game against the Chicago Bears.

October 24, 1975: Nicky Jarvis and Jim Walker exchange the fastest Ping-Pong rally in history, 159 shots in 60 seconds, in a match at Barrow-in-Furness, England.

OCTOBER 25

October 25, 1964: Minnesota Vikings defensive end Jim Marshall picks up a fumble and runs 60 yards the wrong way for a safety against the San Francisco 49ers. Despite the blunder, the Vikings defeat the 49ers, 27–22.

October 25, 1972: Gymnastic darling Olga Korbut of the Soviet Union wins the gold medal in the floor exercise at the Montreal Olympics.

October 25, 1980: Mike Weaver knocks out Gerrie Coetzee in the 13th round to retain his WBA heavyweight title.

October 25, 1985: Seven-foot-seven-inch Manute Bol of the Washington Bullets and five-foot-seven-inch Spud Webb of the Atlanta Hawks play their first NBA game in Atlanta. Webb scores 12 points while the giant Bol is held scoreless, as Washington defeats Atlanta, 100–91.

October 25, 1987: The Minnesota Twins defeat the St. Louis Cardinals, 4–2, to win the World Series in seven games.

OCTOBER 26

October 26, 1911: The Philadelphia A's crush the New York Giants, 13–2, to win the World Series four games to two for their second consecutive world championship.

October 26, 1947: Columbia, sparked by two fourth-quarter touchdowns, defeats Army, 21–20, snapping Army's 32-game winning streak.

October 26, 1951: Heavyweight boxing champion Rocky Marciano knocks out former champ Joe Louis in the eighth round, ending the Brown Bomber's comeback attempt.

October 26, 1980: The St. Louis Cardinals unleash a fierce pass rush that accounts for 12 sacks of Baltimore Colts quarterback Bert Jones, an NFL record. Sparked by the defense, the Cardinals defeat the Colts, 17–10. Until this game, the Colts' eighth of the season, Jones had been sacked only nine times.

OCTOBER 27

October 27, 1912: Indiana's Martin Erehart returns a punt 112 yards for a touchdown against Iowa. In those days, the field was 110 yards long.

October 27, 1967: Quarterback Brooks Dawson throws six touchdowns in his first six completions as the University of Texas at El Paso overpowers New Mexico, 75–12.

October 27, 1973: The University of Alabama Crimson Tide rolls up a record 828 yards in total offense as they flatten Virginia Tech, 77–6.

October 27, 1984: Reuben Mayes rushes for an NCAA

record 357 yards as the Washington State Cougars defeat the Oregon Ducks, 50–41.

October 27, 1985: The underdog Kansas City Royals surprise their cross-state rival, the St. Louis Cardinals, 11–0, in the seventh game of the World Series.

October 27, 1986: The New York Mets defeat the Boston Red Sox, 8–5, to win the World Series in seven games.

OCTOBER 28

October 28, 1922: WEAF in New York transmits the first coast-to-coast radio broadcast of a college football game. Princeton defeats the University of Chicago in a game played at Stagg Field in Chicago.

October 28, 1931: Edmund Burke of Mississippi returns a kickoff 109 yards in a game against Alabama. However, it is the only bright spot for Ole Miss, as they are trounced by the Crimson Tide, 55–6.

October 28, 1950: Pat Brady of Nevada-Reno has a record 99-yard punt in a game against Loyola of Los Angeles.

October 28, 1962: New York quarterback Y. A. Tittle throws for seven touchdowns and 505 yards as the Giants defeat the Washington Redskins, 49–34.

October 28, 1973: Secretariat wins the Canadian International Stakes at Woodbine Racecourse in Toronto in the final race of his career.

October 28, 1981: The Los Angeles Dodgers defeat the New York Yankees, 9–2, to win the World Series in six games.

October 28, 1984: Orlando Pizzolato of Italy wins the New York City Marathon, despite stopping ten times during the race.

OCTOBER 29

October 29, 1908: Ulrich Salchow of Sweden wins the first Olympic gold medal in figure skating. Figure skating will be a part of the Summer Olympics until the Winter Olympics are established in 1924.

October 29, 1921: In what many believe to be the greatest upset in college football history, little Centre College (student body:

300) defeats Harvard, 6–0. It is Harvard's first loss in four years and their first intersectional defeat in forty years.

October 29, 1924: Gene Sarazen scores a hole-in-one on a 246-yard hole at the Briarcliff Manor Golf Course in New York during the first demonstration of night golf. The course is illuminated by a 400-million-candlepower searchlight.

October 29, 1948: Triple Crown winner Citation wins the Pimlico Invitational Special Stakes in a walkover, one of 19 races he wins in 1948.

October 29, 1950: Marion Motley of the Cleveland Browns rushes 188 yards in 17 carries, an average of over 11 yards per carry, in a game against the Pittsburgh Steelers. Elsewhere, the Los Angeles Rams score 41 points in one quarter as they rout the Detroit Lions, 65–17. Detroit's Wally Triplett averages 74 yards per return on four kickoffs.

OCTOBER 30

October 30, 1943: Football star Tom Harmon is shot down over China while flying a combat mission against the Japanese during World War II. Harmon is able to parachute to safety.

October 30, 1943: Toronto Maple Leaf rookie Gus Bodnar scores a goal 15 seconds into his first game, against the New York Rangers.

October 30, 1955: The Cigar Bowl is canceled, joining the Refrigerator Bowl, Ice Bowl, and Salad Bowl on the list of extinct bowl games.

October 30, 1972: Lyudmila Tourischeva of the Soviet Union wins the gold medal in the all-around gymnastic competition at the Munich Olympics. Eventually, Tourischeva will marry 100-meter-dash gold medalist Valery Borzov.

October 30, 1974: Muhammad Ali knocks out George Foreman in the eighth round to regain the heavyweight title. During the fight, Ali unveils his notorious "rope-a-dope" strategy.

OCTOBER 31

October 31, 1925: Red Grange rushes for 363 yards as Illinois defeats Penn, 24–2.

October 31, 1930: Cedartown's Ed Barrett, despite having only one arm, catches four passes and intercepts three in a game against Rome, Georgia.

October 31, 1959: The Nebraska Cornhuskers upset the Oklahoma Sooners, 25–21, to snap Oklahoma's 74-game winning streak in the Big Eight Conference.

October 31, 1964: Kelso wins the Jockey Club Gold Cup to clinch his fifth consecutive Horse of the Year title. His time of 3:19⅕ for the two-mile distance is a world record that still stands.

October 31, 1971: The Cincinnati Bengals are held to a minus 52 yards passing in a 10–6 loss to the Houston Oilers.

October 31, 1983: George "Papa Bear" Halas dies at the age of 88.

NOVEMBER 1

November 1, 1913: Notre Dame defeats Army, 35–13, in the game that first popularizes the forward pass. Quarterback Gus Dorais completes 14 of 17 passes for 243 yards. His favorite receiver is Knute Rockne, who will later gain fame as Notre Dame's head coach.

November 1, 1924: Montana State freshman Forest Peters kicks 17 field goals in 22 attempts during a college football game against Billings Polytech.

November 1, 1938: Seabiscuit defeats Triple Crown winner War Admiral by four lengths in their match race at Pimlico Racetrack in Baltimore.

November 1, 1946: The New York Knicks defeat the Toronto Huskies, 68–66, in the first professional basketball game. The teams play in the Basketball Association of America, forerunner of the NBA.

November 1, 1964: George Blanda of the Houston Oilers completes 37 of 68 passes in an American Football League game against the Buffalo Bills.

November 1, 1987: Golfer Tom Watson wins first prize of $384,000 in the $3,000,000 Nabisco Championships in San Antonio, Texas.

NOVEMBER 2

November 2, 1879: It's man against horse to see which can run farther over a six-day period. The horse named Pinafore covers 559 miles, nine more than his human rival.

November 2, 1935: Notre Dame scores three touchdowns in the fourth quarter as they defeat Ohio State, 18–13. The winning touchdown pass is thrown by a player named Bill Shakespeare.

November 2, 1944: The Montreal Canadiens extend their unbeaten streak to 28 games. The streak includes 24 wins and four ties.

November 2, 1968: Carrying 139 pounds, Dr. Fager sets a track record when he wins the seven-furlong Vosburgh Handicap at Belmont Park in a time of 1:20⅕.

November 2, 1969: The New Orleans Saints defeat the St. Louis Cardinals, 51–42, in an NFL game in which 12 touchdown passes are thrown.

November 2, 1974: Hank Aaron, baseball's all-time home run king, is traded from the Atlanta Braves to the Milwaukee Brewers in exchange for Dave May.

November 2, 1986: Skywalker is a surprise winner of the $3,000,000 Breeders' Cup Classic horse race.

NOVEMBER 3

November 3, 1899: Heavyweight champion Jim Jeffries wins a 25-round decision over Sailor Tom Sharkey at Coney Island, New York, in the first filmed heavyweight title bout. Because filming a boxing match is illegal at the time, the camera is hidden in a cigar box.

November 3, 1942: Even though Boston's Ted Williams wins the Triple Crown, New York Yankees second baseman Joe Gordon is voted the American League's Most Valuable Player.

November 3, 1952: Mickey Mantle of the New York Yankees is turned down for military service because of a knee injury. The injury will not prevent Mantle from going on to hit 536 home runs.

November 3, 1973: Roy Bentley sets an endurance record when he runs 161 miles in one day at Walton-on-Thames, Surrey, England.

November 3, 1973: Catch-22 takes on a new meaning as Brigham Young's Jay Miller sets an NCAA record with 22 receptions in a 56–21 victory over New Mexico.

NOVEMBER 4

November 4, 1884: Wyllys Terry has a record 115-touchdown run as Yale shuts out Wesleyan, 46–0.

November 4, 1890: Princeton's Philip King scores 11 touchdowns in a game against Columbia.

November 4, 1923: Chicago's George Halas picks up a Jim Thorpe fumble and runs 98 yards for a touchdown against the Oorang Indians.

November 4, 1965: Lee Ann Roberts Breedlove drives her rocket-powered vehicle 308.5 miles per hour over the Bonneville Salt Flats to set a women's land-speed record. Eleven days later, her husband, Craig, reaches 600.6 miles per hour to break the existing land-speed record.

November 4, 1974: The shortest fight in boxing history occurs when Mike Collins floors Pat Brownson with the first punch of their Golden Gloves fight in Minneapolis. The referee stops the contest after only four seconds has elapsed.

November 4, 1979: The Los Angeles Rams limit the Seattle Seahawks to a minus seven yards total offense, an NFL record.

NOVEMBER 5

November 5, 1906: The great handicap horse Roseben carries 57 more pounds than Zienap, yet manages to defeat his rival by two and a half lengths. Roseben carries 147 pounds to victory, one of 52 races he will win in his fabulous career.

November 5, 1928: Walter Hagen wins the PGA tournament for the fourth year in a row.

November 5, 1946: Long before Darryl Dawkins was even born, Chuck Connors shatters a glass backboard dunking a basketball while a member of the Boston Celtics. Connors will also play professional baseball with the Brooklyn Dodgers and Chicago Cubs before turning to acting, where he will attain greater fame in roles such as the Rifleman.

November 5, 1966: Roger Taylor of Great Britain defeats Wieslaw Gasiorek of Poland, 27–29, 31–29, 6–4, in the King's Cup tennis tournament in Warsaw. The match, played prior to the adoption of the tiebreaker rule, is the longest, in terms of games played, in tennis history.

November 5, 1987: In the inaugural "Battle of the Sexes" at Meadowlands Racetrack, a team of female jockeys including Julie Krone, Patty Cooksey, Abagail Fuller, Vicky Aragon, and Tammi Campbell defeat their male counterparts.

NOVEMBER 6

November 6, 1869: Rutgers defeats Princeton, 6–4, in the first collegiate football game. The rules are considerably different than they are today, with one-point goals and 25 players to a side.

November 6, 1904: During the first quarter of a college football game against Oklahoma, Oklahoma State is forced to punt from their own one-yard line. The punt, into gale-force winds, is blown 15 yards back over the punter's head into Cottonwood Creek. Oklahoma halfback Ed Cook retrieves the ball and swims upstream to score the game's first touchdown, as the Sooners rout Oklahoma State, 75–0.

November 6, 1934: The Philadelphia Eagles defeat the Cincinnati Reds, 64–0, in a National Football League game. The Reds will lose all their games in 1934, scoring only ten points during the season.

November 6, 1958: The Baltimore Colts defeat Chicago, 17–0, marking the first time the Bears have been shut out in 12 seasons.

November 6, 1966: Philadelphia's Tim Brown returns two kickoffs for touchdowns in a game against the Dallas Cowboys.

NOVEMBER 7

November 7, 1962: Goaltender Glen Hall of the Chicago Black Hawks injures his back in an NHL game against the Boston Bruins. Hall's consecutive-game playing streak ends at 503 games.

November 7, 1963: Elston Howard of the New York Yankees becomes the first black Most Valuable Player in American League history.

November 7, 1968: Red Berenson scores six goals as the St. Louis Blues defeat the Philadelphia Flyers, 8–0, in a National Hockey League game.

November 7, 1970: Carlos Monzon of Argentina knocks

out champion Nino Benvenuti of Italy in the 12th round to win the world middleweight title. Monzon will successfully defend his title 15 times before his retirement in 1977.

NOVEMBER 8

November 8, 1970: Tom Dempsey of the New Orleans Saints kicks a record 63-yard field goal with time running out to give the Saints a 19–17 victory over the Detroit Lions. Dempsey wears a special kicking shoe because he is missing toes on his right foot.

November 8, 1978: The Philadelphia 76ers defeat the New Jersey Nets, 137–133. However, the Nets will protest three technical fouls called on Bernard King and the NBA will agree, ruling that the final 18 minutes of the game be replayed. By the time the game is replayed, three players have been traded between the teams and play on opposite sides. The 76ers also win the rematch, 123–117.

November 8, 1980: In college football, Illinois quarterback Dave Wilson passes for 621 yards in a 49–42 loss to Ohio State.

November 8, 1981: Cincinnati's Louis Breeden returns an interception 102 yards for a touchdown as the Bengals defeat the San Diego Chargers, 40–17.

NOVEMBER 9

November 9, 1912: Jim Thorpe runs 95 yards for a touchdown in leading underdog Carlisle Indian School to a 27–6 victory over Army. In the game, Carlisle coach Pop Warner uses the double wing formation for the first time. Playing halfback for Army is a young man named Dwight David Eisenhower.

November 9, 1946: Notre Dame and Army battle to a scoreless tie in the so-called "Game of the Century." Army had defeated Notre Dame in their previous two meetings by scores of 59 to 0 and 48 to 0.

November 9, 1982: Larry Holmes stops James "Bonecrusher" Smith in the 12th round to win the new International Boxing Federation heavyweight title.

November 9, 1985: Al Unser finishes fourth in the Beatrice Indy Challenge race at Miami, Florida, to edge his son, Al Unser, Jr., 151–150, in the CART-PPG championship standings for the year.

NOVEMBER 10

November 10, 1931: Magnolia A & M defeats Jonesboro-Baptist, 143–1, in the most lopsided women's basketball game on record.

November 10, 1957: A record crowd of 102,368 watch the Los Angeles Rams defeat the San Francisco 49ers, 37–24, at the Los Angeles Coliseum.

November 10, 1962: Dr. Joseph Boydstone, an amateur golfer, shoots three holes-in-one during a single round in Bakersfield, California.

November 10, 1974: Cincinnati quarterback Ken Anderson sets an accuracy record when he completes 20 of 22 passes in a 17–10 Bengals victory over the Pittsburgh Steelers.

November 10, 1983: "Marvelous" Marvin Hagler defends his middleweight title with a 15-round decision over Roberto Duran.

November 10, 1984: The inaugural running of the 10-million-dollar Breeders' Cup is run at Hollywood Park. Wild Again, a 31-to-1 long shot, wins the 3-million-dollar Breeders' Cup Classic in a thrilling three-horse photo finish.

NOVEMBER 11

November 11, 1911: Jim Thorpe leads Carlisle to an 18–15 upset of Harvard. Harvard will not lose another football game for four years.

November 11, 1944: The New York Rangers' winless streak reaches 25 games. During the dry spell, the Rangers lose 21 games and tie four.

November 11, 1944: Led by backs Doc Blanchard and Glenn Davis, Army defeats Notre Dame, 59–0, the worst defeat in Fighting Irish history.

November 11, 1963: Gordie Howe of the Detroit Red Wings scores the 54th goal of his National Hockey League career, breaking the record of Maurice "The Rocket" Richard.

November 11, 1964: After failing on three previous occasions, Kelso wins the Washington, D.C. International.

November 11, 1978: Running back Eddie Lee Ivery of Georgia Tech rushes for 356 yards in a 42–21 victory over Air Force. Ivery has touchdown runs of 80, 73, and 57 yards.

November 11, 1984: Philadelphia defeats Edmonton, 7–5, to snap the Oilers' streak of 15 games unbeaten since the start of the season. During the streak, the Oilers win 12 games and tie three others.

NOVEMBER 12

November 12, 1892: Pudge Heffelfinger, a former All-American at Yale, becomes the first professional football player when he is paid $500 by the Allegheny Athletic Association to play in a game against the Pittsburgh Athletic Club. He scores the game's only touchdown as Allegheny wins, 4–0 (in those days a touchdown was worth four points).

November 12, 1928: Notre Dame is trailing Army, 6–0, when Fighting Irish coach Knute Rockne delivers his famous "Let's win one for the Gipper" speech at halftime. Inspired, Notre Dame rallies to beat Army, 12–6.

November 12, 1955: The smallest crowd in college football history witnesses a game between Washington State and San Jose State in Pullman, Washington. Because of zero-degree temperatures and high winds, only one fan is in attendance.

November 12, 1966: Dick the Bruiser, a former Green Bay Packer lineman, pins Mad Dog Vachon to win the American Wrestling Association title.

November 12, 1982: Aaron Pryor knocks out Alexis Arguello in the 14th round to retain his WBA junior welterweight title.

NOVEMBER 13

November 13, 1875: In a game played in New Haven, Connecticut, Harvard and Yale become the first college football teams to wear uniforms. Harvard wears crimson and Yale wears blue as the Bulldogs drop a 4–0 decision.

November 13, 1921: Jimmy Leach of VMI rushes for eight touchdowns, passes for another, and kicks 12 points after to account for 66 points in a game against Catholic University.

November 13, 1978: McLennan Community College defeats

Kilgore Junior College, 169–165, in four overtimes in the highest-scoring college basketball game.

November 13, 1982: Lightweight champion Ray "Boom Boom" Mancini knocks out Korean challenger Duk Koo Kim in the 14th round in a match carried on national television. Kim died a few days later from head injuries suffered in the bout.

November 13, 1985: In a game played in Spokane, Washington, Lynette Woodard becomes the first woman to play for the Harlem Globetrotters. Woodard scores seven points as the Globetrotters defeat the Washington Generals, 81–65.

NOVEMBER 14

November 14, 1899: The University of the South defeats Mississippi State, 12–0, their fifth win in six days. The tiny school (enrollment: 97) has defeated Texas, Texas A & M, Tulane, LSU, and Mississippi State in succession without allowing a point, an incredible feat, especially considering that the team has only twelve players on the squad.

November 14, 1900: Ban Johnson, president of a minor league known as the Western Association, announces his intention to form a major league to rival the established National League. The Western Association will expand to include eastern cities and will change its name to the American League, which will begin play in 1901.

November 14, 1943: Against the Detroit Lions, Washington Redskins quarterback Sammy Baugh shows his versatility by becoming the first NFL player to intercept four passes in a game.

November 14, 1966: Heavyweight champion Muhammad Ali unleashes a flurry of punches to knock out Cleveland Williams in the third round.

November 14, 1970: Thirty-seven members of the Marshall University football team are killed in a plane crash near Kenova, West Virginia.

NOVEMBER 15

November 15, 1949: Headlines read "Dewey Wins!" as Dewey High School of Wisconsin defeats Avoca High School, 31–20, to snap their 92-game losing streak.

November 15, 1952: Thirteen players foul out in an NBA game between Syracuse and Baltimore.

November 15, 1962: Golfer Larry Bruce scores a 480-yard hole-in-one in Hope, Arkansas.

November 15, 1964: Kansas City quarterback Len Dawson sets a record he'd rather forget when he fumbles seven times in a game against San Diego.

November 15, 1964: Mickey Wright fires a 62 during a round of an LPGA tournament in Midland, Texas, the lowest score ever shot by a woman professional golfer. Wright comes from ten shots behind to win the Tall City Open, one of 11 tournaments she will win in 1964.

November 15, 1969: San Diego State quarterback Dennis Shaw rewrites the record book when he throws nine touchdown passes in a 70–21 victory over New Mexico State.

NOVEMBER 16

November 16, 1912: Dwight Eisenhower, a hard-running halfback for the Army Cadets, suffers a knee injury in a game against Tufts, ending a promising football career. Eisenhower will spend his final two seasons at West Point as a member of the cheerleading squad. Later, Eisenhower will become the supreme military commander in Europe during World War II and the 34th President of the United States.

November 16, 1927: Haven High School of Connecticut defeats Sylvia High, 256–0, in the most lopsided football game in history.

November 16, 1940: Dartmouth defeats Cornell, 3–0, in the famous "fifth down game."

November 16, 1957: Notre Dame halfback Dick Lynch sweeps right end for an eight-yard touchdown with four minutes remaining in the game to give the Fighting Irish a 7–0 victory over Oklahoma, snapping the Sooners' record 47-game winning streak.

November 16, 1968: Michigan's Ron Johnson rushes for 347 yards and five touchdowns in a game against Wisconsin. The same afternoon, University of Cincinnati quarterback Greg Cook passes for 554 yards in a 60–48 loss to Ohio University.

NOVEMBER 17

November 17, 1894: The *Daily Racing Form* is established.

November 17, 1928: Notre Dame loses to Carnegie Tech at South Bend, Indiana, their first football loss at home since 1905.

November 17, 1944: Pitching great Tom Seaver is born in Fresno, California.

November 17, 1954: Boxer Jimmy Carter knocks out Paddy DeMarco to become the first man to win the lightweight title three times.

November 17, 1956: Jim Brown scores six touchdowns and kicks seven extra points to account for an NCAA record 43 points as Syracuse defeats Colgate, 61–7.

November 17, 1959: Syracuse's Connie Dierking has an early exit as he fouls out of an NBA game against New York in the first quarter.

November 17, 1968: The Oakland Raiders defeat the New York Jets, 43–32, in the infamous "*Heidi* game." New York is leading, 32–29, when NBC decides to cut away from the game to air a children's special named *Heidi*. The Raiders score two touchdowns in the final 42 seconds to win the game. As a result, networks adopt a policy never to cut away from a game until it's completed.

NOVEMBER 18

November 18, 1930: The Boston Bruins win their 26th consecutive game at home, a streak dating back to March 12 of the previous year.

November 18, 1954: The New York Yankees and Baltimore Orioles make an 18-player trade, the largest in major league history. One of the players the Yankees acquire is pitcher Don Larsen. Larsen was 3–21 with the Orioles in 1954, but the change of scenery does him good as he is 9–2 with the Yankees in 1955 and pitches a perfect game in the 1956 World Series.

November 18, 1966: At the height of his career, Los Angeles Dodgers pitcher Sandy Koufax announces his retirement from baseball. The 30-year-old southpaw, who was 27–9 in 1966, retires rather than risk permanent injury to his pitching arm.

November 18, 1967: O. J. Simpson breaks away for a 64-yard touchdown run in the fourth quarter to give the University of Southern California a 21–20 victory over crosstown rival UCLA. The game is a matchup of the two best players in college football, Simpson and UCLA quarterback Gary Beban. Beban will win the Heisman Trophy in 1967; Simpson will win it a year later.

NOVEMBER 19

November 19, 1932: Joe Kershella scores 11 touchdowns and a total of 71 points as the West Liberty Teachers College blanks Cedarville College, 127–0.

November 19, 1955: Ted Kennedy catches a seven-yard touchdown pass for Harvard's only score in a 21–7 loss to archrival Yale. It is one of two touchdown receptions Kennedy has for the season. Seven years later, Kennedy will be elected to the United States Senate, representing Massachusetts.

November 19, 1961: Quarterback George Blanda throws seven touchdown passes as the Houston Oilers defeat the New York Titans, 48–21.

November 19, 1966: Notre Dame and Michigan State battle to a 10–10 tie in a college football "Game of the Century." Notre Dame is criticized for running out the clock on their final possession instead of going for the win.

November 19, 1978: Philadelphia defeats the New York Giants, 19–17, in a game played in Giants Stadium. The Giants are leading 17–12 with time running out when they attempt a handoff rather than dropping on the ball. The result is a fumble, which the Eagles return for a game-winning touchdown.

NOVEMBER 20

November 20, 1923: Kentucky Derby winner Zev defeats English Derby winner Papyrus by five lengths in a match race at Belmont Park.

November 20, 1924: Former Detroit Tigers manager Hughie Jennings, Chicago White Sox manager Johnny Evers, and pitcher Red Faber are granted an audience with Pope Pius XI. Topics of conversation range from the St. Louis Cardinals to the College of Cardinals.

November 20, 1969: Pele becomes the first soccer player to score 1,000 goals.

November 20, 1977: Walter Payton of the Chicago Bears rushes for an NFL record 275 yards as the Bears defeat the Minnesota Vikings, 10–7.

November 20, 1982: On the final play of the game, California makes five laterals to score the game-winning touchdown as they defeat Stanford, 25–20. The California players have to weave their way through the Stanford band, which has prematurely come out onto the field.

NOVEMBER 21

November 21, 1902: The Philadelphia Athletics shut out Kanaweola, 39–0, in the first football game played at night.

November 21, 1964: Abebe Bikila of Ethiopia wins his second consecutive Olympic marathon gold medal.

November 21, 1971: The New York Rangers score eight goals in the third period to rout California, 12–1.

November 21, 1973: Fred Dryer of the Los Angeles Rams scores two safeties in a game against the Green Bay Packers. After his football career is over, Dryer will become a successful actor.

November 21, 1978: Wichita State's Joe Williams kicks a 67-yard field goal against Illinois.

November 21, 1981: Running back Marcus Allen of USC rushes for 219 yards against UCLA to set the NCAA single-season rushing record. That season, Allen rushed for 2,342 yards and 22 touchdowns.

NOVEMBER 22

November 22, 1917: The National Hockey League is formed.

November 22, 1943: Tennis great Billie Jean King is born in Long Beach, California.

November 22, 1945: Against the Detroit Lions, Jim Benton of the Cleveland Rams catches ten passes for 303 yards.

November 22, 1950: In the lowest-scoring game in NBA history, the Fort Wayne Pistons defeat the Minneapolis Lakers, 19–18.

November 22, 1951: Jack Christiansen of the Detroit Lions returns two punts for touchdowns in a game against the Green Bay Packers.

November 22, 1967: Wimbledon tennis champion Boris Becker is born in West Germany.

November 22, 1986: George Branham III becomes the first black bowler to win a PBA title when he defeats Mark Roth, 195–191, to win the Brunswick Memorial World Open in Glendale Heights, Illinois.

November 22, 1986: Mike Tyson, 20 years old, becomes the youngest heavyweight champion in boxing history when he knocks out Trevor Berbick in the second round.

NOVEMBER 23

November 23, 1905: The University of Chicago defeats Michigan, 2–0, to finish the season unbeaten and untied. In ten games, they outscore their opponents 495 to 0.

November 23, 1968: The Houston Cougars blow away the Tulsa Golden Hurricanes, 100–6, in a college football mismatch. Houston's Paul Gipson rushes for 282 yards as the Cougars amass 762 yards in total offense. Elsewhere, Harvard scores 16 points in the final 42 seconds to tie Yale, 29–29. It is such a moral victory that the Harvard newspaper carries the headline, "Harvard Beats Yale, 29 to 29."

November 23, 1981: The U.S. District Court in Brooklyn finds five former Boston College basketball players guilty of fixing games during the 1978–1979 season.

November 23, 1984: On the final play of the game, Boston College quarterback Doug Flutie throws a desperation bomb to Gerald Phelan for a 47–45 victory over Miami. Flutie passes for 472 yards in the game, while his Miami counterpart, Bernie Kosar, passes for 447 yards.

NOVEMBER 24

November 24, 1938: Basketball immortal Oscar Robertson is born in Charlotte, Tennessee.

November 24, 1949: In a game against the Chicago Bears, Detroit's Bob Smith returns an interception 102 yards for a touchdown.

November 24, 1949: Officials whistle 122 fouls in a game between Syracuse and Anderson. In those days, players were permitted eight fouls apiece.

November 24, 1953: Walter Alston signs a one-year contract to manage the Brooklyn Dodgers, the first of 23 consecutive one-year contracts Alston will sign. Former manager Charlie Dressen was fired despite winning the pennant in 1953 because he asked for a multiyear contract.

November 24, 1960: Philadelphia's Wilt Chamberlain pulls down 55 rebounds in a game against the Boston Celtics.

November 24, 1984: Bodybuilder Cory Everson defeats Rachel McLish to win the Ms. Olympia title in Montreal.

NOVEMBER 25

November 25, 1937: All-American Byron "Whizzer" White rushes for two touchdowns and scores a third on an interception return as Colorado defeats Denver, 34–7. Years later, White will become a member of the United States Supreme Court.

November 25, 1950: The Michigan Wolverines do not complete a pass or make a first down, yet somehow manage to defeat Ohio State, 9–3, in the infamous "Snow Bowl." The game is played in a driving snowstorm.

November 25, 1951: Dub Jones of the Cleveland Browns scores six touchdowns in a game against the Chicago Bears. A record 374 yards of penalties are called during the game.

November 25, 1971: In one of the greatest college football games ever played, Nebraska defeats Oklahoma, 35–31, in a battle of unbeatens.

November 25, 1973: O. J. Simpson of the Buffalo Bills rushes for 273 yards in a game against the Detroit Lions.

November 25, 1980: Welterweight champion Roberto Duran indicates he's had enough in round eight of the notorious "no mas" fight against Sugar Ray Leonard.

NOVEMBER 26

November 26, 1881: At the Seventh Regiment Armory drill hall in New York, the first indoor tennis match is played.

November 26, 1896: The University of Chicago defeats

Michigan, 7–6, in the first indoor football game. The historic game is played in Chicago Stadium.

November 26, 1902: The Philadelphia Athletics, coached by Connie Mack, win the United States football championship by defeating the Pittsburgh Pros, 12–6. Baseball pitcher Rube Waddell plays for Philadelphia while Christy Mathewson is the starting full-back for Pittsburgh. Mack, Waddell, and Mathewson will soon retire from football to devote their full attention to baseball.

November 26, 1956: American Bob Richards wins his second consecutive gold medal in the pole vault at the Summer Olympics in Melbourne, Australia.

November 26, 1963: Navy quarterback Roger Staubach wins the Heisman Trophy.

November 26, 1968: USC running back O. J. Simpson wins the Heisman Trophy.

NOVEMBER 27

November 27, 1938: Chicago White Sox pitcher Monty Stratton accidentally shoots himself in the leg with a .32-caliber pistol while hunting in Texas. The bullet shatters an artery and the leg has to be amputated. Years later, Hollywood will make a movie of Stratton's life starring James Stewart.

November 27, 1948: Army and Navy play to a 21–21 tie. Entering the game, Army's record was 8–0, while Navy's was 0–8.

November 27, 1966: The Washington Redskins, behind the passing of Sonny Jurgensen, defeat the New York Giants, 72–41, in the highest-scoring game in NFL history.

November 27, 1971: Florida is leading Miami, 45–8, with time running out when all the defenders intentionally fall to the ground to allow Hurricane back John Hornibrook to score a touchdown uncontested. The reason behind the unusual strategy is to give their quarterback John Reaves a chance to break Jim Plunkett's NCAA passing record, which he does.

November 27, 1974: Baseball commissioner Bowie Kuhn suspends New York Yankees owner George Steinbrenner for one year for making illegal contributions to the campaign of President Richard Nixon.

NOVEMBER 28

November 28, 1895: J. Frank Duryea wins the first automobile race in America. Driving an electric car, Duryea averages seven miles per hour in the *Chicago Times Herald* Automobile Race from Chicago to Evanston and back. Duryea's car uses three and a half gallons of gasoline and 19 gallons of water.

November 28, 1929: Ernie Nevers of the Chicago Cardinals scores six touchdowns and all of his team's points in a 40–6 win over the Chicago Bears.

November 28, 1942: Holy Cross upsets Boston College, 55–12. The football defeat proves to be a blessing in disguise as the Boston College players cancel a planned victory celebration at the Cocoanut Grove nightclub. That evening, the Cocoanut Grove burns and 491 people perish in the fire.

November 28, 1971: Ian Colston plays 22 rounds of golf in one day, a grand total of 401 holes, in Bendigo, Victoria, Australia.

November 28, 1974: Dallas quarterback Roger Staubach is injured with the Washington Redskins leading 16–3. Little-used quarterback Clint Longley comes off the bench to lead the Cowboys to a 24–23 victory.

November 28, 1979: In an NHL game against Colorado, Bill Smith of the New York Islanders becomes the first goalie ever to score a goal.

NOVEMBER 29

November 29, 1890: Navy defeats Army, 24–0, in the first Army-Navy football game.

November 29, 1900: Hundreds of fans watch the Stanford-California football game from the roof of the Pacific Glass Works factory across the street from the stadium. The roof suddenly collapses under the weight, and 13 people die when they fall into vats of molten glass.

November 29, 1948: Lightweight boxer Hal Bagwell fights his 183rd consecutive bout without a loss. Bagwell has won 178 fights and has had 5 draws during the streak, which began on August 10, 1938.

November 29, 1984: Wheeling College defeats Waynesburg, 62–57, in overtime, the sixth consecutive overtime game for Wheeling, which acquires the nickname "Cardiac Cardinals."

November 29, 1987: Lee Trevino wins $175,000 for a hole-in-one during the Skins Game. Overall, Trevino comes away the big winner, with $310,000 in prize money.

November 29, 1987: Ivan Lendl wins a record-setting $583,200 in a winner-take-all tennis match in West Palm Beach, Florida.

NOVEMBER 30

November 30, 1956: Twenty-two-year-old Floyd Patterson knocks out 42-year-old Archie Moore in the fifth round to win the vacant heavyweight boxing title.

November 30, 1969: Buffalo recovers seven fumbles as they defeat the Cincinnati Bengals, 16–13, in a game played in a blizzard.

November 30, 1974: Notre Dame has a 24–0 lead in the second quarter when USC explodes for eight touchdowns in the next 16 minutes to defeat the Fighting Irish by the score of 55 to 24.

November 30, 1976: Pittsburgh running back Tony Dorsett wins the Heisman Trophy.

November 30, 1979: Middleweight champion Vito Antuofermo and challenger Marvin Hagler fight to a 15-round draw in Las Vegas. In another important fight, Sugar Ray Leonard stops champion Wilfred Benitez in the 15th round to win the welterweight title.

November 30, 1986: Golfer Fuzzy Zoeller wins $370,000 in the Skins Game.

DECEMBER 1

December 1, 1939: Golfer Lee Trevino is born in Horizon City, Texas.

December 1, 1951: "Showboat" Boykin scores all seven touchdowns as Mississippi defeats Mississippi State, 49–7.

December 1, 1956: Led by center Bill Russell, the United States basketball team defeats the Soviet Union, 89–55, to win the Olympic gold medal.

December 1, 1958: Heavyweight Lamar Clark knocks out

six opponents in one night. Clark will have a string of 44 consecutive knockouts at one time during his career.

December 1, 1982: Jockey Patti Barton rides against her daughter, Leah, in the first race at Latonia Racetrack, marking the first time that mother and daughter jockeys have competed against each other.

December 1, 1984: Greg Page knocks out Gerrie Coetzee in the eighth round to win the heavyweight boxing title in Sun City, South Africa.

DECEMBER 2

December 2, 1896: Bob Fitzsimmons is giving Tom Sharkey a horrendous beating when referee Wyatt Earp stops the bout in the eighth round. To everyone's surprise, Earp declares Sharkey the winner on a foul. When Fitzsimmons protests the decision, Earp pulls a revolver, terminating the debate. Apparently, Earp, a former marshal, had been bribed by gamblers to let Sharkey win. A few months later, Fitzsimmons fights again and wins the heavyweight title. Earp, a survivor of the Gunfight at O.K. Corral, ends his days as a sportswriter.

December 2, 1950: Bantamweight champion Vic Toweel knocks down challenger Danny O'Sullivan 14 times before knocking him out in the tenth round.

December 2, 1972: Anthony Davis scores six touchdowns as the University of Southern California defeats Notre Dame, 45–23. Davis returns the opening kickoff 97 yards for a touchdown and later returns another kickoff 96 yards for a score.

December 2, 1975: Running back Archie Griffin of Ohio State becomes the first player to win the Heisman Trophy twice.

December 2, 1984: Quarterback Dan Marino passes for 475 yards and four touchdowns as the Miami Dolphins defeat the Raiders, 45–34.

DECEMBER 3

December 3, 1949: The Notre Dame football team goes undefeated for the fourth year in a row.

December 3, 1950: Receiver Cloyce Box catches 12 passes for 302 yards and four touchdowns as the Detroit Lions maul the

Baltimore Colts, 45–21. Tom Fears of the Los Angeles Rams celebrates his 27th birthday by making an NFL record 18 receptions in a game against the Green Bay Packers. The same day, the Cleveland Browns play an entire game against the Philadelphia Eagles without attempting a pass.

December 3, 1965: Two-time Olympic gold medalist Katarina Witt is born in Staaken, East Germany.

December 3, 1970: In one of the biggest upsets in boxing history, Billy Backus knocks out champion Jose Napoles in the fourth round to win the welterweight title.

December 3, 1982: Thomas Hearns wins a decision over Wilfred Benitez in a WBC super welterweight title bout.

DECEMBER 4

December 4, 1920: Former Notre Dame quarterback George Gipp dies of pneumonia at the age of 25. Years later, Notre Dame coach Knute Rockne will urge the team to victory in a crucial game with the cry, "Let's win one for the Gipper!" When Hollywood films Gipp's life story, Ronald Reagan will be selected to play the title role.

December 4, 1977: The Tampa Bay Buccaneers are defeated by the Chicago Bears, 10–0, their 26th consecutive loss.

December 4, 1979: Notre Dame of Louisiana is leading Daniel Murphy, 67–61, late in the game when Notre Dame coach Glenn Marx is assessed three technical fouls. The irate coach refuses to leave the court, and the official tacks on nine more technical fouls. Herb Simon sinks 11 of 12 free throws to lead his team to an improbable 72–67 victory.

December 4, 1980: Track legend Stella Walsh is killed when she is caught in a crossfire during a robbery attempt in Cleveland. When an autopsy is performed, it is discovered that the former Olympic gold medalist is really a man.

DECEMBER 5

December 5, 1908: Washington and Jefferson University defeats Pittsburgh, 14–0, in the first football game where players wear numbers on their uniforms.

December 5, 1947: Joe Louis survives a first-round knockdown to win a disputed 15-round decision over challenger Jersey Joe Walcott to retain his heavyweight title. Four years later, Walcott will become the oldest boxer to win the heavyweight title.

December 5, 1971: Willie Ellison of the Los Angeles Rams rushes for 247 yards in a game against the New Orleans Saints.

December 5, 1978: Free agent Pete Rose signs with the Philadelphia Phillies after having spent 17 seasons with the Cincinnati Reds.

December 5, 1981: USC running back Marcus Allen wins the Heisman Trophy.

December 5, 1984: Helena Sukova defeats Martina Navratilova, 1–6, 6–3, 7–5, in the semifinals of the Australian Open, snapping Navratilova's record 74-match winning streak.

DECEMBER 6

December 6, 1873: In New Haven, Connecticut, the first international football game is played, as Yale defeats Eaton, England, 2 goals to 1. (At the time touchdowns were known as goals and counted for one point instead of six.)

December 6, 1960: Rafer Johnson of the United States narrowly defeats Taiwan's C. K. Yang in a dramatic decathlon competition at the Rome Olympics.

December 6, 1966: San Francisco's Rick Barry makes 14 free throws in one quarter in a game against the New York Knicks.

December 6, 1969: With President Richard Nixon in attendance, unbeaten Texas defeats Arkansas, 15–14, in a classic college football game.

December 6, 1985: All-American guard Steve Alford of Indiana is suspended for one game for appearing in a beefcake calendar without permission. The Hoosiers, without Alford, lose to Kentucky, 63–58.

December 6, 1986: Miami quarterback Vinny Testaverde wins the Heisman Trophy.

DECEMBER 7

December 7, 1941: Pittsburgh pitcher Rip Sewell, famous for his blooper pitch, shoots himself in both legs during a hunting accident in Ocala, Florida. Sewell will have an amazing comeback, winning 17 games in 1942 and a league-leading 21 games in 1943.

December 7, 1947: Catching great Johnny Bench is born in Oklahoma City, Oklahoma.

December 7, 1956: Boston Celtics forward Larry Bird is born in French Lick, Indiana.

December 7, 1963: Kansas defeats Cincinnati, 51–47, snapping the Bearcats' 90-game winning streak at home dating back to March 1, 1957.

December 7, 1963: During an Army-Navy football telecast, CBS uses the instant replay for the first time.

December 7, 1977: In a game against the Birmingham Bulls, Gordie Howe of the New England Whalers scores his 1,000th goal.

December 7, 1985: Auburn running back Bo Jackson edges Iowa quarterback Chuck Long by 45 votes in the closest Heisman Trophy balloting in history.

DECEMBER 8

December 8, 1940: The Chicago Bears destroy the Washington Redskins, 73–0, in the most one-sided NFL championship game in history. Incredibly, both teams have 17 first downs and the Redskins have more passing yardage, 223 to 119 yards. The big difference in the game is eight interceptions by the Bears' secondary. Mutual Broadcasting System pays $2,500 for the rights to broadcast the game, the first national broadcast of an NFL championship game.

December 8, 1961: Syracuse's Larry Costello sets an NBA record by scoring 32 consecutive points without missing a shot. Costello hits 13 of 13 from the field and 6 of 6 from the foul line in a 123–111 loss to the Boston Celtics. In other NBA action, the Los Angeles Lakers defeat the Philadelphia Warriors, 151–147, in three overtimes. Philadelphia's Wilt Chamberlain scores 73 points and the Lakers' Elgin Baylor scores 63.

December 8, 1962: In a game against the Washington Redskins, R. C. Owens of the Baltimore Colts blocks a field-goal attempt in a unique way. Standing at the goal line, Owens leaps up and bats the ball away just as it's about to pass through the crossbar.

DECEMBER 9

December 9, 1934: The New York Giants score 27 points in the fourth quarter to defeat the Chicago Bears, 30–13, in the NFL championship game.

December 9, 1941: Minnesota's Bruce Smith wins the Heisman Trophy. The awards ceremony is interrupted by a false air raid.

December 9, 1965: In one of the worst trades in baseball history, the Cincinnati Reds trade slugger Frank Robinson to the Baltimore Orioles in exchange for pitchers Milt Pappas and Jack Baldschun and outfielder Dick Simpson. In 1966, Robinson wins baseball's Triple Crown and leads the Orioles to their first world championship.

December 9, 1977: Houston's Rudy Tomjanovich suffers a concussion, fractured jaw, and broken nose when he is punched by Kermit Washington of the Los Angeles Lakers.

December 9, 1984: Eric Dickerson rushes for 216 yards as the Los Angeles Rams defeat the Houston Oilers, 27–16. Dickerson will break O. J. Simpson's single-season rushing record, finishing the year with 2,105 yards.

DECEMBER 10

December 10, 1896: Yale defeats Wesleyan, 39–4, in what is frequently acknowledged as the first major college basketball game. The rules differ slightly, with seven players to a side.

December 10, 1939: The Green Bay Packers shut out the New York Giants, 27–0, in the NFL championship game.

December 10, 1958: Light heavyweight champion Archie Moore is floored three times in the first round by challenger Yvon Durrelle. Moore rallies to knock out Durrelle in the 11th round to retain his title.

December 10, 1971: The New York Mets trade pitcher Nolan Ryan to the California Angels for infielder Jim Fregosi. Ryan will pitch a record five no-hitters and will become baseball's all-time strikeout king.

December 10, 1982: Michael "Dynamite" Dokes lives up

to his name by knocking out Mike Weaver in only 63 seconds to win the heavyweight boxing title.

DECEMBER 11

December 11, 1938: Despite being outgained 379 to 212 yards, the New York Giants take advantage of two blocked punts to defeat the Green Bay Packers, 23–17, in the NFL championship game.

December 11, 1960: Johnny Unitas of the Baltimore Colts fails to throw a touchdown pass for the first time in 47 games, as the Colts lose to the Los Angeles Rams, 10–3. The record streak dates back to December 9, 1956.

December 11, 1966: Al Nelson of the Philadelphia Eagles returns a missed field-goal attempt 100 yards for a touchdown against the Cleveland Browns.

December 11, 1977: Kansas City's Gary Barbaro returns an interception 102 yards for a touchdown against Seattle. Elsewhere, the Tampa Bay Buccaneers defeat the New Orleans Saints, 33–14, for their first NFL victory after 26 consecutive losses. Some Saints fans are so humiliated by the loss that they wear paper bags over their heads.

December 11, 1985: Wayne Gretzky has seven assists as the Edmonton Oilers defeat the Chicago Black Hawks, 12–9.

DECEMBER 12

December 12, 1937: Sammy Baugh passes for 335 yards as the Washington Redskins defeat the Chicago Bears, 28–21, in the NFL championship game.

December 12, 1959: Twenty-two-year-old Bruce McLaren wins the United States Grand Prix to become the youngest driver ever to win a Grand Prix race.

December 12, 1965: Rookie Gale Sayers of the Chicago Bears scores six touchdowns in a game against the San Francisco 49ers. Elsewhere, Paul Hornung scores five touchdowns as the Green Bay Packers defeat the Baltimore Colts, 42–27.

December 12, 1982: The New England Patriots defeat the Miami Dolphins, 3–0, with the help of a snow sweeper. The game is a scoreless tie in the fourth quarter when the Patriots line up for a 33-yard field goal attempt on the snow-covered field. At that moment, maintenance man Mark Henderson drives a snow sweeper on the field to clear the spot where the ball will be kicked. The field goal by John Smith is good and the Patriots score a controversial win.

December 12, 1986: James "Bonecrusher" Smith knocks out "Terrible" Tim Witherspoon in the first round to win the WBA heavyweight title.

DECEMBER 13

December 13, 1887: Jack "Nonpareil" Dempsey knocks out Johnny Regan in the 45th round to retain his world middleweight title. The fight is held near the waterfront on an island in Long Island Sound. Soon the ring is engulfed by the rising tide, and before long Dempsey and Regan are fighting in waist-deep water. The bout is moved farther inland, but by that time a cold front has passed through the area and the rest of the fight takes place in a raging snowstorm.

December 13, 1936: The Green Bay Packers defeat the Boston Redskins, 21–6, to win the NFL championship. The next season, the Redskins will move to Washington.

December 13, 1942: The Washington Redskins defeat the Chicago Bears, 14–6, in the NFL championship game.

December 13, 1983: The Detroit Pistons defeat the Denver Nuggets, 186–184, in the highest-scoring game in NBA history. Kiki Vandeweghe leads all scorers with 51 points.

December 13, 1985: You can bet it's a lucky Friday the 13th for 66-year-old Frank Judson, who wins $1,132,466 on a Pick Six wager at Bay Meadows Racetrack.

DECEMBER 14

December 14, 1901: The first table tennis tournament is held at the London Royal Aquarium. R. D. Ayling wins the competition.

December 14, 1952: Washington quarterback Sammy Baugh announces his retirement from football. Not only is Baugh at the time one of the greatest passers in football history, he is also the NFL's all-time leading punter.

December 14, 1972: Ice skater Roger Wood jumps a record 29 feet, 2 inches over barrels. Coincidentally, the distance is almost exactly the same as Bob Beamon's record leap in the long jump.

December 14, 1985: Undefeated boxer Craig Bodzianowski knocks out Francis Sargent in the second round of their fight in Palos Heights, Illinois. What makes the feat remarkable is that Bodzianowski fights with an artificial leg. The boxer had lost part of his leg as the result of a motorcycle accident. Bodzianowski had fought Sargent before the accident and won a ten-round decision.

DECEMBER 15

December 15, 1935: The Detroit Lions defeat the New York Giants, 26–7, in the NFL championship game. The winners' share is $313 per player, while the losers receive $200.

December 15, 1946: The Chicago Bears intercept five passes and defeat the New York Giants, 24–14, in the NFL championship game.

December 15, 1969: Jockey Chuck Baltazar rides seven consecutive winners at Laurel Racecourse.

December 15, 1974: Quarterback Bert Jones of the Baltimore Colts completes 17 consecutive passes in an NFL game against the New York Jets.

December 15, 1982: Alabama coach Paul "Bear" Bryant announces his retirement from football. Bryant, who has spent 38 years as a head coach, retires as the winningest coach in college football history. Ray Perkins will replace Bryant as Alabama head coach.

DECEMBER 16

December 16, 1930: Golfer Bobby Jones receives the first Sullivan Award as the nation's outstanding amateur athlete.

December 16, 1945: The Cleveland Rams defeat the Washington Redskins, 15–14, in the NFL championship game.

December 16, 1966: Dick Tiger wins a 15-round decision over Jose Torres to capture the world light heavyweight boxing title.

December 16, 1973: O. J. Simpson of the Buffalo Bills gains 200 yards in a game against the New York Jets to become the first NFL player to rush for over 2,000 yards in a season. Simpson finishes the season with 2,003 yards.

December 16, 1984: Washington wide receiver Art Monk catches 11 passes against the St. Louis Cardinals to set a single-season record with 106 receptions. The Redskins defeat St. Louis, 29–27.

December 16, 1985: Morganna, baseball's "Kissing Bandit," becomes a part owner of the Utica Blue Sox, a minor league affiliate of the Philadelphia Phillies. Morganna, who sports some interesting stats of her own, 60-24-39, gained notoriety by kissing baseball stars such as Pete Rose and George Brett during games.

DECEMBER 17

December 17, 1933: The Chicago Bears defeat the New York Giants, 23–21, in the first NFL championship game.

December 17, 1944: Fullback Ted Fritsch scores both touchdowns as the Green Bay Packers defeat the New York Giants, 14–7, in the NFL championship game.

December 17, 1967: Nolan "The Flea" Smith of the Kansas City Chiefs returns a kickoff 106 yards for a touchdown against the Denver Broncos. At 5 feet, 6 inches and 154 pounds, Smith is one of the smallest players ever to play professional football.

December 17, 1974: Chris McCarron rides his 516th winner to set a single-season record for jockeys.

December 17, 1978: Fran Tarkenton throws three touchdown passes in his final NFL game, giving him 342 for his career. His finale is spoiled as the Oakland Raiders intercept five passes in a 27–20 victory over the Minnesota Vikings.

December 17, 1984: Dan Marino throws four touchdown passes as the Miami Dolphins defeat the Dallas Cowboys, 28–21. Marino sets NFL single-season records for most touchdown passes (48), completions (362), and passing yards (5,084).

DECEMBER 18

December 18, 1886: Baseball immortal Ty Cobb is born in Narrows, Georgia.

December 18, 1932: The Chicago Bears defeat the Portsmouth

Spartans, 9–0, at Chicago Stadium in the first NFL game played indoors. The stadium floor is covered with dirt because a circus had just appeared there, and the field is only 80 yards long.

December 18, 1943: Triple Crown winner Count Fleet is named Horse of the Year. Count Fleet wins the Belmont Stakes by an incredible 25 lengths.

December 18, 1949: Steve Van Buren rushes for 196 yards on a rain-soaked field as the Philadelphia Eagles defeat the Los Angeles Rams, 14–0, in the NFL championship game.

December 18, 1979: Stan Barrett becomes the fastest man on wheels when he drives the Budweiser Rocket 739.666 miles per hour in Mojave, California.

DECEMBER 19

December 19, 1917: Joe Malone scores five goals as the Montreal Canadiens defeat Ottawa, 7–4, in their first NHL game.

December 19, 1948: In a game played under blizzard conditions, the Philadelphia Eagles defeat the Chicago Cardinals, 7–0, to win the NFL championship.

December 19, 1970: Ken Houston of the Houston Oilers returns two interceptions for touchdowns in a game against the San Diego Chargers. He sets an NFL record by returning four interceptions for touchdowns during the season.

December 19, 1982: Garo Yepremian kicks a 42-yard field goal with four seconds remaining to lift the Miami Dolphins to a 15–14 victory over the New York Giants. It is Yepremian's 21st consecutive field goal.

December 19, 1983: CBS sportscaster Tom Brookshier causes a controversy when he suggests on the air that the Louisville Cardinals basketball team has a collective IQ of 40. Brookshier later apologizes for his remarks.

December 19, 1984: The Buffalo Sabres defeat the Chicago Black Hawks, 6–3, as Scotty Bowman becomes the winningest coach in NHL history. At the time, Bowman's record is 691 wins, 285 losses, and 202 ties.

DECEMBER 20

December 20, 1946: Sugar Ray Robinson wins a 15-round decision over Tommy Bell to win the world welterweight boxing title.

December 20, 1982: The San Diego Chargers defeat the Cincinnati Bengals, 50–34, in the highest-scoring game on *Monday Night Football*. Quarterbacks Dan Fouts of the San Diego Chargers and Ken Anderson of the Cincinnati Bengals combine to set numerous single-game passing records, including most completions (66) and passing yards (883).

December 20, 1985: Dennis Potvin of the New York Islanders scores his 916th point, breaking Bobby Orr's NHL career scoring record for defensemen.

December 20, 1987: Jerry Rice of the San Francisco 49ers has his 12th consecutive game in which he catches a touchdown pass. Rice finishes the season with an NFL record 22 touchdown receptions.

DECEMBER 21

December 21, 1941: The smallest crowd in football playoff history, 13,341, watch the Chicago Bears defeat the New York Giants, 37–9, in the NFL championship game.

December 21, 1954: Tennis champion Chris Evert is born in Fort Lauderdale, Florida.

December 21, 1969: The Dallas Cowboys defeat the Washington Redskins, 20–10, in Vince Lombardi's last game as head coach.

December 21, 1974: In one of the greatest games in NFL history, the Oakland Raiders defeat the Miami Dolphins, 28–26, in an American Conference playoff game. Kenny Stabler's desperation eight-yard touchdown pass to Clarence Davis with 26 seconds remaining is the game winner.

December 21, 1981: Doug Schloemer sinks an 18-foot jumper with one second remaining to give the University of Cincinnati a 75–73 victory over Bradley in seven overtimes, the longest game in college basketball history.

December 21, 1984: In a 110–82 victory over the University of Charleston, Georgeann Wells of West Virginia University becomes the first woman to dunk a basketball.

DECEMBER 22

December 22, 1894: The United States Golf Association is founded.

December 22, 1944: Pitching great Steve Carlton is born in Miami, Florida.

December 22, 1951: Golfer Jan Stephenson is born in Australia.

December 22, 1957: The Detroit Lions overcome a 24–7 halftime deficit to defeat the San Francisco 49ers, 31–27, in a Western Conference playoff football game.

December 22, 1985: Three NFL records are set on the same day. San Francisco running back Roger Craig becomes the first player to go over 1,000 yards rushing and receiving in the same year. Kansas City wide receiver Stephone Paige catches passes for a record 309 yards in a game. San Diego's Lionel James amasses a record 2,535 all-purpose yards in a season.

DECEMBER 23

December 23, 1928: Golfer Horton Smith shoots a four-round tournament record of 245 in the Catalina Open. Smith shoots rounds of 63, 58, 61, and 63.

December 23, 1951: Tom Fears catches a 73-yard touchdown pass from Norm Van Brocklin to give the Los Angeles Rams a 24–17 victory over the Cleveland Browns in the NFL championship game.

December 23, 1962: The Dallas Texans defeat the Houston Oilers, 20–17, in two overtimes to win the American Football League championship.

December 23, 1972: With Oakland leading 7–6 and time running out, Pittsburgh quarterback Terry Bradshaw throws a desperation pass intended for Frenchy Fuqua. Fuqua is leveled by Raiders defensive back Jack Tatum and the ball deflects to Pittsburgh's Franco Harris, who runs for a touchdown to give the Steelers a 13–7 playoff victory over Oakland on a play christened the "immaculate reception."

December 23, 1977: Tight end Dave Casper catches a 10-yard touchdown pass from Ken Stabler to give the Oakland Raiders a 37–31 playoff win over the Baltimore Colts in two overtimes.

DECEMBER 24

December 24, 1950: Lou Groza kicks a 16-yard field goal with 20 seconds remaining to give the Cleveland Browns a 30–28 victory over the Los angeles Rams in the NFL championship game.

December 24, 1961: The Houston Oilers defeat the San Diego Chargers, 10–3, in the American Football League championship game.

December 24, 1962: General Douglas MacArthur is selected to arbitrate a dispute between the NCAA and AAU.

December 24, 1967: Boston Red Sox pitcher Jim Lonborg injures his knee in a skiing accident. The Cy Young winner, who won 22 games in 1967, will slump to 6–10 the following season.

December 24, 1968: Hockey star Garry Unger plays the first of 914 consecutive games. His consecutive-game playing streak will not end until 11 years later.

DECEMBER 25

December 25, 1866: Henrietta wins the first transatlantic yacht race, in a time of 13 days, 21 hours, and 55 minutes.

December 25, 1888: Seventy-seven years before the opening of the Houston Astrodome, the first indoor baseball game is played in Philadelphia. Two thousand spectators watch the Downtowners defeat the Uptowners, 6–1, in the main building of the state fairgrounds.

December 25, 1945: Raiders quarterback Ken Stabler is born in Foley, Alabama.

December 25, 1971: Garo Yepremian kicks a 37-yard field goal in the second overtime to give the Miami Dolphins a 27–24 victory over the Kansas City Chiefs in the longest game in NFL history.

December 25, 1985: The New York Knicks overcome a 25-point deficit to defeat the Boston Celtics, 113–104, in overtime.

DECEMBER 26

December 26, 1902: Oscar Nelson knocks down Christy Williams 42 times before knocking him out in the 17th round of their bout.

December 26, 1908: Jack Johnson knocks out Tommy Burns in the 14th round to become the first black heavyweight boxing champion.

December 26, 1943: Sid Luckman throws five touchdown passes as the Chicago Bears defeat the Washington Redskins, 41–21, in the NFL championship game.

December 26, 1954: Quarterback Otto Graham scores three touchdowns and passes for three more as the Cleveland Browns bury the Detroit Lions, 56–10, in the NFL championship game.

December 26, 1955: The Cleveland Browns defeat the Los Angeles Rams, 38–14, in the NFL championship game. Quarterback Otto Graham throws two touchdown passes in his final NFL game.

December 26, 1960: The Philadelphia Eagles defeat the Green Bay Packers, 17–13, in the NFL championship game.

December 26, 1964: The Buffalo Bills, led by quarterback Jack Kemp, defeat the San Diego Chargers, 20–7, in the American Football League championship game.

DECEMBER 27

December 27, 1892: North Carolina Biddle defeats Livingston College 4 goals to 0 in the first black college football game. The game is played in Salisbury, North Carolina.

December 27, 1953: Jim Doran catches a 33-yard touchdown pass from Bobby Layne with two minutes remaining to give the Detroit Lions a 17–16 victory over the Cleveland Browns in the NFL championship game.

December 27, 1959: In a rematch of the famed 1958 NFL championship game, the Baltimore Colts, behind the passing of Johnny Unitas, defeat the New York Giants, 31–16, to claim another NFL crown.

December 27, 1964: Quarterback Frank Ryan throws three touchdown passes to receiver Gary Collins as the Cleveland Browns shut out the Baltimore Colts, 27–0, in the NFL championship game.

December 27, 1987: Seattle Seahawks wide receiver Steve Largent catches six passes to pass Charlie Joiner as the NFL's all-time leading receiver with 752 catches.

DECEMBER 28

December 28, 1902: The Syracuse Athletic Club defeats the Philadelphia Athletics, 6–0, in the World Series of Football played in Madison Square Garden. The first baseball World Series will not occur until the next year.

December 28, 1947: The Chicago Cardinals defeat the Philadelphia Eagles, 28–21, in the NFL championship game, the only championship in Cardinals history.

December 28, 1952: The Detroit Lions defeat the Cleveland Browns, 17–7, in the NFL championship game. Surprisingly, Cleveland has 22 first downs, compared to 10 for Detroit.

December 28, 1958: Alan Ameche scores on a one-yard run to give the Baltimore Colts a 23–17 victory in overtime against the New York Giants in the NFL championship game. The game will often be cited as the greatest game in NFL history and will help popularize professional football.

December 28, 1975: Drew Pearson catches a 50-yard "Hail Mary" touchdown pass from Roger Staubach with 24 seconds left on the clock to give the Dallas Cowboys a 17–14 victory over the Minnesota Vikings.

DECEMBER 29

December 29, 1934: In college basketball's first double-header at Madison Square Garden, New York University defeats Notre Dame, 25–18, and Westminster defeats St. John's, 37–33.

December 29, 1945: Despite refusing to jump the fourth hurdle, Never Mind II wins a steeplechase race. The horse and rider had already returned to the paddock when the jockey was informed that all the other horses had fallen. They return to the course and win the two-mile race in 11 minutes and 28 seconds, nearly three times the average clocking.

December 29, 1957: Quarterback Tobin Rote throws four touchdown passes as the Detroit lions overpower the Cleveland Browns, 59–14, in the NFL championship game.

December 29, 1963: The Chicago Bears defeat the New York Giants, 14–10, to present coach George Halas with his sixth and final NFL championship.

December 29, 1978: Clemson defeats Ohio State, 19–15, in the Gator Bowl. Buckeyes head coach Woody Hayes is fired after he punches Clemson middle guard Charlie Bauman on the sidelines following his game-clinching interception.

DECEMBER 30

December 30, 1935: Hall of Fame pitcher Sandy Koufax is born in Brooklyn, New York.

December 30, 1936: Stanford defeats Long Island University, 45–31, to snap LIU's 43-game winning streak in basketball. The star of the game is Stanford forward Hank Luisetti, who revolutionized basketball by being the first player to shoot the ball one-handed. Before Luisetti popularized the jump shot, players had used the two-handed set shot.

December 30, 1956: The New York Giants defeat the Chicago Bears, 47–7, in the NFL championship game. To get better traction on the frozen field, the Giants wear sneakers.

December 30, 1962: Jerry Kramer kicks three field goals as the Green Bay Packers defeat the New York Giants, 16–7, in the NFL championship game. The players brave 13-degree temperatures and 40-mile-per-hour winds.

DECEMBER 31

December 31, 1961: On leave from the army, Paul Hornung scores a touchdown and kicks four field goals and four extra points as the Green Bay Packers defeat the New York Giants, 37–0, in the NFL championship game.

December 31, 1967: Bart Starr scores on a quarterback sneak with 13 seconds remaining to give the Green Bay Packers a 21–17 victory in the NFL championship game. The historic game is played in 14-degree-below-zero weather.

December 31, 1971: Sixty-four-year-old golfer Weller Noble shoots his age when he fires a round of 64 on the Claremont Country Club Course in Oakland, California.

December 31, 1973: Notre Dame defeats Alabama, 24–23,

to win the Sugar Bowl and the national championship in football.

December 31, 1985: Jockey Jorge Velasquez misjudges the finish line by a mile in the Display Handicap at Aqueduct Racetrack. Velasquez urges his mount, Southern Sultan, to the finish line first, only to discover that there is one mile left to go in the two-and-a-quarter-mile race. The exhausted horse is beaten 42 lengths by the eventual winner, Erin Bright.